/HOW TO AVOID BEING KILLED IN A WAR ZONE/

/HOW TO AVOID BEING KILLED IN A WAR ZONE/

ROSIE GARTHWAITE

B L O O M S B U R Y

LONDON • BERLIN • NEW YORK • SYDNEY

First published in 2011

Illustrations by Oxford Designers and Illustrators Ltd

Bloomsbury Publishing Plc, 36 Soho Square, London W1D 3QY
Bloomsbury USA, 175 5th Avenue, New York, NY 10010

www.bloomsbury.com
www.bloomsburyusa.com

Bloomsbury Publishing, London, Berlin, New York and Sydney
A CIP catalogue record for this book is available from the British Library
Library of Congress Cataloging-in-Publication data has been applied for

ISBN 978 1 4088 1682 0 (UK edition)
ISBN 978 1 60819 585 5 (US edition)

10 9 8 7 6 5 4 3 2 1

Designed by Will Webb
Printed and bound in China by C&C Offset Printing Co. Ltd

All papers used by Bloomsbury Publishing are natural, recyclable products made from wood grown in well-managed forests. The manufacturing processes conform to the environmental regulations of the country of origin

This book is for the parents – mine and yours – and for lovers left behind.

To Mum and Dad for their sleepless nights and support for my act-first-think-later adventures.

/CONTENTS

/ACKNOWLEDGEMENTS

If ever there was a book that was the sum of its parts, this is it. I cannot thank enough all the people who contributed, whether in name or behind the scenes. You are all street-smart geniuses. Never mind a war zone, I would carry you in my bag everywhere I went if I could.

Chris Cobb-Smith has acted as my personal encyclopedia of all survival knowledge. There'll be a crisp, cold lager waiting for you at the Windsor Castle whenever you want one, Chris – thank you.

And I am especially grateful to Mark Brayne, psychotherapist and former BBC correspondent (www.braynework.com), whose invaluable work with trauma and journalism forms the backbone of chapter 15.

I am indebted to Kathy Rooney for her faith in both me and the idea for this book. And to Nigel Newton and the rest of the Bloomsbury team for their ability to see past my terrible driving and lectures on the delights and doldrums of Doha to a potential author lurking inside. It has been a fantastic privilege to watch Bloomsbury Qatar Foundation Publishing grow from seed and now be a part of it.

My lifelong partner in crime and now agent Alice Lutyens, thank you for teaching me the language of this new world and helping me over the hurdles.

MÉDECINS SANS FRONTIÈRES

Everyone who has ever worked with, travelled alongside or filmed Médecins Sans Frontières (MSF) has come back with stories of how impressed they were by the organization. My friends and colleagues say that MSF stands apart from other charities in their view because there are no pennies wasted. MSF provides free medical care to people in desperate need in war zones, disaster areas and other utterly forsaken places, often where no one else is willing or able to go.

That's why I decided to give them 30 per cent of the royalties from this book. They were happy with the idea and put me in touch with several very experienced current and former staff who have made generous contributions to the book, especially Dr Carl Hallam, who was kind enough to check over my medical knowledge whilst holed up in bed with a freshly broken back in his New Zealand home.

However, MSF do want me to make it extremely clear that any input here from MSF people is their personal advice and is not to be confused with the strict rules and procedures to be found in the official MSF handbooks.

/CONTRIBUTORS

Without the help and advice of the people below and dozens of anonymous voices, this book would have been impossible. I have leaned heavily on these contributors in order to make this book stand up. Thank you, all of you, for being so generous and thoughtful with your experiences.

Hoda Abdel-Hamid, correspondent for Al Jazeera English. A three-time Emmy Award winner, Hoda has covered stories from Saudi to Sarajevo, Morocco and Pakistan, and won an award from the Monte Carlo Film Festival for her documentary *Koran and Kalashnikovs*. She spent years making brave journalism with her team on the front line in Iraq, a month of it with me.

Tim Albone, journalist, documentary-maker and author of *Out of the Ashes* (Virgin Books, 2011), his account of following the progress of the Afghan cricket team around the world for a year in the lead-up to the World Cup.

Shadi Alkasim, my former colleague at the *Baghdad Bulletin*, worked with the United Nations Mission in Sudan and then Liberia as a radio producer and journalist until moving to China. He has also covered the war in Lebanon and has worked with www.aliveinbaghdad.org.

Helen Asquith is a doctor who trained at Oxford University and University College London. Her particular interest is public health, and she has travelled widely in her study of it, including to southern Afghanistan and Bangladesh.

Qais Azimy, Afghan journalist and Al Jazeera English producer in Kabul.

Samantha Bolton, former world head of press and campaigns for Médecins Sans Frontières.

James Brabazon, journalist and documentary film-maker, author of *My Friend the Mercenary* (Canongate Books, 2010).

James Brandon, former colleague at the *Baghdad Bulletin*, now head of research at the Quilliam Foundation, a counter-terrorism think-tank.

Julius Cavendish, Kabul correspondent for the *Independent* newspaper.

Chris Cobb-Smith, former artillery commando officer in the British Army, now a media security expert, founder of Chiron Resources, which provides specialist security support to news and documentary teams reporting from war zones; also carries out investigations into the deaths of journalists in the field, as well as examining human rights abuses and war crimes allegations.

Tom Coghlan, defence correspondent for *The Times* newspaper, formerly based in Kabul as a freelance reporter for various British newspapers, including *The Times*, the *Daily Telegraph* and the *Independent*.

Stefanie Dekker, producer and reporter for Al Jazeera English.
Marc DuBois, executive director of Médecins Sans Frontières – UK since 2009.
Jane Dutton, senior presenter for Al Jazeera English, formerly at CNN as a presenter and 'Hotspots' girl, and at the BBC and ETV.
Alina Gracheva, camerawoman for Al Jazeera English, but a television journalist since the collapse of the Soviet Union, covering many notable events, including the Chechen wars. She won an Emmy for her work as part of the team covering the fall of the Taliban in Kabul in 2001, and was nominated for an Emmy for 'Aneta's Choice', a report about a Beslan mother.
Carl Hallam, doctor, formerly in the British Royal Marines, now a volunteer for Médecins Sans Frontières.
Jonny Harris, captain, Light Dragoon Regiment, British Army.
Sayed Hashim, captain, No. 1 Kandak S2, 3/205 Atal Brigade, Afghan National Army.
Ralph Hassall, founder of the *Baghdad Bulletin* newspaper in Iraq. On its closure, he became involved in disaster management on an international scale, training governments and emergency services in key skills for post-conflict. His main area of expertise is landmines, and at the time of writing he was the manager for the UNDP Mine Action Capacity Development programme in southern Sudan.
Caroline Hawley, formerly the main BBC correspondent in Iraq, was named Broadcaster of the Year by the London Press Club in 2006. She is now based in London as a special correspondent for the BBC.
Patrick Hennessey, former British army officer and author of *The Junior Officers' Reading Club* (Allen Lane, 2009).
Chris Helgren, editor-in-charge at the Reuters UK pictures bureau; was formerly chief photographer for them in Baghdad and Rome.
Mohammed Hersi, former pirate off the coast of Somalia, 2001–9.
Tom Hudson, former soldier, now legal counsel for a Middle East security company that provides services in 'hostile' environments.
Kamal Hyder, journalist who has spent many years working in the tribal lands of Pakistan and Afghanistan with CNN and now Al Jazeera English.
Sebastian Junger, journalist and author, most famously of *The Perfect Storm* (Norton, 1997) and most recently of *War* (Fourth Estate, 2010). In 2009 he made his first film, the award-winning feature *Restrepo*, based on one year working with a US platoon in Afghanistan's 'deadliest valley'.
Wadah Khanfar has worked for Al Jazeera since its inception, progressing from cameraman, correspondent and Baghdad bureau chief to director-general, and seeing almost every war along the way. In 2009 *Forbes* magazine listed him as one of the most powerful people in the world.

Zeina Khodr began her career with local radio in Beirut, working through the civil war there. She then moved to Dubai TV, Al Arabiya, Al Jazeera Arabic and now Al Jazeera English. In 1999 she won best feature of the year for CNN's *World Report*.
Donald Kirk, Korea correspondent for the *Christian Science Monitor*, has also written a number of books on Southeast Asia and Korea, most recently *Korea Betrayed* (Palgrave Macmillan, 2010).
Marc Laban, co-founder of AsiaWorks Television, an independent production company.
Mohammad Tahir Luddin, Afghan freelance journalist.
Ian Mackinnon, freelance journalist, now based in Bangkok, where he was formerly the *Guardian* newspaper's Southeast Asia correspondent.
Kathleen McCaul, journalist, formerly at the *Baghdad Bulletin*, now a freelance radio and TV producer, and author of *Murder in the Ashram* (Piatkus, 2011).
Laura McNaught, freelance film-maker and founder of Sam's College Fund for children in the developing world (www.samscollegefund.com).
Leith Mushtaq, senior Al Jazeera cameraman.
Monique Nagelkerke has worked for Médecins Sans Frontières for 20 years and currently travels the world as a head of mission. Her last four posts were in Liberia, south and north Sudan, and Papua New Guinea.
Rageh Omaar, news presenter for Al Jazeera English, has covered over 15 conflicts and 40 countries for the BBC and other broadcasters. He was nicknamed the 'scud stud' of the Iraq war in 2003.
Mary O'Shea, former staff member with both the EU and UN, now working for them on a freelance basis as a governance and human rights specialist.
Leigh Page, film-maker and poker pro from Cape Town.
Jacky Rowland, correspondent for Al Jazeera English. Her 16 years of covering conflicts in the Balkans and the Islamic world have won her several awards, including the Royal Television Society Award in 2001. She joined Al Jazeera from the BBC, where she held a number of high-profile foreign postings.
Nazanin Sadri, producer for Al Jazeera English.
Mike Sawatzky, Congo bush pilot and volunteer at the Goma-based charity Kivu Kids (www.kivukidsfoundation.org).
Imad Shihab, Iraqi journalist, once driven underground because of his courageous reporting, is now out of hiding and working for the BBC Arabic channel as an occasional reporter.
Subina Shrestha, journalist and film-maker based in Nepal; she was nominated for a Rory Peck Award for her work undercover in Myanmar after cyclone Nargis hit in 2008.

John Simpson, world affairs editor and long-time senior correspondent at BBC News. He has reported from around 30 war zones, winning an International Emmy award for his work, and has written a number of books, most recently *Unreliable Sources* (Macmillan, 2010).
Jon Snow, chief presenter, Channel 4 News in the UK.
Peter Stevens, freelance newsman.
Jon Swain, journalist, writer and one-time recruit to the French Foreign Legion, has worked as a correspondent for the *Sunday Times* for 35 years. His best-selling *River of Time* (Heinemann, 1995) was the book that made me want to be a journalist.
Sherine Tadros, correspondent for Al Jazeera English, was one of only two international television journalists broadcasting from inside Gaza during the 2009 war.
Shelley Thakral, senior news producer for BBC World, who has covered Iraq, the Indonesian tsunami, the Pakistan earthquake, Benazir Bhutto's assassination and a dozen other disasters and war zones.
Nick Toksvig, former foreign editor at Sky News, and now a senior news editor for Al Jazeera English.
Giles Trendle, spent over 10 years in Beirut reporting for, among others, the *Economist*, the *Sunday Times*, CNN and CBS radio. He became an award-winning film-maker and now heads up a part of the programming department for Al Jazeera English.
Laura Tyson (née Conrad) worked for Save the Children and is a former senior media officer at the Department for International Development.
Terry Waite, CBE, conflict negotiator and former hostage.
Sebastian Walker, journalist for the *Baghdad Bulletin*, then Reuters and Al Jazeera; covered the Haiti earthquake in January 2010.
Sue Williams, a trained hostage negotiator since 1991 and former regular contributor to meetings of COBRA, the UK government's emergency taskforce, while head of the Hostage Crisis Unit at New Scotland Yard.
Vicki Woods, contributing editor at US *Vogue* and columnist for the *Daily Telegraph*; mother of my colleague and friend Sebastian Walker.

/FOREWORD BY RAGEH OMAAR

'How do you cope with it all? Weren't you terrified? What's the one thing you always pack? What do you do about food and electricity? Who or what protects you in a place like that?' Confronted with questions like these after each assignment in a conflict zone or amidst a humanitarian crisis, journalists, diplomats and relief workers face the dilemma of glossing over the truth, or trying to tell it but failing to do it justice. The answers either take quite a bit of rehearsal, or you just admit that some things are very difficult to convey to those who haven't experienced them.

This book gives a vivid glimpse into the experiences and thought processes of war correspondents as they try to answer these questions, but it also goes much further. It punctures a number of myths that have existed around the work of war reporters; and for me, one of the most dangerous myths is that with each experience of working in a dangerous or even just plain difficult place, you somehow build up layers of immunity until, after many such experiences, you can consider yourself (I can't stand the phrase) 'an old hand'. If only it were true. The list of highly experienced, dedicated and professional reporters who have been killed on assignment is every bit as tragically long as the one of young, inexperienced and dedicated journalists who go to war zones in search of a break into foreign news reporting. For war correspondents, the next assignment is always the first assignment.

Rosie's book is a great collection of essays, reflections, memories, anecdotes and self-counselling confessionals by reporters, many of them friends and colleagues of both of us. They are at times funny and revealing, and at other times both sobering and refreshing. But above all else they are useful. It's as though a bunch of war reporters, diplomats, travellers and aid workers have got together and collectively brewed their own extra-strength version of *Schott's Almanac*.

Most importantly, Rosie's book punctures the myth that being a war reporter means you have to be more than a mere mortal to do it, and dispels the idea that you need a bewildering array of skills to deal with a million and one situations. The truth, of course, is that people who cover conflicts and upheaval are not only human, but often find themselves unprepared for the experience. From what to pack to how to deal with checkpoints, from what to wear in the midst of a dispute between rival religious groups to the best phone to take, this book has all the facts you need, and much, much more.

It's the kind of book that will inform, educate and entertain, and you will find yourself coming back to it again and again. Enjoy.

/INTRODUCTION

I do not agree with people who say that if God wanted you to die this day, you will, no matter what precautions you take. I believe God gave me a brain to do my best to avoid getting into such situations. **Imad Shihab,** Iraqi journalist

SOMEONE YOU LOVE is heading off to a war zone and you are saying goodbye. You want to give them a last piece of advice. Something that will come to them when they most need it. A moment of clarity in all that mess.

'Don't be a hero,' you say. Or, 'Remember, nothing is worth your life.'

Trite. Not very useful and trite.

I want to say, 'Put me in your hand luggage and I'll protect you while you get on with whatever you need to do.' But I don't – either fit in their hand luggage or have the ability to fight off the enemy with one hand while holding onto them with the other.

So I usually hand them my lucky bracelet, which is a string of Buddhist prayer beads from northern India, though it could be mistaken for Muslim or Catholic beads, depending on the religion of the person who taps on your car window with their gun at a checkpoint. 'They've got me out of a couple of sticky situations before,' I nod reassuringly, waving the loved one goodbye. What I don't say is that I would be there with a pop-up emergency-room doctor and missile defence shield if I could.

But that just ain't enough.

My friend Sherine Tadros was heading to Gaza. She's a reporter for Al Jazeera English and had the hostile-environment training we all need in order for our insurance to work in conflict areas. But that was three years before.

'I can't remember how to do mouth-to-mouth, Rosie. Is it 30 breaths to two pumps?'

'The other way round...I think.' And she's gone, to Jerusalem and then Gaza, before I can find anything more helpful to tell her.

Her one-night visit to Gaza turns into a four-month stint and a 23-day war. She's deep into her first war zone, while me and my few meagre tips for survival are a time zone away.

There is a wealth of knowledge out there, but for some reason the vault of advice for people like Sherine and me was locked in other people's memories and experience. This book aims to tap into that knowledge and bring it to a wider audience – to people who find themselves running towards bombs rather than away, to those surrounded by disaster rather than watching it on TV. This book is for doctors, charity volunteers, NGO workers, engineers, government contractors, journalists, human rights lawyers and so many more of the world's curious and curiouser who find themselves drawn to these places.

It's not just visitors who have to adapt. There are millions of people living in the midst of what has become routine conflict – from Bogotá to the Baltimore backstreets, from downtown Mogadishu to uptown Johannesburg, the West Bank and Beirut. They have learnt to adapt.

Over a shot of tequila you hear, 'Of course everyone knows that's a sure-fire way to get yourself killed.'

The nervous laughs of others echo my thoughts – 'I didn't.'

People who return to war zones again and again listen to a story about someone who didn't survive, and their instincts tell them, 'That would never have happened to me. I would never have done that.' It's what they tell their friends and family. A person would have to be suicidal to put themselves in a situation where they thought they might die every day. For people like them it's a risk – but a calculated risk.

Hostile-environment courses fit you with some armour to help you make that calculation. But they are textbook while war is messy. You can never be prepared. You don't know how you will react until it happens, and then it might be too late.

Courses are particularly bad at preparing you for the mundane issues that can be just as deadly as guns and bombs in a war zone – boredom, hunger, lack of sex, too much sex, alcohol, lack of alcohol, getting fat and unfit, adrenalin rushes with nowhere to go.

What you *can* do is listen to as much advice as possible from people who have spent years dodging bullets and dancing through minefields.

Here's the disclaimer. You'll find while reading this book that different people's experiences can lead them to opposite conclusions. The tips are rarely what you might find in an average instruction booklet. They sometimes break rules and protocol, but they worked for the individuals in this book and they could work for you. Treat it as a guide to help you make the choices that are right for you.

I have dipped my toe into a semi-war zone, spending around six months in Basra after the Iraq war in 2003. I was 22 years old and straight out of Oxford University, earning the local rate of $10 a day as a Reuters stringer. How did I survive? I poached a translator off the British Army. He was the size of a tank, a body builder. When I refused to let him bring a gun inside the battle-broken house where we lived, he brought life-size posters of Arnold Schwarzenegger to scare off potential intruders. Armed with my blonde hair and a practised smile, I tried to remember everything I had picked up during a year working as a British Army officer after leaving school.

I learnt how to avoid getting killed by my mistakes. There were many. And some very narrow misses. If I'd had something like this book to flick through at night, it might have helped, just a little.

And finally, because attitudes, cultural values and even national borders change with time – dangerous places become top holiday destinations, just look at Vietnam – do send your own experiences, ideas and suggestions to me at howtoavoidbeing@gmail.com, or follow my Twitter feed, @Rosiepelican, for updates.

1/PLANNING, PREPARING AND ARRIVING

Never go in blind. Don't move until you know everything about where you are going. **Leith Mushtaq**, senior Al Jazeera cameraman

I WAS VERY UNPREPARED for my trip to Baghdad. For a start, I thought I was going for six weeks, but ended up staying for five and a half months. This was no holiday: there were things I should have sorted out before I left, but just didn't.

You need to take control of your own destiny. Don't go along for the ride. You need to have thought through all the risks before you go in, and made sure you have done everything possible to minimize them.

You need to keep your family or friends informed and get them involved in your preparations.

/BEFORE YOU LEAVE HOME

Here is a list of stuff you need to think about before you go, but I'm sure others will offer useful suggestions too.

Prepare your grab bag (see page 41).

Begin your medical preparations – ideally about six weeks before you're due to leave. You need to find out if you should be taking any pills or having any vaccinations. Go to your local doctor or a reputable travel website to find out which ones.

Dr Carl Hallam, MSF volunteer and former British Royal Marine doctor, advises: 'Get yourself vaccinated for everything possible. Don't die from something you could have been saved from. I was shocked to find workers in Aceh in Sumatra who had not been vaccinated for rabies. I think that's crazy. One little prick in the arm can save your life.'

Pack at least a month's supply of any prescription medication required. Carry it in your hand luggage.

Pop into the dentist for a check-up if you are going to be away for more than a few months.

Get decent medical insurance, making sure you have cover for your destination country, and check if your activities there require any extra cover. Make a separate note of how to contact the insurers in case of an emergency. Put your insurance contacts along with your medical history somewhere you can easily find it.

Prepare a medical kit (see page 103), or check your old one for 'best before' dates.

What kind of contraception would you like to take? Even if you think you won't need it, take some for your friends. Condoms are valuable things in dangerous places (see page 104).

Find out your team's pre-existing ailments and allergies. If you are travelling with a team of people, you need to know where they keep their medicine and how to administer it if they can't do so themselves. Everyone should write down their medical history and everyone should know where that is kept.

Choose your next of kin, and remember that whoever you choose needs to be asked rather than told. You need to give them all your details: medical history, insurance details, bank account numbers, where your will is kept (if you have one), the password to get into your safe...anything they'd need to know if something goes wrong. It isn't morbid to do this. Next of kin are a first port of call in an emergency, such as your kidnapping or arrest, not just in the event of death. Don't leave them unprepared.

In my experience, tragedies happen at the worst times: your primary contact – news editor, producer, partner – must have immediate and 24-hour access to your next of kin and medical details.

/ON THE WAY IN

You are at your most vulnerable on the way into a country because you are unfamiliar with the procedures, the language and the culture. Here are some useful tips.

Know who is picking you up. Get their phone number and call them in advance for advice on what you need to do to smooth your way into the country. (I remember asking my boss whether my pick-up would bring my body armour, and getting pretty nervous when he shrugged and said, 'You'll find out when you get to the airport.' My next stop was Baghdad.) Take the initiative and make sure you know all the answers before you go.

Arrange a meeting place and, if necessary, a code word to identify that the right person is picking you up. Get their phone number and give them yours.

Take all essentials in your hand luggage – some clothes, a washbag, valuables and your grab bag (see page 41).

Find someone friendly enough to be your temporary translator so they can help you through any problems on the journey. The person who smiles at you when you struggle to buy a ticket will usually work.

/ON THE WAY OUT

Leaving a country is another vulnerable time because you tend to let your guard down. It might sound strange, but you need to know your way out before you go in.

Call people who are already there and discover your options. You need to find out the following things:

What are the emergency and medical evacuation procedures (often shortened to 'medevac')? Your embassy will know. Your travel agent will also know. And, if you have one, your employer should know. If they don't, then make sure they do before you go.

> I've frequently found the embassy rather unhelpful and unreliable when it comes to planning for a possible evacuation. Both 'Medevac' and 'Emergency Evacuation' should be sorted out prior to deployment. It's always worth a call to the insurers to find out where the nearest airport would be if they had to come and get you. **Chris Cobb-Smith**, security expert

What are your alternative routes out if the road, railway, airport or sea route you arrived on is closed down? You need to be informed in order to make a decision if everything goes wrong.

/CARRYING CASH

On my first trip to Iraq with Al Jazeera I was asked to take a large amount of money with me because we needed to put a down-payment on our bureau. Suddenly I was a walking ATM for any criminal who managed to find out. It was a dangerous situation in which to be placed.

My friend Nick Toksvig, senior news editor for Al Jazeera English, recalls the perils of carrying huge wads of cash: 'The Iraq war of 1991 saw the old Iraqi currency fall prey to hyperinflation. Suitcases of bills were required to pay even for small things. Paying local fixers was like taking part in some massive Las Vegas poker tournament. Be careful not to flash the money at any stage.'

Don't tell anyone in your destination country that you will be carrying large amounts of cash. If it slips out at the wrong time to the wrong person, you will become a target.

When it comes to your daily cash, carry just enough for the day and try to spread it around your body. Also carry a credit card for emergencies.

Former EU and UN staff member Mary O'Shea has some good ideas for things you can do in case of a mugging: 'I have been robbed twice in my life. Once in the Paris Métro and once in an airport in Cameroon. In Paris it was a clever knife slit along the bottom of my bag in a crowded carriage. Presumably another bag was positioned underneath to catch my things. In Cameroon it was a good old-fashioned set-up – electricity cut, surrounded by men, etc. In terms of a confrontation, I would advise you to carry two wallets – one being a dummy wallet that can be handed over with a small amount of cash inside and some out-of-date cards.'

Keep around $1000 plus a few hundred in local currency in your grab bag at all times.

Cheque books, backed by a cheque card, can be used in many countries.

Be especially cautious at ATMs and coming out of banks and money exchange places.

Carry some low-denomination notes for tipping. Dollars will work for the first day or two until you can get your money changed. Store this money separately from your main cash so you are not flashing it every time you open your wallet.

/EMERGENCY NUMBERS

Always carry a list of contact numbers (sometimes known as a 'call sheet'). It should include your hotel, your embassy, the local hospital, the airport, police, colleagues, local contacts, your next of kin and whoever it is you are calling into back at base, wherever that may be. This information might be in your phone, but remember that you could lose your phone or it might be stolen.

/COMMUNICATION

Make sure you have a point person – someone back at base, be it a colleague from your company, a family member or friend, who will be responsible for noticing when you don't call in. But remember that *you* are responsible for making sure you can call. This means always taking your phone and charger, or a satellite phone if you are likely to be out of network coverage.

Give your point person some idea of your itinerary at all times and let them know if it changes.

Give your emergency numbers to your point person.

Ensure you have two working and charged methods of communication. It's a good idea to take your home mobile phone and a back-up (both with all numbers). I take my UK phone, a back-up UK phone, a cheap mobile for use with a local SIM card, and, when necessary, a satellite phone. If working with the media, ensure that the M4/BGAN can also be used as an alternative. Do make sure your SIM card has enough cash on it if it is pre-paid, and always carry a mobile phone charger: car chargers can be life-savers, as can wind-up phone chargers, or solar-powered ones that sit on top of your backpack. Also make sure everyone in your team is aware of how to work your communications system – whether it be a phone, e-mail, VHS two-way radio or a satellite mast – so that they can step in during emergencies.

> The call-in should be a rigorous procedure – according to area or threat – every three or six hours. In the event that the call is not received, the procedure should be equally rigorous: no call for an hour – alert people that there may be a problem; no call for two hours – start emergency procedures. **Chris Cobb-Smith**

Choose communications equipment you understand. Simple is usually best because a phone that has a hundred gadgets will simply eat up the battery. It could also get you into trouble as people might assume it is something more exciting than it is – some sort of new-fangled spy system or secret camera. It is less likely to get stolen if it's similar to what everyone else in the country has.

/YOUR PAPERWORK

Senior Al Jazeera cameraman Leith Mushtaq says it loud and clear: 'Get your papers in order and do not move until they are sorted.'

Your passport should be valid for at least six months and have at least three empty pages. Some countries are fussy about these things when it comes to giving out visas.

Check and double-check visa procedures and make sure you do it right. Getting it wrong can cause delay, cost money and get you into trouble.

If you have an Israeli stamp in your passport, you should get a second passport if possible. Many countries will not let you in with an Israeli stamp. If you are arrested or caught by kidnappers, it is the sort of thing that might get you into trouble, so it's not worth the risk. Ask Israeli border guards to stamp a separate piece of paper rather than your actual passport. Equally, if you are travelling to Israel, be careful about what stamps you have in your passport. Friends of mine with Iranian and Syrian stamps have had difficulties.

Use your least offensive passport, if you have more than one nationality, choosing the best one for your destination. Take the other passports with you, unless they might get you in trouble. In some countries a US or a UK passport could get you killed if found in your luggage, or they might be a 'Get out of Jail Free' card in the right hands. Take advice from the ground before you go in.

Get visas for neighbouring countries too if you think you might need to escape quickly.

Make multiple colour photocopies of your documents: passport, ID card (if you have one), driving licence (back and front), insurance papers, emergency numbers (including next of kin) and credit cards (back and front). Keep them in a separate place from the originals. Give copies to your team, your company and friends or family back home.

Pay your bills before you go so that you don't get stung with a late payment fee or, even worse, have your utilities cut off while you're away.

Check your credit cards will remain valid throughout your trip, and give your bank a call to let them know you will be travelling so that you don't get cut off for unusual purchases that look like fraud. They will put a note in the system.

Update your will or write one. I found it quite therapeutic, and others say they found it helped them to sleep better knowing it was written.

/LOCAL KNOWLEDGE

Your most important investment when working in a foreign place is in local knowledge. Think about this ahead of time. Who will be your friend and fixer on the ground? Have you done as much groundwork as possible ahead of your visit for making those key connections?

Find a trustworthy and knowledgeable local who is able and willing to look after you – and do it quickly. To do this you must understand the cultural divisions of the place you are going to. Your fixer has to be from the right part of town if he is going to be able to help you – and in Baghdad, for example, that could change from day to day. We hired four translators – one Shia, two Sunni and one a Christian Kurd. Most of the time they got on, but when things went wrong or events by one side damaged another, we discovered they hated each other more than they hated us, and that was a comfortable position to be in. But you must be aware of the rivalries and jealousies involved in running a team of people who have never worked together before.

By the time I got to Basra I knew I wanted less tension among my colleagues, so I chose a man who came from a tribe with mixed religious affiliations – a tribe that always seemed to be in the middle. I didn't necessarily get everything I needed done as quickly without other key connections, but at least our two-man team didn't offend people.

Read up about the local culture and don't stop until you touch down back at home again. Leith Mushtaq says: 'Books about the area are a key piece of your kit. You could read something the night before that saves your life.'

/LOCAL TRANSPORT

You need to think about how you are going to get around the country (see page 63) and make sure it is sorted from the beginning. Don't jump into a taxi on the first day only to find out it's been waiting for someone like you to put their hand up and volunteer for a kidnapping.

Laura McNaught, a freelance film-maker and founder of Sam's College Fund for children in the developing world, told me about a narrow escape she'd had as a result of too little forethought: 'It was my first morning in Baghdad. We were getting a lift into the Green Zone with an old Iraqi dude driving a red sports car. He's chatting merrily with his foot flat down on the gas when I see a Checkpoint – No Entry sign flash past us. I'm about to scream "Stop!" when a series of No Stopping signs whip past the window. Our driver won't slow down, so in desperation I grab my hair, press pass in hand, and hold it as far out of the tiny back window as I can. We're greeted by a far from impressed US army officer chastising, "We were about to open fire there, ma'am, if I hadn't seen your hair..."

'What I learnt...when Plan A doesn't work out, an improvised Plan B involving a driver you don't know is not acceptable. A good driver can save your life; a bad driver can get you killed. Never trust men driving sports cars.'

On the other hand, if you are absolutely certain that taxis are a safe way to travel, save money by using them rather than hiring a car and a driver.

/LANGUAGE ESSENTIALS

Take a basic book of the local language – the one that most people speak. It needs to show how it is written, not just how it sounds to your ear. That way you can point to phrases or words in the book if local people don't understand what you are saying. You need to learn how to say your name, your job and where you come from. If you will need to lie because your identity isn't especially popular in that country, please practise and practise that lie. In Iraq I always said I was Swedish until I realized that many Iraqis had escaped to Sweden under Saddam and I didn't know my rollmops from my pickled herring. Be careful who you lie to. Get your name, address and next-of-kin phone number written down somewhere in the local language as soon as you get there. And finally, if you have a medical condition, learn its name in the local language and how to ask for a hospital or whatever you need in order to make it better.

Marc DuBois, executive director of MSF–UK, offers some useful advice about getting to grips with the local language: 'Try to learn a few words as this sets you apart from other strangers. But a word of caution: I was mimicking the language of those around me in one African village. Most of the people there during the day were women, so I was using all the feminine greetings. It didn't work too well as a 6-foot 3-inch guy.'

This next piece of advice, from Samantha Bolton, former world head of press and campaigns for MSF, has been repeated again and again by people, Muslims and Christians alike: 'In Islamic areas make sure you know the words of the call to prayer, or at least one other full key paragraph from the Koran. It saved the life of one MSF kidnap victim, a Serbian aid worker from Sarajevo, when she was in Chechnya. She was tied up and about to be shot when she suddenly remembered the call to prayer, which she had heard so many times in her childhood. The kidnappers started arguing about how it was a sign from God and decided not to shoot her. She was eventually released.'

/TEAMWORK

The team you find yourself working with might have been put together by a human resources department who have chosen people for their individual strengths and qualities. On the other hand, it might be made up of a band of brothers and cousins, chosen because someone wanted to keep the money in the family. Or it could have been scrambled together as you were going out the door. There is no guaranteed way of assembling the best team. But there *is* a lot of groundwork you can do to put your team in the best possible position for working together.

Try to make contact with the rest of your team before you travel. If you get into trouble during your first tentative steps in the country, it is best if they know your name and the sound of your voice rather than just a flight number. And similarly, you need to know their names and who is in charge rather than just an address.

Get to know your team. There will likely be a clash of cultures, not least in the way they work. Some cultures like to work late in the night, leaving time for a three-hour siesta in the afternoon. Others like to have everything wrapped up by 5 p.m. in time for an early dinner and bed. In intense situations there will always be personality clashes, so it is a good idea to have ironed out some of your differences before arriving.

Get the best team to ensure success. This might not always be as simple as choosing the best. You need to choose the most appropriate. One MSF volunteer told me: 'In Yemen we chose not to bring Americans into the team because there was a high level of anti-American feeling.' This person also gave me some other interesting information: 'For the Yemenis their names give away their tribal history, but we outsiders had no clue when we were moving into different territory. You need to know someone locally who can tell you about it. One translator we hired was half-Ethiopian, half-Yemeni. That made him very low-ranking in society. He was our translator in the women's section, and that was sensitive enough to create problems. It became extremely difficult and we reached a point where we were risking his life, so we had to evacuate him from the area.'

Create systems where everyone is responsible for everyone else in case the real or natural leader is not around to tell you what to do. Nick Toksvig illustrated the importance of this with the following story: 'At one night-time checkpoint four of us were ordered out of the vehicle at gunpoint while the car was searched. We were then told we could go. I was driving and just before setting off realized only three of us were in the car. The fourth was having a slash nearby. Count them out and count them in.'

Create equality in your team. Even if people are treated differently outside the team, within the team they should be served the same food and sleep in the same beds. Apart from anything else, griping and whining about the hideous situation you are all in will bring a team together. If someone is receiving better treatment than others, it causes problems. Another point Nick Toksvig makes is: 'Make sure everyone has a flak jacket. The whole team should have the same level of security or insecurity.'

A team that eats together stays together. One MSF volunteer told me: 'When I first got to Yemen we used to eat our breakfast separately from our national staff – us with bread and chocolate spread, and them with the local food. But I decided it would be better for the team if we ate together. Then we discovered they had some amazing food. Honey and meat and their own type of pancake. It was delicious. Now, wherever I am, I seek out Yemeni restaurants, I love the food so much.'

Be upfront about pay. In my experience, transparency is the best way forward when it comes to money. If everyone knows what everyone else is getting and they choose to stay in the job, they cannot complain. It is a good idea to set aside some cash to use later as tips for the lower-paid workers in the team. It should be a surprise, not expected. Make that prize-giving transparent too and everyone will strive for that one goal.

Nick Toksvig discovered the hard way that paying team members should not be delegated: 'I was paying our translator in Kabul $150 per day, 50 of which was meant to go to the driver. In the end I found out that the translator was giving the driver only 10 bucks a day, and this was the guy driving us to some dodgy areas. Pay each person separately or they might get pissed off.'

Make sure everyone understands the point of your trip and agrees with the chosen method of getting there. When lives are in danger it is not fair to impose rules on people. Everyone needs to be in agreement. On the other hand, if someone is stubbornly refusing to toe the line, the team needs to make clear that it will not be tolerated.

Clearly define roles within a team so there is no clash of responsibility. When lives are at stake it is sometimes difficult to delegate, but it must happen or people will not be fully invested in the task and will begin to feel sidelined.

Sherine Tadros was one of the only international reporters inside Gaza during the war between Hamas and Israel in 2009. She was there for several months, just her and dozens of boys in a building stuck in the heart of the conflict. In the build-up, then during and after the war, they all witnessed more horror than I can ever imagine. She says one of the hardest things was learning to allow individuals their own response to a situation they were experiencing as a team. She drew a comparison with a near-tragedy from her childhood:

'When I was 15 years old, my baby cousin fell in the swimming pool and started drowning. My aunt froze, my mother screamed, my dad jumped into the pool. At a moment of extreme stress everyone has different ways of reacting and coping. You need to recognize that each of your colleagues is coping in their own way and respect their mechanism for dealing with stress, even if you don't think it's healthy or it's not what you are doing.

'During the Gaza war I had a lot of men around me; most were incredibly robotic, seeming almost unaffected by what was going on, or in some kind of bubble. I was the opposite. I felt every day of that war and the suffering around me, and I didn't hide my fear or distress. A lot of the time my colleagues would walk out of the room when I was emotional. I felt they were being unsympathetic and unkind. What I realized later was that I was disturbing their coping mechanism. Just as I needed to cry and feel to stay sane, they needed *not* to cry or feel at that moment.

'There is no right way to cope. In the end we are there to do a job, to perform, and you must do whatever you need to do in order to do your job. Respect that and don't take things personally.'

/EXIT PLAN

Understanding that everyone responds in different ways is important when it comes to planning for the worst.

Make an exit plan. Talk through the exit plan with your team as thoroughly and as early as possible. Everyone needs to know how they are going to exit the hotel or area where you are meeting, and should know each other's numbers, as well as those for the emergency people. Do you have a reliable driver who will pick up the phone at any time of night? Does everyone have his number? Does everyone know where everyone else is staying so they can go and find them if they are not responding to a phone call?

Don't assume that everyone understands the situation as well as you do. Make things crystal clear to those around you. Remember, everyone on the team has a responsibility to make sure the rest know what is going on.

Don't assume you always have the best ideas. Be prepared to listen and learn.

Check and double-check that everyone knows the risks and exactly what to do in a disaster because you might not be there to shout instructions.

Zeina Khodr, an Al Jazeera English correspondent, talked to me about looking after the weakest link: 'You need to have thought and talked about the worst eventualities. I was in Kandahar during the election in Afghanistan in 2009. We were well staffed. We had two local guys, but also two guys from our head office to help work the satellite. They had never been anywhere dangerous before and nobody briefed them about what to expect. They were terrified that the Taliban were going to take over the town. They would hear mortars and they would panic. We sat down with them and I explained what was going to go on. We talked through the worst-case scenarios – from suicide bombing, mortars landing and car bombs to major armed assault and take-over. Everyone in the team should know what's going on. That was the first time

I realized that we didn't have an exit plan. I had started to take it for granted that everyone knew what was going on. So we worked out a plan.

'I come from Lebanon. I grew up in a civil war. We don't think of insurance, we don't think of exit plans. We used to film fighting in the morning and go clubbing in the evening. It is only recently I have realized that we need to ensure the safety of the whole team – to look after the weakest link. You should have an exit plan before it happens: this is damned important.'

When thinking about your exit plan the place you decide to stay is key.

/WHERE TO STAY

I arrived at our house in Baghdad late one afternoon after a 16-hour drive from Amman. I had been told it was in a leafy Christian suburb, away from the hectic dangers of the capital's centre. We parked up. I was very excited about being able to pee after so many hours on the road. A white van drove slowly past on my right. On my left a man started running and the van sped up. Inside I could see men in black masks. Shots rang out, the man stopped running and fell to the ground. The van sped away and we ran to see the body of what we were told was the local booze shop owner. It was my first dead body, my first picture on my new camera. A man murdered in broad daylight on my quiet suburban street. We were, in fact, not very far from what became Sadr City – the heartland of the Shia militia run by a man most of the press were calling the 'renegade cleric', Moqtada al Sadr. The Mehdi army were our neighbours.

But we stayed in our chosen house, preferring to be amongst people who would protect us and our reputation as a 'paper of the people' than be sitting targets in a hotel. That was our decision and we made it work.

Choosing the right place to stay is the key to being able to sleep at night, eat well during the day, and open a window without fear of being burgled. It should be researched and thought about properly before you arrive, and constantly checked thereafter.

Check the location of the building and find out what key official buildings are nearby. Does the threat of their being targeted outweigh the usefulness of their proximity?

What kind of security is there at night? Outside lighting is a minimum, CCTV is good, but guards and a checkpoint are even better.

Who else is staying in the building? There are no hard and fast rules about who the ideal occupants are. If there is no one at breakfast and lots of shady-looking businessmen making deals at night, you probably want to avoid it. If it is a well-known hang-out for one side or another during a war, and therefore a potential target, you should probably avoid it. Strange as it sounds, I was once told that any hotel where prostitutes feel safe to hang out is often a safe one...for women at least.

Where are the nearest police station and hospital? You need to know how to get to both these places, so find out where they are and drive the route. Being close to a police station is almost always a good idea – unless the police are part of the problem.

Ask about the local area. Find out if it is known for being safe. If it isn't, find out what the locals do to avoid trouble. It might mean not travelling at night or knowing which streets to avoid on your morning jog.

Check room security. The locks on the doors and windows need to be secure.

Avoid having a room on the ground floor – it is the most easily burgled. And avoid any rooms with balconies that can be reached from the ground.

Never let anyone know where your room is. If you're staying in a hotel, meet visitors in the lobby. Tell the desk that you are staying in a different room – the one where your security man is staying.

Choose a room for its proximity to an emergency exit. How close is the fire escape? Check the route for padlocks and work out a way to avoid them.

For the sake of your sanity there are several things you can do to improve your day-to-day life...

Nick Toksvig says, 'It's a good idea to hire extra rooms for offices and equipment. Otherwise some poor person's room will become the de facto office till the wee hours of the morning, everyone smoking and drinking.'

Mary O'Shea and I originally met on a sweaty floor mat under a tent near Timbuktu, both of us doubled over with food poisoning, but that's another story. She now works as an election observer, moving hotel every two months all year round. When choosing a room, she recommends: 'Never higher than the third floor. Soviet-manufactured fire engines in developing countries do not reach higher than this. Never ever stay in a room with bars on the window (tricky in south Asia). Avoid any room with windows facing onto the street or the hotel entrance. I was once advised never to get into a lift with anyone else. This is nearly impossible, however. Ideally, stay on the outskirts of a town so that you are not trapped if there are street protests.'

My personal phobia in hotel rooms is cockroaches. I once found five on my bed in a shockingly bad hotel in southern Nepal. The whole town was on an electricity blackout, and as I crunched across the floor in flip-flops, my head-torch flicked down from my crawling bed to the shiny, wriggling black carpet around my feet. I hadn't slept for a couple of days, so I took two sarongs from my bag, swept the roaches off my pillow and made myself a stripy head-to-toe shroud to keep 'em out till morning. Next time my grumpy correspondent recommended a hotel, I pretended I couldn't hear him. Sarongs are a key piece of kit.

In her years spent filming dodgy and dangerous diseases in the outback of the Democratic Republic of Congo, Filipino slums and all sorts of other glamorous locations, Laura McNaught has picked up some key things to avoid. 'Make sure you get a room that is away from the entrance, the restaurant, the bar, the pool, the barking dogs, the Chinese take-away, the nightclub next door... Alternatively, bring earplugs.'

Other great tips from Laura include: 'Bring a T-shirt that can double up as a second, protective pillowcase. Bring a silk sleeping bag and never sleep naked, no matter how hot it is.' She also notes: 'A mini bottle of Cif goes further than alcohol handwash when you're cleaning the doorknobs, light switches and phone.' It's wise to do this if you're in an area where sickness is spreading as the cleaners rarely remember to do it.

My colleague and friend Jane Dutton is a genius of security tricks designed to thwart thieving fingers. Brought up in Johannesburg and weaned as CNN's 'Hotspots' girl, parachuting into 35 countries a year, she can spot potential hazards a mile off. She has even persuaded me to travel with a suitcase that padlocks shut these days. When it comes to hotel rooms these are her tips:

'Before you leave the room always check that your windows are locked, and double-lock the door on the way out. If there is no safe, hide valuable or important things around the room in the least obvious places. Put them in your shoes, in your pants, in your dirty washing. Zip and lock your bag with your stuff still inside to act as a temporary safe.'

In some places you will have little choice about where you can stay. Even if you are not in a war zone, it can still feel like one if there is a high enough crime rate. In those cases, you must take every precaution to make your house secure. Change your locks and take advice from neighbours. Don't use the first security firm that knocks on your door.

Nick Toksvig points out that there are many times when it is a good idea to have a different 'safe house' to return to in case something goes wrong. 'Covering the volcano eruption on the island of Montserrat, I rented two houses, with the second closer to the "safe" zone. It meant we could move our operation quickly if things got out of control close to the mountain. Another time, during Israel's war on Lebanon in 2006, we had local hotel accommodation, but also a safe house down by the harbour in case things got heavy and the Israelis invaded.'

> I always carry a simple little wooden wedge. Just slide it under the door as an additional lock: the harder the door is forced, the more it jams. And remember, your 'Do Not Disturb' sign is a simple deterrent. I'd much rather a grubby room than some cleaner snooping around my belongings.
> **Chris Cobb-Smith**

/SAFE ROOM

I first met Chris Cobb-Smith in a favourite London pub with the mad but fantastic BBC reporter John Sweeney. We were investigating the deaths of six British 'Red Caps' (military policemen) during a riot in southern Iraq. I was ex-army and so was Chris, an artilleryman from the 29 Commando regiment. After working in Kosovo as a weapons inspector, he founded Chiron Resources, which provides specialist security support to news and documentary teams reporting from war zones. We have been bumping into each other on various jobs ever since. Name a conflict or disaster and you will find Chris was a visitor.

He says that in addition to having a safe house, a 'safe room' should be prepared in advance – somewhere to go when evacuation is impossible:

'Offices, bureaux and accommodation in high-risk areas should have a safe room – a secured area that could be used as a last resort for sanctuary in the event of an attack or attempted abduction. The aim of a safe room is to provide a hardened sanctuary that will at least buy additional time until help arrives, and may even act as a deterrent to an aggressor.

'Ideally, the safe room should not have any outside walls, be of substantial construction and have a solid and securable door. If the room does have windows, external or internal, they should be armoured. The room should also have power and, ideally, be equipped with a panic button connected to the agency responsible for responding to an emergency. A safe room can be specially constructed, or created by enhancing a bathroom or possibly the space under the stairs.

'It is essential that there is a reliable quick-response force capable of responding to any emergency calls for assistance. Whoever that security agency is – police, army or private contractor – it should conduct a thorough survey of the facility and be shown the exact location of the safe room so their procedures can be comprehensively planned.'

Chris says the room must contain the following:

- At least two methods of communication – a telephone of some sort (landline, mobile or satellite) and walkie-talkies or two-way VHS radio if possible. Note that satellite phones and some radios will not work inside, so antennas will need to be 'remoted' to the outside to maintain a strong signal.
- A good supply of water.
- Non-perishable food (tins, dried fruit, etc.).
- Medical pack.
- Radio – for news, information and entertainment.
- Sleeping bags and blankets.
- Fire-fighting equipment.
- Personal protective equipment: body armour, helmets, eye-protection and gas masks.
- Reading material.
- Torches and spare batteries.
- Bucket and tissues in case you are there longer than expected, or someone gets caught short.

/THE LAW OF THE LAND

> Never go in blind. Don't move until you know everything about where you are going. **Leith Mushtaq**

Getting to know your destination starts with understanding the culture, but then you have to learn the laws of the country. And finally, there's international law.

You probably break laws every day where you are right now. I do. I have stuffed my pockets full of bacon on flights back to Doha on more than one occasion. I drive far too fast, and badly. And I drink when I shouldn't. Not proud, not clever.

These are rules I reckon I can get away with most of the time in a place where the rules are relatively stable. In a less forgiving place – one where the rules are changing all the time, or where there are none at all – breaking those rules could get you chucked in jail for some time, or even executed.

If there are any rules at all in a war zone, they are often made up on the spot. Wherever you are going, one of the most important things you need to do in preparation for arrival is to get a basic grasp of any awkward laws. Something as simple as failing to carry your correct ID card around can be an excuse for authorities to slam you in jail just to keep you 'out of trouble' for a while.

Tom Hudson has done many an extra hour's stag (watch) for me while I slept my watch out in the frozen woods during army training. We were in the same troop at Sandhurst, and he shared his sleeping bag with me when mine was wet. He used to work as a lawyer for Linklaters, and is now the legal counsel for a Middle East security company that provides services in Iraq, Afghanistan and other 'hostile' environments. He offers the following expert advice.

/HOW TO AVOID BREAKING THE LAW IN A WAR ZONE

War zones, by definition, can seem entirely lawless, so describing the legal position might seem hypothetical at best. However, there is a complex matrix of laws that might apply to any war zone. Understanding these is a surprisingly difficult but key step.

The 'law of war' is considered a part of public international law. It's a broad body of law concerning everything from acceptable justifications to engage in war (*jus ad bellum*) to the limits of acceptable wartime conduct (*jus in bello*). Humanitarian law plays its part. And, as 'modern' warfare evolves, the convergence and overlap with criminal law and civil law becomes more apparent.

Given the varied nature of people's roles, territories and actions, the information here will not be a comprehensive guide as to what one can and can't do. But it should get you asking the right sort of questions and give some pointers as to what law might apply to you.

Military personnel

If you are in the military, you will be well aware of military law. Taking the position of British soldiers as an example, the Military Criminal Justice System is seen as an essential part of the British Army, both at home and abroad. The Adjutant General has said that 'it often serves where there is no law or where UK standards of law and justice are not applied. Self-regulation is therefore a prerequisite for military operations.'

The overview provided by the Armed Forces Bill Team serves as a useful summary of the legal position for the British military in war zones: 'UK courts cannot generally try offences which are committed outside the UK. The Service system of law ensures that, as far as possible, Service personnel are dealt with by a familiar system if they commit an offence when serving overseas. They can expect a consistent and fair hearing wherever they find themselves. Without such a system, they would be dealt with under the law of the country in which they are serving or escape justice altogether. At a practical level this means that they are dealt with in a language they understand. They are also dealt with fairly by a system judged to be fully compliant with the European Convention on Human Rights (ECHR).'

A soldier will have to be cognisant of his position under military law in addition to his position under civilian law.

In September 2009, Steven Green, accused of raping and murdering an Iraqi girl, became the first former soldier to be prosecuted in the United States for crimes committed overseas. Had he been sentenced to execution, he would have been the first American soldier ever tried for war crimes in a civilian court to receive that sentence, but he was given life imprisonment instead.

Government contractors

Aside from the military, much public attention has focused on armed private security contractors. The legal treatment of the Blackwater contractors who were accused of killing 17 Iraqis in Baghdad's Nisour Square in September 2007 caused an international media storm.

According to a December 2009 report to Congress, the US Department of Defense (DoD) workforce in Iraq and Afghanistan comprises roughly comparable numbers of contractors (218,000) and uniformed personnel (195,000). But it is estimated that less than 10 per cent are security contractors, and the rest are doing just ordinary jobs, working as electricians, engineers, canteen staff and suchlike.

Paul Bremer, head of the Coalition Provisional Authority, controversially signed Coalition Provisional Authority Order 17, which stated that 'Contractors shall not be subject to Iraqi laws or regulations in matters relating to the terms and conditions of their Contracts.' It provided effective 'immunity' for contractors in the eyes of the Iraqis for them to do what they wanted.

In late 2008 a new law was approved by the Iraqi government, and Bush's announcement of it was made more famous by a displeased Iraqi journalist throwing a shoe at him. It was agreed that 'Iraq shall have the primary right to exercise jurisdiction over United States contractors and United States contractor employees', so US contractors working for US forces would be subject to Iraqi criminal law. If US forces committed 'major premeditated felonies' while off duty and off base, they would be subject to the still undecided procedures laid out by a joint US–Iraq committee. However, the agreement is not totally clear and the immunity question is still being talked about.

Contractors are also subject to international laws, such as the Geneva Convention. This refers to 'supply contractors', which could include defence and private military contractors. Provided they have a valid identity card issued by the armed forces that they accompany, they are entitled to be treated as prisoners of war if captured. If they are found to be mercenaries, they are unlawful combatants and lose the right to prisoner of war status. This means that US contractors to the coalition forces in Iraq are subject to three levels of law – international, US and Iraqi.

Other commercial companies

There are many difficult aspects to operating a commercial company in a war zone. Among those that foreign nationals working for them should be aware of are the international anti-corruption measures, which will still be applicable to them. Perhaps the best known, thanks to rigorous enforcement and hefty fines, is the US Foreign Corrupt Practices Act (FCPA), but there are also measures laid down by the Organization for Economic Cooperation and Development (OECD) and UN conventions. The UK Bribery Act (in effect since April 2010) is an interesting development as the UK has been relatively poor at investigating and prosecuting corruption offences in the past. This new law is wider in scope than the piecemeal ones it replaced, and it has extra-territorial reach.

Some of the red flags one should look out for as an employee working for commercial companies are requests for cash payments, requests for payments to third parties or offshore, requests for hospitality for government officials, or in fact any request if you are in a country with a reputation for corruption. The penalties can be quite substantial. Under the new British Act, for example, individuals guilty of one of the principal offences are liable on conviction to imprisonment for up to 10 years, or a fine, or both. If a deal 'smells wrong', it probably is, so it's best to seek legal advice.

Journalists

In areas of conflict journalists are considered civilians under Additional Protocol I of the Geneva Conventions, provided they do not do anything or behave in any way that might compromise this status, such as directly helping a war, bearing arms or spying. Every journalist should ensure that they are not put in a compromising situation in relation to any of these things. A deliberate attack on a journalist that causes death or serious physical injury is a major breach of this Protocol and deemed a war crime.

Journalists should also note in what capacity they are travelling to a country in terms of Employment Law. Are they considered an employee or are they freelancing? Some media corporations have been criticized for preferring freelancers in order to save money or abdicate themselves of legal responsibility.

Medics

The First Geneva Convention of 1864 established that a distinctive emblem should be worn by medical personnel on the field of battle as an indication of their humanitarian mission and their neutral status. This is still the case today, and whether you're wearing the Red Cross or the Red Crescent, make sure it's visible to afford yourself this protection.

And a final thought from Tom… 'Before travelling to any hostile environment, spare some thought for your legal position there and what laws apply. Remember, though, that the "rule of law" is often the very thing being fought for, so don't expect it always to be upheld.'

/WHEN TO LEAVE

James Brandon, a journalist who was kidnapped in Iraq in 2004, offers the following advice: 'Deciding when to leave a war zone is as important as deciding when to arrive. Many people are killed or kidnapped because they stay too long. Typically, people arrive in war zones feeling wary, suspicious and paranoid. In many cases, however, they become more relaxed the longer they are there. Danger becomes so omnipresent that people sometimes become fatalistic ("Everybody dies one day" is a typical refrain you hear in war zones). For example, a person new to a war zone might estimate the chances of being killed while doing such-and-such activity and decide that if the odds of getting killed are more than 1–1000, they won't do it. But after a few months they might say that a 1–50 chance of being killed on a particular mission is "do-able". A few more months, however, and a 50:50 chance of being killed starts to look like playable odds. That's when it's time to leave.'

It might seem strange to plan your exit before you arrive, but for the sake of friends, family and your own sanity, it is a very good idea.

/GRAB BAG

Also known as a 'sac d'evac' or 'crash bag', this is the bag you will grab when the bombs are raining down and you head to a bomb shelter. It is the *only* thing you will have with you if you are evacuated in a rush. It is the one bag you will put in a safe or a friend's hotel room if you think someone uninvited might be coming into yours when you pop out for dinner later.

Nick Toksvig recalls how important this bag can be: 'During the Russia–Georgia conflict, a car with four Sky News people was stopped by armed men. They were forced out and the car was stolen. Inside was their luggage and camera equipment. One guy had got out with his shoulder bag still around his shoulders. It contained money, passport and water. It got them out of there.'

A grab bag is not optional. Everybody needs one. It can be as small as a bum bag, but it had better be bloody good. The stuff you put in there can save your life.

YOUR GRAB BAG MUST INCLUDE...

/ Passport(s)

/ Means of communication, fully charged and ready to go, plus charger. There are now some great solar-powered phones on the market.

/ Emergency contact list

/ Pocket knife – make sure you take it out of your hand luggage at airports or security will take it off you. I have lost about 10 this way.

/ Airline tickets

/ Cash – $1000 plus several hundred dollars-worth of local money

/ Credit cards

/ Water for a day

/ Torch – I find head-torches the most useful for day-to-day use

/ Medical kit, including all your prescription medicines

/ Food – some dried food, such as granola bars and raisins, and some tinned food, in tins that don't need a tin opener

/ Matches and/or a lighter – buy these at your destination, and discard before boarding any planes.

You should check your grab bag every evening before you go to bed. You should put chargers and passports straight back into their assigned pocket the moment you have used them. You might also decide to put a packet or two of cigarettes in there, or a book; you'll have your own priorities.

I went into Baghdad with a backpack full of ugly baggy clothes, a book about Iraq by Dilip Hiro, a lot of tampons, a very good Berlitz Arabic phrasebook, a head-torch, a corkscrew/bottle opener (I never travel anywhere without a corkscrew) and a couple of hundred dollars. They all came in useful at one time or another. Having been in the army, I am pretty good at packing a lot into a small space.

I thought I was well prepared, but if I had thought for a bit longer, there was so much more I could have done to help my journey. It is better to carry more than less if you can. The most experienced people in war zones tend to come with a house-load of stuff and then dump it all in an emergency. Of course, the amount you take also depends on your mode of transport. The not-so-funny stories I have heard about people getting killed on the way to buy a razor, or getting pregnant because all the local condoms were out of date should be a lesson to all.

Note: Whether you are a girl or a boy, there are some quick lessons to learn about underwear under fire. You need to be able to get up and go straight from your bed to the fire escape if necessary. Leave your posh pants at home. Stefanie Dekker, an Al Jazeera English producer, remembers: 'I was in Kurdistan and in most of the hotels guys do the laundry. I put all my pretty G-strings in the laundry and came back to my room to see them lined up, drying on my windowsill. Then two guys arrived at my door, one of them from the laundry, big grins on their faces: "Anything else you need, madam?" It felt very awkward. Now I travel with only big pants.'

Optional extras

On top of the essentials there are some other bits and bobs I always take along on any trip to make life a little easier:

- Baby wipes – several different brands so that no particular smell becomes associated with a bad time. If that happens, it will limit your choices next time.
- Couple of sarongs – as quick-dry towels, emergency headscarves, skirts (manly ones too, as per David Beckham), dresses, cover-ups, pillows, curtains, extra blankets, useful medical equipment for bandaging and tying on splints, and a crucial layer between you and dirty, smelly hotel sheets when you need one.
- Hot-water bottle – can be your best friend in a cold climate. Boil up your water, wait 30 seconds, then pour it into the hot-water bottle. When you wake up in the

morning you have water that is safe to drink and at body temperature rather than freezing cold.
- Space blanket – useful to stay warm, and the orange-gold side can be used as a signal (that colour doesn't occur naturally in the wilderness). Plus, they fold to the size of a hankie.

And, depending on where you are travelling, some other useful things that can be difficult to find in a hurry should also go in your bag:

- Tin opener
- Duct tape
- String
- Bin bags
- Puritabs/water sterilizing tablets
- Toilet paper
- Vaseline or the cure-all Australian remedy Lucas' Pawpaw Treatment
- Tweezers
- Eyedrops
- Soap
- Candles
- Washing liquid
- Sewing needles (of different sizes) and thread

Tips from the top

There are plenty of other optional extras, not so much for your grab bag, but equally important for remaining safe and sane.

'Good pair of sunglasses.' **Shelley Thakral**, senior producer, BBC World

'Books – lots of them. Also cigars and good whisky.' **John Simpson**, world affairs editor, BBC News

'iPod – being able to take photos of family and music on my travels has changed my life.' **Jon Snow**, chief news presenter, Channel 4

'Booze – great for winding down after a day of human suffering and hopelessness. Also Vegemite – it makes anything taste better.' **Laura Tyson**, former media officer, Department for International Development

'Plenty of aspirin and painkillers.' **Subina Shrestha**, journalist and film-maker

'Remaining professional-looking can be a struggle when there is little water to wash with for weeks on end. I usually take dry shampoo with me. It is a powder spray, which absorbs all the dirt and gives your hairdo a little extra oomph. It's like a shower in a can!' **Stefanie Dekker**, Al Jazeera English producer

'Cheque book. This works a treat with the *hawala* system [an informal money-loaning system based on honour and found mainly in the Arab world]. Go to a money-changer and write a cheque – just the sterling amount and a signature are required; the payee and date are left blank – and you are given the equivalent in US dollars. The system works across south Asia and much of the Arabic world.' **Ian Mackinnon**, freelance journalist

'Penicillin, two passports and a means of communication.' **James Brabazon**, journalist and documentary film-maker

'Sat nav and maps, but leave the sat nav behind if you are off to somewhere sensitive. Small generator that produces 220 volts of electricity. Gifts to win people over: chocolate is great for kids, while small solar-powered panels to charge mobiles are cheap and priceless to adults. Camelbak-style water container. Torches with plenty of batteries for when the electricity is down.' **Leith Mushtaq**, senior Al Jazeera cameraman

'Condoms, peanuts, water-bottle, torch, long- and short-sleeved shirts, anti-mosquito repellent, a small bottle of gin or vodka that will not get spotted in a Muslim country where booze is forbidden. Vodka in an IV bag is the best!' **Monique Nagelkerke**, MSF head of mission

'Good book and a head-torch to read it by. Sleeping mat and a sleeping bag as it can get very cold at night.' **Tim Albone**, journalist

'Music on my iPhone, shortwave radio, snakebite kit (in the wilds of Southeast Asia), and a US army escape kit (in Vietnam).' **Jon Swain**, journalist and author

'Army tourniquet, clean needle, antiseptic, water purification tablets and portable chess set.' **Sebastian Junger**, journalist and author

2/AVOIDING MISUNDERSTANDING

There is no such thing as an enemy. You are independent in a war zone: you should be able to deal with everyone and everything. Understand that the people outside are just men and women. How are they thinking? What part of them can you understand? In the end they are all human. You need to find the kernel of humanity. **Leith Mushtaq**

AT THE RISK OF SOUNDING LIKE a beauty pageant contestant, if everyone could approach the unfamiliar with the same sensitivity and lack of preconceived judgement as Leith Mushtaq, a world of violence and death could be avoided.

Unfortunately, when two people meet they bring their baggage with them – fears and notions of otherness that lead to dangerous misunderstanding. All we, as visitors, can do is to try to bridge the canyon of difference. There are many different ways to do that, from speech to looks and body language.

John Simpson, the BBC correspondent who has sat on many a front line, says you always need to retain your 'self'. 'Act naturally, don't allow yourself to be scared; be friendly, look people in the eye and never, ever try to pretend you're not who you are.'

Kamal Hyder has spent years working as a journalist in the tribal lands of Pakistan and Afghanistan. His reports are as popular with the Taliban as they are with the Pakistani Army. He advocates learning how to blend in with people in any way you can. 'Even if you can't assimilate, you can learn how to treat people, show respect for their culture. You should aim for them to respect you as much as you respect them. Engage them on their level.'

/TO BLEND IN OR NOT?

There are two very different schools of thought about blending in, and both sides feel equally strongly.

I spent a lot of time in Iraq struggling with my *abia*, a long black robe that is worn with a headscarf. Initially, I wore it to travel when visiting scary places in town, and to funerals, but while other girls could go through an assault course in their headscarves, mine would not stay on. It was like the material and my head were magnetized at polar opposites. Wearing this outfit just meant that people looked twice and often came up to me and asked who I was – the last thing I wanted. I quickly learnt that it was never going to help me – a blonde-haired, blue-eyed girl – blend in.

A friend of mine, however, was able to wander freely around Baghdad without anyone batting an eyelid because she had brown eyes and brown hair. She had also perfected the art of dressing to blend in – carrying only plastic bags, never a smart laptop case. She wore local clothes, bought on arrival, and, most importantly, local shoes, and went quietly about her business. Our Muslim translators thought it was fantastic. The Christian was furious.

I ended up wearing the *abia* only out of respect, never for disguise. If I was meeting a member of the Badr Brigade – the Shia armed group who clashed with the Mehdi army just after I left town – I would wear an *abia* so that he was able to talk to me. If I was meeting a recently bereaved family, I would cover my head to show I understood their values. They would often tell me to take it off. But they knew I was willing to try upholding their culture, even if my efforts didn't work very well.

I think I was saved more than once by people wanting to protect me because I stood out. As one of the only blondes in Basra – the only one I ever saw – and a journalist who was listening to their stories, I was apparently dubbed 'the angel' by some people in the town. They would bang on the ice-cream parlour window, where I chose to interview all the most dangerous people I met, to let me know if trouble was coming. They would stand in front of my car window if we got stuck in a crowd so that no one would see who was inside. They would run into the Internet café I used every day and tell my translator when we needed to move on.

Then there was the British Army – the only people who knew where I lived in town. When I was with them I had to blend in too. I needed to be respectful, smart and familiar – I needed them to trust me. It was a difficult balance, especially given the complete lack of running water during my whole stay in Basra. A daily 'baby wipe shower' just didn't cut it.

My advice would be that if you *can* blend in, then try to do so, especially for one-off encounters, such as checkpoints, or travelling on public transport. But if you are staying for a while, blend in only out of respect for the local culture, not to hide. In the long run you will be found out.

Others have different advice. James Brandon was in Iraq and Yemen for several years and found going undercover worked best for him. 'The number one rule is to try to blend in with the locals. Wear a cheap shirt. Grow a beard. Go to a local barber's and demand the latest style. If locals don't wear seatbelts, then you shouldn't either. The exception is footwear. Even if most locals wear sandals, you should stick to trainers (in a local fashion of course) because if people start shooting, you might need to run. Unless you can run in sandals, don't wear them.

'Remember that disguises that work in one part of the world won't work in another. Heading up into northern Yemen to report on the civil war in late 2004 with an American journalist, I travelled in a battered pick-up truck with some sympathetic Yemenis. The other journalist and myself were dressed in the traditional Yemeni outfit of long grey *thoab* and Arab-style headdress, plus a belt and traditional curved tribal dagger. To complete the image, we chewed *qat*, the local drug beloved by Yemenis. As we neared our destination, we were flagged down in a stretch of barren, volcanic desert by two tribesmen carrying AK-47s. They asked for a lift and we were happy to oblige – two armed men in the back of our truck only added to our authenticity. As a result, we made it through over a dozen army checkpoints to get into this remote region declared strictly off-limits to foreigners. We were later arrested and thrown into prison, but that's a different story.'

If you are in a location as part of a team, you must realize that the actions of one individual could harm the whole group, so you should lay down some rules. One (female) MSF volunteer explained to me how they went about it in Yemen during the battle between government forces and tribes in the north in 2007. Peace talks were under way, but it was very tense and one of the hardest places to work as an outsider. The tribal, social and religious divisions are incredibly complex in Yemen. Everyone carries weapons.

'We established a strict dress code…to find a way to be respected by the tribal leaders and respect their culture at the same time. It is a completely patriarchal society. Women are not considered to have any value. If we looked just like the Yemeni women, we would be dismissed immediately, so we went halfway – we covered our heads. We wore long shirts down to our knees and over our trousers. We also avoided flashy colours. Once we had established what we thought was sensible, we wrote a behaviour code and no one was allowed into the country to work with MSF unless they agreed first to stick to it. It risked putting us in danger if they stood out or gave the group a bad name. No NGOs had worked in the area before us, so we decided to go low profile in the beginning. Our logo would not have offered us any protection.

'When we were at home we had an understanding that we could do what we wanted inside our own four walls. We didn't cover our heads. We wore T-shirts. And if people didn't like it, they could leave. People respected that. We had a complete ban on alcohol. There was zero tolerance on that. And if you had a tattoo, you had to keep that covered. It is an extreme culture.'

Clothes are a uniform, and every choice you make is a sartorial sign of your tribe, whether it be a teenage traveller, an off-duty security guard or a group that is friendly to the Taliban. In Pakistan a millinery mistake could get you into trouble.

Kamal Hyder advises: 'Be aware of the signals given by your clothes. In tribal areas I often carry several different types of turbans and hats, known locally as *pakols*. When you cross front lines you have to know which one to wear. In some areas the other side will just shoot at you if you are wearing the wrong one.

'Foreigners should try to blend in too. They shouldn't feel silly. There are many European-looking people in Afghanistan and Pakistan. Once upon a time, it didn't matter what you wore. Many of these places used to be very hospitable to foreigners wandering around in T-shirts and trousers (never shorts). But because of the "War on Terror" the attitude has changed and you have to understand that. Xenophobia has crept into what used to be the easy-going hippy trail.

'When I first started working in the tribal areas of Pakistan I was clean-shaven. I stuck out like a sore thumb. I was an outsider. Many people asked me why I didn't have a beard given that I was speaking their language. So I grew one and started to blend into the local population.'

Kamal is now famous for his beard. It used to have its own fan club on Facebook.

Zeina Khodr has been working in dangerous places as a journalist for nearly 20 years. She says you should be careful of trying to 'be' one of the locals. A nod of respect towards their culture should be the aim:

'Your "look" is important...there is no way to look exactly like the locals. It should be a balance. You don't want to appear as if you are trying to be one of them; you might be taken for a spy. Don't overdo it. I usually buy something from the local market. I want to look like I am a foreigner showing respect for the local customs. So while I might use a *burka* to travel in disguise, I can't work in one because that would be showing a lack of respect to their local culture.'

I have worked with Sebastian Walker my whole career in one way or another. From the *Baghdad Bulletin* to Reuters in Iraq through to Al Jazeera, where he is now a star reporter, flying from his base in Washington DC out to one story or another. An open and unthreatening approach has won him many friends out of potential enemies. In Iraq his wide eyes and brown hair helped him get by as a young whippersnapper swimming around in a bowlful of sharks. He describes our first encounter as follows:

'By late 2003, with the insurgency raging, there were only two field-based Western stringers working for the wire agencies in post-invasion Iraq. One was the author of this book, in Basra, and the other was me, in Mosul. Neither of us spoke Arabic, and the day job consisted of taxi rides around two cities quickly spiralling out of control, stopping frequently to interview witnesses at the scene of car bomb explosions, riots, attacks on coalition soldiers, and so forth. I have no idea how the blue-eyed, blonde-haired, young British girl got back in one piece.

'As for me, the strategy was to try to blend in. As ridiculous as that sounds, it was the advice I was given by an Iraqi colleague while mulling the offer of $200 a month plus expenses and a satellite phone. "If you want to survive as an *ejnebi* [foreigner] in Mosul for six months, start wearing clothes like mine," he advised. So I went to Baghdad's second-hand clothes market and purchased several nondescript nylon shirts, cheap trousers and some faux-leather shoes. As I checked into Mosul's finest budget hotel, the manager peered over the counter and studied me carefully: "Kurdish?"

'Over the next few months, as Iraq's second city descended into violence, with death squads cruising the city in search of anyone collaborating with the occupation, the only occasions anyone gave me a second look was when I opened my mouth. Traipsing the streets with translator in tow, we looked like a pair of unsuccessful Iraqi businessmen. As we pushed our way through crowds thronging the scene of one of the many US military slayings I witnessed while down there, I took notes while he did the talking.

'A low profile isn't always going to be possible. But for a lone stringer living in a flat in Mosul and filing text reports for Reuters from Internet cafés over the winter of 2003, managing to avoid attention – at first glance at least – was the difference between being able to do my job, or ending up like Nicholas Berg, who was staying at my hotel before being kidnapped and then apparently beheaded live on the Internet. It was four months before I started being followed and had to leave town... I've still got those awful clothes in my wardrobe at home.'

/BODY LANGUAGE

If you want to blend in, it starts and ends with an integral understanding of the local body language, down to the smallest detail. As Tom Coghlan, defence correspondent for *The Times*, told me: 'Southern Afghans don't cross their arms, nor do they move their hands and bodies when they are talking. These they regard as a peculiar Western sort of acting. So if you are being Afghan, don't do it either. Afghans also walk at half the pace of Europeans. Being shy and modest is quite normal, so looking at the ground is fine if you don't want to be engaged.'

Doing what the locals do will often mean going against your instincts. James Brandon told me: 'People in developing world war zones frequently look as if they have seen it all before. If you can mimic this quality, when necessary, it will increase your chances of staying alive. If you are walking down a street and see trouble brewing ahead, whatever you do don't turn around, stare, run or slow down. Do what a local would do: keep your nerve and don't panic. Trudge on past the incident, ignore everything and don't catch anyone's eye. You need to act as if you've seen everything before: after all, most locals probably have.

'I once saw a Jordanian man kidnapped from his hotel in central Baghdad. As two men with guns fired warning shots over his head and forced him into a car, I stood at a tea stand no more than 10 yards away and calmly watched, sipping tea as this unknown man was forced into a car and driven away to his possible death. Keeping cool in such situations might save your life. By watching this incident with an Iraqi-style air of bored indifference, I escaped the attention of this particular kidnapping gang.

'Unfortunately, after too many months of acting like this, the coldness stops being a mask: this aloofness from humanity becomes part of your character. I sometimes wonder what happened to that unknown man. Five years later I wonder if I should have intervened or somehow done something to help him.'

No matter what you look like or what presents you take, it is your body language that shows respect for the local culture. I have no fluent languages other than English, but all around the world there is a common language of humanity. You just have to learn the local dialect of body language and your message will be a lot clearer.

Zeina Khodr enlarges on this point: 'They need to know that you are one of them. As a human, show them that you can relate to them. I went to meet a Taliban commander. At first I was shocked when 30 or 40 men emerged from nowhere with guns. But I remembered he had invited me as a guest. They wanted to talk to me, so I should assume the best. I told them I came from a place of conflict in Lebanon. We discussed something we had in common. That way it's not like I am coming from Paris to talk to them about fighting in the jungle.

'As a visitor to the area, I would be regarded as a guest by the local tribal elder in Afghanistan, and he would see me as his responsibility. Those feelings are even stronger if you are a female visitor. Having a woman in the team helps.

'Little things help to show your respect. In Afghanistan don't look men straight in the eye at checkpoints. They are not used to that from a woman.'

Fitting in is all about knowing how to approach people so that they forget the barriers that might otherwise exist outside that room. Monique Nagelkerke, MSF head of mission, told me: 'When dealing with UN peacekeepers or with officials, and when trying to break the ice, look at the name on their shirt pocket and address the man with his name as printed on his uniform. Often it is long and difficult to pronounce, so you can always ask what his mother or wife calls him. This always worked for me until I met a sharp officer from India, who looked me straight in the eye and answered, "My mother always calls me Sweetheart." Oh well, it did break the ice!'

Jon Snow is the chief presenter of Channel 4 News in the UK. He is as famous for his socks and ties as his challenging interviews. He was a long way from the studio in 1982 when he had a brush with a group of fighters north of the capital of El Salvador. 'I had my life saved by a small gesture at the right time...by a man with a packet of Marlboro. A Dutch film crew had been killed and we wanted to find out what happened. We went to the area they had been murdered and found what seemed to be the same death squad. We looked into their eyes and thought we'd had it. My Italian fixer Marcelo Zinini got out a packet of cigarettes and handed them round. They put down their weapons and never picked them up again.'

And sometimes, says one former UN worker, who prefers to go unnamed, you need to know the body language in order to avoid offence. 'Gestures for implying "Would you like a drink?" are not universal. The hand rounded, as if holding a glass, and tilting back into your mouth can imply something quite different in different cultures. This was a lesson I learnt when working as a cocktail waitress, with limited Spanish, in Buenos Aires many moons ago. The drink gesture in that part of the world is in fact a thumb gestured towards the mouth. I did well on tips however.'

Knowing the right gesture to make at the right time could save your life. Leith Mushtaq told me: 'I am a white-skinned Arab. I was sitting having coffee in a teashop in Kandahar and there were some men who looked like Taliban. The tea boy told me they thought I was a kaffir [non-believer]. I got up and started saying a prayer, something I knew from childhood. It worked – they came and shook my hand.'

/TEA AND COFFEE

Countries of the Middle East, Asia and the Orient each have their own obsession with tea and coffee. It varies from country to country, and even from town to town.

In the Arab world the tea might come in a tiny cup, but after hours of brewing and often ladles of sugar, it will pack a punch. The coffee is delicious, cardamom-rich stuff in some areas, and just plain strong in others. It is not usually filtered, so don't gulp down the muddy end of the cup. They will tap it out when you are offered more...and you will be offered more, and more and more until you can barely remember what it was like not to have every half hour and meeting punctuated with the ritual of pouring. It was when I totted up eight strong, sweet coffees in a day in Iraq that I knew it had to stop.

Ian Mackinnon is a freelance journalist, now based in Bangkok, where he used to be the *Guardian* newspaper's Southeast Asia correspondent. Before that he spent years earning his stripes as Jerusalem correspondent for *The Times* newspaper, and as a Delhi freelancer in and out of Afghanistan and Pakistan. He told me about his various tea and coffee experiences:

'Accepting *chai* (in India), hot sweet tea in Afghanistan, tea with mint in the Palestinian territories, or sweet 'mud' coffee is an occupational hazard. You've no choice but to accept as it's part of the hospitality, and to refuse would be impolite and rather militate against breaking the ice. In martyrs' mourning tents accepting seems doubly important. Drink slowly if sweet "anything" would be your last choice because your cup will be refilled again and again. You'll get used to it eventually and may even develop a taste for it.

'The problem is that after the fifth or tenth interview of the day, and many more during the week, you'll risk getting fat. Worse, in the short term you'll be bursting for a pee, even in the heat of an Afghan or Gazan summer when you're sweating buckets. It's a bigger problem for women, as they're forced to brave filthy loos. Even for men there are perils to peeing al fresco. In Afghanistan don't be tempted to wander off the road to pee modestly under a tree. The lurking landmines might take off your

FAILSAFE RULES IN ISLAMIC COUNTRIES

/ Do not enter a house, mosque or hospital without asking the permission of whoever is in charge. You will be causing more offence than just trespassing.

/ Men should not wear shorts, and should stick to long sleeves in religious areas.

/ Women should wear loose-fitting clothing that covers from head to toe. In some countries that also means no sandals or flip-flops.

/ Women should carry something that can be used as a headscarf in case they feel it is needed.

/ Take off your shoes when entering a mosque, and offer to do so when entering someone's home.

/ Showing the soles of your feet is rude – don't sit with them on show; sit cross-legged if you are on the floor.

/ Sunglasses, cameras and binoculars can be misconstrued in some remote places as aids to see through clothing or walls. Avoid them, even if it means a few extra wrinkles.

/ Dogs are not man's best friend in Islamic countries. They are often considered dirty. If you have one with you or choose to adopt one, do not take it into people's houses or anywhere near a religious site.

/ Men can touch men and even hold hands, women can be close to other women, but the opposite sexes should not touch each other in public. No kisses, no hugs. Even in a medical situation, you will need to ask permission to touch.

/ Check locally to see if any other rules also apply.

foot and spoil the whole day. Standing to pee against a wall is offensive too in Afghanistan and Pakistan, and risks offending local modesty, where it's polite to squat down. It's no mean feat.'

/WORKING WITH THE MILITARY

There are two options when dealing with the military: blend in with them and be a legitimate target in the eyes of any opposing force, or stand out from the green or khaki crowd and potentially become a target just because you look different. You might be targeted just because you are a medic, teacher or journalist, and your injury or death is more valuable than the average soldier.

You have to find a way to remain independent while firmly hugged in the arms of the army. I always chose to wear my scruffy press uniform – an enormous shirt and sagging trousers – when I was out on the occasional foray with British forces. Another essential piece of kit was the look I perfected of sympathetic innocence any time we went through the badlands of Basra. I would try to catch the eyes of boys throwing stones and smile as they bounced off my helmet. When it came to winning the troops over, I always worked on making myself very small, almost invisible and out of the way. That is not always easy if you have a lot of kit. You are often reliant on the military for your safety. Don't piss them off.

Tim Albone told me: 'Nothing, I imagine, annoys the military more than a scruffy journalist. Soldiers have to wear uniform, shave daily and have their hair cut above the collar: journalists don't. Having someone hanging around asking lots of questions must be annoying enough. When they are dressed in baggy clothes, with long hair and unshaven, like I often am, it must be worse. When I first went on an embed [an attachment to a military unit in combat] an older, much more experienced journalist told me to cut my hair, tuck my shirt in and have a shave. It was pretty good advice. The more you blend in, the more likely it is that soldiers will open up to you.'

Julius Cavendish is the *Independent* newspaper's correspondent in Kabul. He spends a lot of time under canvas on embeds with the military of one sort or another. And, as he explained to me over lunch one day in London, he is learning how to adapt all the time. 'Putting sniper tape over shiny karabiners and wearing more military-issue clothing so you blend in better with soldiers works. It's a matter of making the people around you feel comfortable because part of your job is, like a doctor, asking them to lie down and take off their emotional clothing. Otherwise, just try to be nice, despite whatever frustrations Western armies throw at you as you try to report. Being a pushy pain is the best way to alienate people.

'And take booze. It's an easy way to buy yourself some friends, especially in countries like Afghanistan, where it's hard to obtain. This doesn't hold when you're interviewing Al Qaeda-inspired fighters, who may be put out by the gesture.'

Patrick Hennessey graduated from being a fellow cider fan with me at university to becoming the youngest captain in the British Army. He has served in Iraq and Afghanistan, and his bestselling book, *The Junior Officers' Reading Club*, describes fighting the Taliban in 2007 and how his experiences actually pushed the army to change their rules of engagement. He's now a civilian studying to become a barrister, and revisiting Afghanistan for various publications – a bit of an unnerving experience, given what he knows about the way the Taliban fight:

'We find ourselves in an age of messy and complex conflicts in which the lines between combatant and non-combatant are blurred. Listening to intercepts of Taliban radio communications in southern Afghanistan provides chilling insight to how ruthless a modern enemy can be. Having noticed that medics often carry scissors somewhere immediately accessible, snipers are instructed to target anyone carrying first-aid kits or scissors at the start of an ambush. Perhaps of even greater concern to civilians is that the same commanders are well aware that anyone in "blue armour" is likely to be either press or some sort of visiting VIP, and is also to be targeted where possible. The highest protection in some conflict zones, it seems, is now afforded by looking as much as possible like a regular soldier, and although I was cursing that I no longer had a rifle, I was very glad I had my old, desert-cam body armour.'

And Tom Coghlan offers one last tip for travelling with the 'Allies': 'If you embed with US forces, one way to ingratiate yourself immediately is to turn up with packs of Copenhagen Black tobacco – the ghastly chewing stuff. Most American soldiers from the Deep South love it. They tend to be the majority in any army or marine unit. You are "in like Flynn" if you turn up with this stuff. British units are delighted with cheap cigarettes of the Lambert & Butler type.'

/MAKING FRIENDS

'In any foreign country,' says Patrick Hennessey, 'particularly one that may be hostile, making a friend might be the smartest tactical move available, which is why talking to anyone and everyone you meet is a good start.'

Everyone I have ever known who went to a war zone talks of the friends they made there – quick friendships forged in fear, and slow-burning ones developed over many, many months stuck in the same foxhole...or hotel. Those friendships will inform your stay, help you remain sane and maybe even save your life.

Zeina Khodr recommends: 'Win over the people of the area. They are the ones who will save you, no one else. Except God, of course. In Tripoli, in Lebanon there are so many factions that it is hard to convince them you are independent. We took the time to get to know the hierarchy locally, in the shops, on the street. Halfway through a gunfight some people came up and put guns to our heads. A shopkeeper approached the men and said that we were good people and told them that I had been filming kids who were shot and that we were on the side of the people. They put down their guns and went away.'

The locals have to know that you are on their side, as James Brandon discovered: 'In mid-2004 I found myself stuck in traffic in a taxi near the Iraqi oil ministry. US troops nearby had set up an impromptu roadblock on a main road that was holding up the traffic ahead. With the windows wound down, the Iraqis caught in the jam soon started talking to each other from car to car. Before long, they discovered I was a Westerner. To make friends, I joined them in complaining about the US troops who were holding us up. Temperatures rose and the traffic showed no sign of moving. Tensions soon began to mount. Complaints that were initially addressed towards the soldiers and towards the West in general were increasingly being addressed to me personally by the increasingly pissed-off Iraqis in the traffic jam. I had to show the Iraqis that I was in the same situation as them, and defuse the growing anger against me.

'Taking a deep breath, I got out of the taxi and walked up to the US roadblock. In full view of the backed-up traffic jam, I had a loud argument with the troops on the inequities of their traffic policy, ignoring the soldiers' guns that occasionally wavered towards my chest. The soldiers were, of course, unmoved by my arguments, but as I walked back towards the traffic jam, Iraqis gave me the thumbs up, patted me on the shoulder and offered me cigarettes. The moment of crisis had passed.'

But remain wary of fake friends. People will lie to you in order to get close to your fat wallet of dollars. They'll tell you the stories you want to hear, rather than the truth, in order to win you over. They'll lie about fellow workers in order to see them fired. They will lie about their qualifications and background in order to get a job they think might get them out of the country. And, worst of all, they might get paid to be your friend, in order to spy on you or lead you down a path to danger. Hoda Abdel-Hamid, an Al Jazeera English correspondent, told me about her dodgy experience:

'I went to Iraq thinking, "I speak Arabic. I look like an Arab. No one will get me," but I was just as vulnerable. We almost got kidnapped and killed on an empty university campus. Some guys circled us as we were interviewing someone. A professor called out of a window to warn us. She told us they were mujahideen [guerrilla fighters]. So we had been talking politely to our potential kidnappers. They were well dressed, well spoken and they had no weapons. We were going to follow them. Then all hell broke loose.'

Afghan jokes are impenetrable, so don't try to make them. However, if you want to get in with a bunch of Afghans and they ask you any sort of question you don't know the answer to, shrug and reply: 'Because the sky is blue and the sea is green.' When it is translated to them they will all fall about laughing and think you are quite the wit.
Tom Coghlan

3/GETTING AROUND IN A DANGEROUS PLACE

Be careful what you carry in a war zone. Take no detailed maps, no compass and no binoculars.
Sebastian Junger, journalist and author

'LET'S MAKE IT A JOURNEY,' I said to my friend as we looked at the map of Mali and decided how we were going to get to Timbuktu for a music festival in the Sahara. There was a flight that would have plopped us a two-hour jeep ride away across the dunes. But instead it was adventure we sought, and boy did we pay for it.

A price agreed over the Internet was dismissed by our guide Aly Guindo when he picked me up from the airport. He had 'forgotten to include the petrol' and that was going to cost us $800 extra. Haggling was worthless; his gang had a monopoly on four-wheel drives, so we had little choice but to pay and go.

It was a beautiful morning as we rode through town, watching people set up their markets, crossing rivers busy with fishermen, passing mosques and churches sitting on top of each other. Aly talked of a four-hour drive to a world-famous mud mosque followed by four hours till dinner and sleep. Fourteen hot, sticky hours later he showed us our bed – a rooftop without a mattress or anywhere to hang a mosquito net. Or, we were told, 'You can pay more money for a room.' More money it was. And raucous laughter when we assumed the food was included (as they had told us when we made the deal).

The next day it was 16 hours at 100 kph across a ridged desert road. We turned orange in the dust that flowed in waves through the door. It was like being tied to a mechanical digger with five other people, relieved intermittently by river crossings in the scorching sun.

The final push was to Timbuktu. And our guide knew it was his last chance to get a tip. He told us he hadn't been paid and that we needed to give him money so he could feed his family...and what seemed to us all to be a very heavy drug habit. We refused. Now everyone felt ripped off.

Eventually we made it, paying again at the door for our pre-paid tickets, and walked into what felt like a refugee camp. Tuareg families huddled around fires. Fat tourists, wearing blue Tuareg scarves to cover their burnt foreheads, stumbled around in the sand. We joined them, looking for our part of the camp. I had the name scribbled on a piece of paper, but had no idea where it might be, or who I could call to find out. But we did find it and thought the organizers were lovely until they charged us double too.

On the last morning, when our red-eyed driver turned up to take our bags to the car, we told him that he could give our seats to one of the six extra people we found sitting on the roof of our jeep. We had managed to get ourselves two precious tickets for a flight to Bamako, the capital of Mali. After three bone-rattling days on the road, followed by four in boiling-hot Sahara sunshine during the daytime and freezing temperatures at night, plus a good dose of food poisoning, we felt we deserved them.

I broke every rule I know about travelling during that holiday, all for the romance of the journey. It started with not following my instincts when Aly Guindo began to barter with me from the moment I left the airport.

/USE YOUR INSTINCT

Your first and last tool should be your instinct. When you are on the move in a dangerous world you have to make snap judgements. Trust your instincts. If you feel something isn't right although it looks like the perfect day for it, whatever it is, stop and turn back.

Sherine Tadros told me a story that she attributes to diet-spurred guilt, but is probably as much to do with instinct: 'Dr Atkins [of diet fame] saved my life. On the first night of the war in Gaza – 27 December 2008 – we were filming live shots from the main hospital in Gaza City. When we were done I was starving; we hadn't stopped for 12 hours, since the first bombs started falling. There's a great falafel stand next to the hospital, so I asked the team if we could stop and get a sandwich. When we got there I had an attack of food guilt: it was 11 p.m. – I shouldn't be eating fried food and carbs. So we left it and went back to the office. A few minutes later we heard a huge explosion. The falafel stand and everyone in its proximity was blown up. Had we got the sandwiches, we would almost certainly have been killed. They say you should always trust your gut. Suffice to say that every decision you make in a war zone is vital and has consequences. Go with your instincts but realize that when it's your time to go it's your time to go.'

/COMMUNICATION IS KEY

You should have a communications system in place from the moment you arrive. And even if all is quiet, it needs to be enforced from day one. Regular calls into base and from base should be established, even if it is just to say hello three times a day. This is especially key when you are travelling. Your point person should know where you are going, when you expect to arrive, the route you are travelling, and the plane, train or vehicle you are using to get there. You should arrange a time to call them when you arrive, and if you haven't arrived by that time, you need to find a way to call in before they begin to panic. Communication is a priority.

Leith Mushtaq told me about the arrangements he made: 'I made a deal with my base: "I will text you every hour. If I stop sending you texts, you must send help and try to find me." And I keep drafts of two text messages, saying "We have been arrested" and "We have been kidnapped". When we get stopped, before they take away the phone, I can send it.'

Being able to communicate is also vital if or when your vehicle breaks down. Make a note of a safe taxi number, along with your hotel address in the local language. Use your hotel's taxi service when possible.

/TAP INTO LOCAL KNOWLEDGE

The people you rely on from the area you are visiting will provide you with invaluable guidance on how to live your life in their world. You need to create a careful balance between respect for their opinion and faith in your own instincts.

Tom Coghlan spent five years in Kabul as a freelance reporter. He worked with Afghan journalists, who risked their lives on a daily basis to bring news from their country to the world. As Tom admits, over time and through the forest of a long-established beard, it is all too easy forget that you are only a visitor:

'In 2006 I pushed my fixer to come with me into a market in the town of Maiwand, near Kandahar, which he said was full of Taliban. I wanted a vox pop [soundbites from the man on the street] on the day the British announced their deployment to neighbouring Helmand. (It seemed appropriate because the town had seen the great defeat of British troops in 1882, during the Second Afghan War.) I overruled my fixer's misgivings and we went in there, though I persuaded two local militiamen to come too.

'The first person we tried to speak to looked at us with incredulity and terror, and said his shop was now closed. Although I was dressed as an Afghan and trying to be discreet, few locals seemed to be fooled. We quickly found a crowd building around us. Our so-called bodyguards looked increasingly frightened. A man gestured at me and I tried to shake his hand. He continued to talk and gesture, as a look of increasing panic and indecision came into the eyes of our bodyguards. My fixer explained later that the man and other members of the crowd were trying to persuade the guards to shoot me as a spy and enemy of Muslims. The guards were unsure what to do, but my fixer was assertive and quick-witted, and dominated the indecision within the crowd for the crucial minute it took to pull me out of there.

'The obvious lesson to draw from this is to think very carefully and really weigh the costs and benefits before you overrule local knowledge. It is, unfortunately, a lesson that I have learnt a few times.'

Zeina Khodr had the opposite struggle. It was sticking to her instincts and overriding the local advice that saved her life, she says.

'Your life should be in your hands, no one else's. Take advice, but also follow your instincts. My team and I were travelling to Helmand from Kandahar in late 2009 along a single-track road. We passed an area that was in the middle of an attack by the Taliban, and continued as far as we could until we came to a bridge that they blew up. There were three choices: go back on the single track; go off-road through the Taliban-controlled villages; or stay put. I said we should head back along the single track – we were all disguised, so there was no reason for them to suspect us. But after 500 metres, we saw Taliban fighters coming out of civilian homes. They were approaching the highway. A bus was stuck and there was a traffic jam. I said, "Don't panic. Go forward." The last thing I wanted was to go back and be a sitting duck. The rest of the team disagreed with me, reversing backwards until we had a police checkpoint full of drugged-up officers on one side, the bridge in front of us and the Taliban all around. We were stuck there for seven hours. We hadn't brought water, so dehydration alone could have killed us. Reversing had been the wrong decision.

'We called the office to ask for help from the US and British military. Then the NATO helicopters came and we realized we were at risk of being bombed. We looked the same as everyone else in our disguise. So we decided we had to leave. We waited for two or three cars from the village to come through and we followed them.'

/DRIVING

I am a terrible driver. However, I have been on a few of the courses – driving in a hostile environment (mud) and driving on a skid board – and, as a result, I'm pretty certain that under pressure we all become better drivers. The key is to remember just a few simple things.

- If you skid, turn the steering wheel into the skid rather than against it and this will bring it under control.
- Lower gears give you more control going up and down hills, and along muddy tracks.
- Listen to your car. It will tell you when to change gear and when to give up.

That's it, really, the basics of driving in extreme conditions. Oh, and don't drink and drive – that is one extreme condition that will not make you a better driver.

/PLANES, TRAINS AND AUTOMOBILES

When you are in a dangerous country there are several important matters you must address before you make a journey anywhere.

Decide whether to drive yourself or let others do it for you. This means choosing between hiring a car, employing a driver, or using buses and taxis. This needs to be thought about before arrival (see page 27).

If you opt for taxis, use the hotel's service if possible, and build up a happy mutual relationship with tips. That way there is a limited number of people who know your movements and where you are staying. Also, the hotel will already have trusted drivers *and* know where they live.

If you opt for a local driver, make sure you choose the right one. An MSF volunteer told me about the checks they tried to make before hiring in Yemen: 'Did they have any revenge issues? Were they from the right tribe for crossing the area? Would anyone take against one of them?'

Even if you have a driver you trust, you can never be sure about their friends. Shadi Alkasim, a freelance radio producer and journalist, recommends: 'If you have an interpreter or driver, never give him accurate information about where you will be on the following day. For example, tell him you want to go tomorrow to such and-such a place to cover the news there in the morning. But the next day tell him you have changed your mind and want to go to another place. Also change your route every day. Someone may be following you, and then you will be a very easy target.'

But even if you are using a local driver and relying on their know-how, you need to stay in control of your situation. If there is something you are not sure of or do not understand, always ask. As Ian Mackinnon told me:

'When it all goes quiet you're probably between the front lines in no man's land. If the local populace has shut up shop, abandoned streets and there are no cars around, take heed. With colleagues from the *Daily Telegraph* and *Independent*, I was approaching the southern Gaza town of Rafah, surrounded by Israeli troops and tanks who were waging ferocious battles with Palestinian militants down the road that had already left more than a score dead. Our fixer, accompanied by a driver new to us, blithely announced that he knew how to thread a way through the tank cordon down some back roads through the sand dunes. To our dismay, he then proceeded to yack away on his mobile as we proceeded down ever-quieter roads, without even bothering to ask the one car coming the other way what lay down the lane ahead. Only then did my *Telegraph* colleague scream at our fixer to get off the phone and stop the car. He rightly expressed reservations despite the fixer's none-too-reassuring assurances that he knew the way and all would be fine. But, spooked, the *Telegraph* man asked to be taken back to the main road and life, where he would find a taxi back to Gaza City. After lunch the rest of us decided we'd give Rafah a miss for that day too.

'The *Telegraph* man's decision illustrated, for me, the importance of being in control and doing what you feel comfortable with. Easier said than done when in a group of competitors each under their own pressures to reach the story. He made it back to Rafah without incident, as did we the following morning.'

It's very important to choose the right car – one that fits into the local area. Tom Coghlan tells you how to do that in Afghanistan:

'Don't use SUVs unless absolutely necessary. Toyota Corollas in Afghanistan are almost as durable as SUVs, a fraction of their cost to run and maintain, and the parts are available everywhere. They also attract a fraction of the attention. If you go somewhere dangerous, make sure you are the driver (if you are male). Nobody ever looks at the driver in Afghanistan because he has the lowest status in the car. Make sure the car is dirty. Girls should all wear *burkas*. Put all your identity documents in the back of the cover of the front seat. Play Afghan music on the stereo. Get a grubby look going and don't wash your hair. To be honest, if people look in the car, they will probably identify you as foreign, but Afghans are quite polite and won't harass you.

'*In extremis* the best thing to do is pretend to be physically disabled or mentally disturbed. It probably won't help much, but there are lots of mentally disturbed people in Afghanistan, so you stand a chance of getting away with it. Because of the high instance of very close intermarriage, deaf and dumb people are quite frequent, and that's an obvious option for the non-Pashto speaker.'

If you must drive yourself, learn how to drive in the local way. Nick Toksvig remembers: 'We did a lot of our own driving during the 2006 war. What worked best was adapting to the way locals drove, whether through the use of lights or hand gestures or whatever. Adapt and you won't stand out so much.'

According to journalist Sebastian Junger, though, your driving should be local in all but one way: 'Wear a seatbelt! Every reporter I've ever met is cavalier about wearing a belt in a war zone, which is crazy.'

If you are driving in a dangerous place, you need to have a plan, make it known to everyone who needs to know, and stick to it. As one NGO worker told me, even small deviations from the plan can get you killed:

CHOOSING YOUR CAR

/ When hiring a car, choose something everyone has locally. You won't stand out and it won't look so much like a rental.

/ Ask your driver or your hotel to have the car checked over by a local workshop. Check you have a spare tyre and that it's inflated, plus a jack, handle and wheel wrench.

/ Air conditioning is not just for extra comfort – it's a safety feature because it allows you to close the windows.

/ Get central locking, if possible. It gives the driver more control over the situation. Electric windows are a plus too.

/ Make sure you know the rules of the road and which ones locals break so that you can fit in...up to a point.

/ Always carry your driving licence and local documentation.

/ Keep in contact with your base about where you are going before you set out, even the roads you are planning to use, if necessary.

/ Always keep a torch, water, blankets, a first aid kit and some food in the car in case of emergencies.

/ Spare oil and water, a tow rope and jump leads should be carried, plus spare bulbs and fuses, and even spare fuel, depending on how remote you'll be.

/ In cold climates make sure you have snow chains, and learn how to fit them somewhere warm so that you can do it later in the dark with frozen fingers.

'In Yemen we had strict laws on movement. It would take 4–8 hours to get from one town to another. To avoid tribal checkpoints, we would leave at four in the morning. On one occasion we decided to stop for a cup of coffee – a stupid, simple cup of coffee – so our driver pulled over at the nearest café. We then found we were in one of the most dangerous places we could be...it was a tribal zone with the highest risk ever. About 40–50 armed men surrounded us and they looked at us like we had dropped from heaven. As they were getting their weapons ready, one approached us to say we could leave if they could keep the car. We explained it was an ambulance, but they said they didn't care – that we were working with another tribe and weren't curing their people and they wanted it. The local driver told us to go back to the car and he would negotiate. He told them he would race them in the car and if they managed to catch us, they could keep the car. Thankfully, ours was better than theirs and we got away.'

HOW TO HOT-WIRE A CAR

I'm not encouraging you to start a career in crime. You just need to know what to do if you lose your car keys. Be aware that with hot-wiring there is a risk of a big electric shock if you get it wrong, and of course it's illegal without the car owner's permission. Plus it's often impossible to hot-wire modern cars because some engines are fitted with kill switches and new-fangled plastic coatings. I'm no expert, but a team of near-naked Namibian bushmen once managed to hot-wire an ambulance in front of me, so I know it can be done. Here's how:

/ Open the bonnet and find the red coil wire, most often at the back of the engine.

/ Now find the battery – that's the rectangular boxy thing with red and black terminals.

/ Run a wire from the red (positive) side of the battery to the red coil wire.

/ Find the starter solenoid (sometimes called starter relay or motor). It's a solid cylinder shape, best found by following the red wire of the battery, but you might need to check under the steering wheel too, depending on the make of the car.

/ Unlock the steering wheel by pushing a flat-bladed screwdriver into the crack between the wheel and the column holding it. The unlocking mechanism should be at the top. It might take a bit of effort.

/ Connect the two pins on the solenoid with something metal. The pins are connected to the positive battery wire and a smaller starter wire. There is a third wire on the solenoid, so you might have to experiment a bit.

/ The engine will fire up and you are free to drive to your nearest garage and order some more keys. Or free to make a quick getaway if the car ain't yours...

/CRIMINAL ATTACKS

The threat of criminal attack obviously applies to places such as South Africa, where there is a high level of crime directed at homes and cars. But it also applies to places such as Mexico City, and Colombo in Sri Lanka, where kidnappers may be staking out your house. The information given here is not just for war zones.

The most fundamental piece of advice is never take the same route to work two days in a row. Never let your pattern become predictable. Leave at different times of the day if you can. One day have breakfast at work, the next have it at home. Have dinner out and return home late, but not every night. Look for any unusual cars outside your accommodation. Note down number plates so you can see if someone is returning again and again out of the blue. And if your instincts tell you to be scared, go to a hotel, or stay with a friend for a few nights.

Mary O'Shea had some interesting experiences as a new driver: 'I moved to South Africa having driven for all of two weeks of my life. I landed in Johannesburg, bought a beat-up Ford Fiesta Flite (a tin can on wheels, specially manufactured for the African market) and had it kitted out with shatterproof windows, a tracking system and so forth, which ended up costing more than the actual car itself. Having diplomatic plates and being instructed never to stop at traffic lights is perhaps not the ideal starting point as a first-time driver. We were always reminded that most "incidents" take place as you get home, so the idea was to speed into the garage and get the gate shut behind you asap. Perhaps it's not surprising that I managed to ram into my garage wall twice. Always keep an eye on cars around you to check if you are being followed. And if you see people lurking outside your house, drive past.'

/CAR-JACKING

The threat of being car-jacked is not confined just to those times of going into and out of your driveway, or to and from work. It could happen along the road too.

Qatar, where my Al Jazeera colleagues and I now live, is the kind of place where you can leave your keys in the car for days on end and no one will even think of stealing it. But back at her home in South Africa, senior news presenter Jane Dutton lives in a different world, where a simple trip to the shops can mean risking an attack from violent criminals. She explains the everyday precautions her colleagues, friends and neighbours take in order to minimize the risk:

'I live next to the beautiful Vall River outside Johannesburg. The road heading there is one of the worst in the area for hijackings. The police have cut all the trees

PRECAUTIONS AGAINST CAR BOMBS

/ Ensure your car is parked in a secure compound or well-lit area near your accommodation.

/ Inspect your vehicle for suspicious objects every time you use it. In order to do that, you need to become familiar with the normal shape of your car. What does the underneath look like, the wheel rims and interior?

/ Look for explosive devices around the wheels and on the windscreen – they might be disguised as rubbish.

/ Carry a torch with you to check underneath the car for anything unusual.

/ Always keep your door locked, even if you leave the car for just a minute.

right back. And my family all drive very defensively, hyper-aware of the rear-view mirror – looking for cars that might be following, driving too close, or just behaving in a threatening way. Attackers used to put bricks out on the road to slow you down, so you have to watch for that too.

'Everyone knows not to stop at traffic lights, and never to pick up hitch-hikers. You must put your bag on the floor of the car and lock the doors and windows before you leave. In some areas further north from where I live, near Pretoria, they actually have signs warning passing drivers of a "Hijack Corner" coming up ahead.

'Once I had a flat tyre while driving past the edge of a township with a particularly bad reputation. There I was in my high heels, vulnerable as anything. It was the fastest wheel change in history. You hear alarming stories all the time. Just last week my brother was driving home and a car rounded off on him to slow him down. He followed his instincts and sped onto the wrong side of the road until he came to a police car parked nearby. The policeman kicked a girl out of his car, popped his siren on and gave chase. That's what it's like in South Africa – more often than not you have to rely on yourself rather than the law.'

/CONVOYS

If the roads are dangerous, it's a good idea to move in carefully organized convoys. Nick Toksvig has worked with teams carrying valuable camera equipment and potential hostages around all sorts of hostile environments. He explains how it's done:

PRECAUTIONS AGAINST CAR-JACKING

/ Keep your windows closed at traffic lights, and stay back from the lights if groups of people are waiting there.

/ Know how to operate the central locking system. If there isn't one, make sure all the doors are locked before you set off.

/ Avoid fuel stations unless absolutely necessary. Drivers should fill up alone, without passengers.

/ Leave enough space between you and the car in front to turn around if necessary.

/ Stick to main roads and avoid driving at night.

/ Vary your route and always call in to base before and after a trip, and even during it.

/ If attacked, keep calm, hand over your keys and valuables, and keep your hands in sight.

'During Israel's war on Lebanon in 2006, Sky News and Fox News teamed up when moving by car. We always travelled in a five-car convoy with radio contact between the vehicles. We kept the vehicles spaced about half a kilometre apart in case of bombing from the air. It meant that in all likelihood we would lose only one car.

'Driving from Beirut to the south we had one car filled with 250 litres of fuel, another filled with personal belongings, and a third with technical equipment. We let the fuel vehicle go in front – if a car was attacked, that would be the least valuable cargo – and the rest of us kept well back on the journey down.'

That said, a convoy can also be a target. On my way out of Baghdad for the last time I was looking for a cheap ride home. A group of gorgeous Italians offered me a seat in their car and told me to meet them at 4.30 a.m. outside our hotel the next day. (We always left before curfew as the streets were safest then.) I woke up at 4.25, my alarm having failed to go off for the first and only time in my life. As I huffed and puffed with my bag to the front door downstairs, the Italians were shutting their doors and about to head off. They shouted at me to jump into the car behind them and the whole convoy left on time. Instead of being surrounded by beautiful men, I found myself alone with a Canadian human shield, clicking on her knitting needles over murmured stitch counts.

We drove safely through the pitch-black, empty streets of Baghdad and onto the main road to Jordan. Dawn was breaking, and through the fudge of the grey morning I saw something that looked like a tank pull up onto the side of the road. It was still curfew and these were US forces, so our driver began to slow down. The Italians' car, though, was still heading fast towards the tank when it was pumped full of bullets and came to a screeching halt. We slowed to a crawl and I leant out my window to wave to the soldiers as we approached the vehicle that was now more of a sieve than a taxi. The driver was dead – I could see that. The others, I have no idea, because the US soldiers shouted at us to move on as we were driving through the middle of an operation. We had broken curfew, as almost everyone did, in order to make it out of the city safely, and that car of happy men on their way home had borne the brunt of that calculated risk. It was a shocking day.

At times like that you realize nowhere is safe. Technology is never as advanced as it needs to be when it comes to identifying one person from another – the 'enemy' from the Red Cross or Red Crescent; the press van following an exit plan from a van full of fighters heading to the border; the refugees huddled around a fire from the locater flare for an artillery bombardment.

Historically, one-third of all deaths during war are from so-called 'friendly fire', and that statistic is getting no better. John Simpson, a BBC news correspondent, remembers one terrible occasion:

'In 2003, during the invasion of Iraq, I thought it would be safe if my team and I tacked ourselves onto a convoy of American and Kurdish special forces. I remember saying to the others, "The Americans aren't going to attack us if we're with them." But they did. A US Navy plane dropped a 1000-lb bomb right in the middle of our group. Eighteen people died, most of them burnt to death. My translator, who was standing close to me, had his legs blown off and died of blood loss. The rest of us were injured in different ways, none seriously. The fault was mine, and I still feel the guilt strongly.'

Apart from that occasion, John had always avoided travelling with the military for protection. It's known as embedding and carries its own risks. You are travelling with the military and subject to their whims. You are, to all intents and purposes, enlisted in the army for those days and must forfeit your independence of movement and choice. The people the army are fighting regard you as just another soldier. Embedding can provide you access to a fight or an area you would never otherwise have seen, but it keeps you away from what is really going on. And John believes (rightly in my view) that it destroys the objectivity of your position as a journalist.

/CHECKPOINTS

You'll come across checkpoints along the road, at border crossings, or even in an airport. The road checks are the ones that pose the most danger, but being aware of your body language and using a skilled approach to people during any meeting will help ease your journey anywhere you travel.

Authority breeds arrogance, and that can be dangerous in a place where laws mean little. Before travelling through Yemen as tourists in 2005, my friends and I had a pile of travel passes printed off to give out to each checkpoint along the way. There were maybe 40 stops over four days of driving through the Hadramaut valley. At each one we were asked for a different level of search or bribe, even though our papers were in order. As frustration grew with the sticky heat of the day, it was difficult to approach each new checkpoint as a new conversation. When our car radiator fizzled out in the middle of a scrubby desert on day three, we looked ahead and saw a well-manned checkpoint about a kilometre away through the desert heat. They saw us and didn't help. We wanted to scream and shout, but we eventually started the car again and chugged to their barrier, where they handed us water with big smiles and waved us through – no bribe, no search. It's difficult to avoid judging one experience by your last, but you must.

When I met the senior news producer Shelley Thakral in Iraq she was a point of calm in all the madness, and the first visiting journalist in Basra who looked me in the eye and asked me if I was all right. It had been months since someone did that. She makes the following observations:

'Your personality changes the more you work in these areas. You become more laidback. When it comes to checkpoints and crowds, calmness, patience and an understanding of the local culture are the way forward. Whatever you do, the guards will still insist on going through the whole frustrating procedure and you have to be very patient to put up with it. In Sri Lanka we were crossing back and forth into the Tamil Tiger region. We were tired and hot, struggling with heavy cases full of camera kit, but the guards don't help to haul them up onto the table to be checked, even if you're a woman. You feel resentful as they ask you to open them. But whatever you may think, it is necessary. You have to be calm and laidback.'

Assuming the guards are not actually hostile, there are some tried and tested ways to win them over. It starts with driving slowly and without your lights on full glare. Some countries may require you to have the lights on inside the car as you approach. Check the local guidelines.

Leith Mushtaq recommends: 'Be friendly, but not too friendly. Give them some cigarettes, offer them something for tomorrow, but don't give them everything.

Make a deal. Ask them to be your escort today and offer them something for the next time. Go out of your way to find information about what is up ahead.'

Marc DuBois says: 'The key is drinks. Often you find guys out in the middle of nowhere and a little cold water goes a long way. It opens a conversation. We also used to ask people if they had any mail to deliver to checkpoints further up the road. Nothing better than arriving at a checkpoint with mail from a little further back. If that doesn't win over their trust, nothing will.'

As Dr Carl Hallam observes: 'Checkpoints are interesting if they have a gun and you haven't. You have to be very, very humble and avoid eye contact altogether. Don't rush them, be patient. Take off your dark glasses and turn off your VHF radio, if you have one. If it blurts out at the wrong moment, it could frighten the person checking your papers. And always wait for the second car if there is more than one of you. Don't drive off without the others.'

If a checkpoint isn't a direct confrontation, it is always a negotiation. Marc DuBois has spent 12 years travelling round the world with MSF. Visiting Sudan in 2009, after 13 NGOs had been expelled by the government, was one of his more difficult recent projects. As he explains, all negotiations begin with one question – where should you target your efforts?

'You have to know who is in charge. One of the biggest problems in negotiating is the failure to understand who is in charge in a given situation – whether it be a village, a checkpoint, a border or a government office. Often I see a person negotiating in vain with someone who doesn't have the capacity to make a decision. With officials, it's not always very clear. You can be in a meeting with someone whose political rank and title are correct, but in terms of real power it might be the national security person sitting in the corner that you need to win over. You need to understand that dynamic because it can be dangerous if you get it wrong.'

> I like to have my documents handy – I don't like rummaging around in pockets and glove compartments at checkpoints manned by jumpy individuals. You want to spend as little time there as possible; they're notoriously dangerous places. **Chris Cobb-Smith**

/FAKE CHECKPOINTS

There are times when you need to be more than cautious, such as at fake checkpoints. Faking a checkpoint is an easy way to make a quick buck out of bribes, or robbery or kidnapping. Sometimes the fake checkpoint will have a particular target, so you might get through, but it is not worth trying your luck at getting through unless your pass has been previously negotiated by whoever is your local fixer on the ground with the right know-how and contacts.

Samantha Bolton recalls: 'You are always told that you should turn on your lights and slow down. That's the correct procedure. But I have also followed my instincts and run a checkpoint. In the Democratic Republic of Congo I was in the car with another girl. We were slowing down for a checkpoint, but even from a distance we could see they had bloodshot, bleary eyes and were moving around like they were drunk. We were out late after curfew and I didn't feel right about it, so when they lowered their guns and surrounded our car, we suddenly sped up and went through the tin cans that were supposed to be the barrier. They tried to shoot at us, but I knew they were so drunk that it would be hard to hit us.'

HOW TO SPOT A FAKE CHECKPOINT

/ The guards might be wearing the same uniforms and have the same cars as the real police or army, but often they have different weapons.

/ Fake checkpoints never stay in the same place for a long time.

/ They appear in places where you do not expect them – not on borders and not near a back up point, but in the middle of a street or a bridge, or on highways.

/ The guards do not check every car; they choose, depending on the name of the province on the number plate, or the make of the car.

/ They are often in a hurry and ask for IDs to be shown quickly.

HOW TO DEAL WITH A FAKE CHECKPOINT

/ Ask the locals where the latest fake checkpoints are before you head off, and avoid them.

/ Know where you are so that you know what kind of people the guards are targeting. Just being you, a visitor to the country, might make you a target.

/ Have several different IDs made up if you can pass for a local. You should know which ID is in which pocket so that when you hand it to the guards it is with confidence and without confusion. In Iraq you would need four IDs – Shia, Sunni, Christian and Kurd. Perfect your accent to match the ID before trying to speak.

/ Appear to be travelling alone if taking a bus, even if someone is with you. The same is true if you are in a private car with friends: you (or whoever is driving) can claim to be a taxi driver hired by them. You should agree on a story in advance. The point is to avoid different answers when being interrogated separately.

/ If you know the various types of fake checkpoint you might face, be prepared for the questions you might be asked before you set off so that you can provide answers without confusion. In Iraq and many Arab countries they will ask you the name of your tribe's sheikh, or the names of famous people in the area you claim to come from. They sometimes ask religious questions, or ask you to pray. You should be prepared for all of this.

/ Keep fake contacts on your mobile phone to reflect people from a certain sect, and keep them right at the top of your list alphabetically. Code any names that give away your real identity. If you are a Sunni, for example, you should avoid the name Omer. I changed every Omer in my phone to Ammar when I was in Baghdad. Give your family members other names in your phone – for example, not 'Mum' or 'Home' but 'Vicki' or 'London'.

Imad Shihab is an Iraqi journalist I worked with in Baghdad and Doha. In 2007 we evacuated together to the Green Zone when our entire office of local cameramen and producers were kidnapped. Some time later we found out that our largely Sunni staff had been arrested by the mainly Shia police forces, but the Interior Ministry, which was in charge of the police, was not the best communicator at the time.

Imad fled Iraq in 2009, when he became a target for trying to bring fair and balanced reports to the world. But he spent the worst years of the fight there, talking his way around the country street by street. He managed to stay safe, and from his hiding place he told me how to approach the most deadly of checkpoints. The advice can be applied to any country, not just to Iraq.

Imad Shihab knows the perils very well. He says: 'I think that many of the victims of fake checkpoints and random arrests did not do their homework well enough. I did some strange things that people thought were funny, but they saved my life. Like having a Shia friend pretending to be a member of a fake checkpoint and asking me questions. These exercises were very helpful for me as a Sunni. A lot of victims would not have been killed if they had done the same.'

Of course there are other, more unorthodox, ways to get around checkpoints, as Nick Toksvig recalls: 'After a bomb explosion in India an enterprising cameraman hired a fire engine to take him to the scene that had been cordoned off.'

/SIGNS

> Aid workers don't have body armour. The logo on our T-shirt is our protection, but can become a target too.
> **Samantha Bolton**

Take advice locally on what type of identification to put on your car. I have been in the middle of many riots where press and tourists were supposed to be able to travel freely, but that isn't always the sentiment on the ground. Even the authorities may not be on message. Don't expect legal protection where the law is under pressure from a popular movement or challenged by a resistance movement.

Nick Toksvig told me: 'Spelling out "TV" or "Press" in gaffer tape on your vehicle used to work, but now many refugees fleeing battle zones do the same, as do local militias. Think about where you are before you attempt this type of vehicle identification. It can be meaningless.'

/TRAINS AND BUSES

The road from Baghdad to Basra was notoriously dangerous after the US-led invasion of Iraq. There were frequent shootings, car-jackings and kidnappings. Fake check-points were set up along the route, and there was no way to get around them. If someone saw you in a car, they would call ahead for their friends to stop your car and target you. The road took six hours to drive very, very fast. The trip cost $6. I was being paid $10 day, so I thought I would try the train at just 50 cents.

The railway station in Baghdad was heaving with people – families getting ready for the long ride. The train left almost on time and off we went. We were told it would take six hours – in fact it took 16. There were no windows, and the train frequently stopped for hours at a time in the middle of nowhere or, even worse, in the middle of towns where people could look in and see my blonde hair. It was scary, but it felt like I was travelling under the radar. My friend Sebastian and I became mini-celebrities on the train, not exactly what we were aiming for. The journey ground on, we ran out of water in the 50°C heat, and the hot, sandy wind rushing past our faces like the ultimate exfoliator. We had time to make friends with a family who gave us water and went on to have me to stay with them for the next two months.

All along the way people slipped coffins onto the train, sitting on them to eat their sandwiches. And at the city of Najaf they jumped off, wailing with grief as they took their family member to the holiest Shia burial site.

Goats were lifted onto the train by boy herders, who stepped off with them an hour later, apparently aiming for a distant flapping tent in the desert.

We passed through the soggy marshlands and, at last, chugged slowly into Basra – safe and with enough change from our ticket to buy dinner for a week.

The problem with trains and buses is that the situation is beyond your control. If there are criminals on board, you will be their target. On the other hand, they won't be expecting you to use the train or bus, so maybe they won't be looking. However, take the following precautions:

- Lock your compartment if you can. I have used a luggage strap to fasten it in the past.
- Sleep in shifts if you are with others. Stay awake if you are alone.
- If you have to sleep, tie yourself to your valuables and sleep on top of your luggage.
- Try to travel during the day rather than at night.

James Brandon remembers a difficult journey: 'Once I had to travel from Baghdad to

Iraqi Kurdistan during a time of particularly bad unrest in Iraq. The 100-odd miles of road passed through several Sunni districts that were heavily infested with Al Qaeda and Baathist fighters. Despite this, I decided that the safest way to travel was by public bus. After all, I reasoned, a taxi or a private car was no safer, and might even be less so. No self-respecting bandits would bother with robbing a bus – they would assume that the passengers were too poor to make it worthwhile. Sunni fighters or Al Qaeda operatives looking for new hostages, meanwhile, would never expect a Westerner to travel through Iraq by bus. There was one problem, however: how could I carry my clothes, camera and notebook without attracting attention? Eventually I hit on the solution. I packed my stuff into cheap plastic grocery bags and headed to the bus depot. Once I got there, nobody looked at me twice. To the casual onlooker, I was just another down-on-his-luck Iraqi guy, his worldly possessions crammed into a couple of grimy plastic bags, saving a few precious dinar by taking the bus. As a result, the journey up to Kurdistan was entirely uneventful – and cheap! When it comes to blending in, you can never blend in too much.'

/TAXIS

When taking a taxi, sit in the back. That way you can sort your money out in secret. Never flash your cash, and try to keep controversial chat to a minimum. Remember, the driver knows where you live.

If you want to keep your address a secret, get the driver to stop at a hotel or restaurant nearby, wait until he's gone, then walk the rest of the way.

/BRIBERY

I am sure that being able to bribe people is a skill you are born with – or not, in my case. There are six-year-olds who are better than me at bribing officials to get what they want. I know how to flirt my way into most things, including trouble. But that is not always the most sensible option. In many, if not most, developing countries bribes oil the wheels. And knowing when you need to pay *baksheesh*, as it is called in Arabic-speaking countries, who to pay and how to do it effectively is something learnt over time. I can but imitate the masters who are born with a fully developed bribery muscle.

Marc DuBois, who works for Médecins Sans Frontières, says: 'MSF doesn't use bribery, but in my earlier travels I sometimes found small gifts useful.

However, you need to be subtle and approach with caution. Maybe suggesting a brand new pair of sports socks are “difficult to fit into your bag” as a security guard goes through your luggage. It's understood what the bargain is, but isn't clearly stated.

'Don't embarrass people by trying to bribe them openly – it can backfire. They can pretend to be highly upset, charging you with the crime of bribery in order to jack up the amount. On one occasion, when I was working with the Peace Corps, I had a visa or permit that wasn't quite right. I was prepared with a $20 bill neatly folded in my pocket. I slipped it into the right page and asked the guard to check my permit again to see if it was in order.'

Samantha Bolton has some other tips: 'When it comes to getting that last seat on a plane, girls should wear a short skirt or deep v-neck – if dealing with disciplined soldiers. Be friendly, polite and respectful with others. Offering corporate gifts, pens or trinkets also helps. This last one is more for getting through roadblocks. Medicine too is always in demand – antibiotics, antiseptic, painkillers. And, of course, cigarettes.'

In the United States tipping is a sport. But in many parts of the world it's an art. An open display of generosity is frowned upon in some parts of the Middle East and China, while other places applaud displays of wealth and philanthropy, on however small a scale.

People in many parts of the developing world are often paid little and kept on a tight employment leash through a bonus system (just like those who wait tables in the USA). As a visitor, you will be expected to tip. But as my good friend and colleague Stefanie Dekker found out on her first trip to Iraq, it is how you do it that counts:

'I was in Halabja with two Peshmerga bodyguards. I wanted to give them both a big tip after a long day in the mountains. I handed over the money – it wasn't obvious, but it wasn't subtle in the slightest. They shouted, “No, no, no – we couldn't!” I know now that you have to fold the cash into a tiny square or scrunch it into a ball and hand it over very carefully at the right time to avoid offence. Of course, they took the money later.'

/DEALING WITH SURVEILLANCE

One former UN worker tells me: 'In countries such as Sudan they like to observe in a very obvious 1970s' sitcom way – vehicles with blacked-out windows, kerb-crawling behind you, aviator sunglasses... It can be fun to lead them on a merry little dance.'

But keeping an eye on people doesn't always mean cloak and dagger stuff: it's as much about your nosy neighbours or a potential house burglar as it is about government surveillance. If you think anyone would be interested in your movements and you are a potential target, there are some obvious first precautions to take.

Make your movements unpredictable: change your routes and travel times daily; find six routes to work and roll a dice each day to choose one; switch vehicles occasionally; send out your normal vehicle as a decoy; occasionally stay in a hotel or with a friend overnight.

Use several different phones and SIM cards. Keep one of each purely for emergency calls that the surveillance people will never have heard you use before. Avoid using a landline.

Whenever possible, use third parties to meet people. Send written or recorded messages via your carefully chosen go-between.

If you have to meet people yourself, do so in public places – a park, or a café or restaurant with large windows on three walls.

Open and close new e-mail addresses every day if you have to. Communicate a code to your contact so they know what the next e-mail address will be.

Radio producer Shadi Alkasim recommends: 'Try to send any important documents, video or audio clips you have acquired out of the country immediately. Do not keep them with you as they may put your life in danger, or get you arrested.'

Turn on loud music before making any calls if you suspect the line is bugged.

Assume that your computer and instant messaging are insecure. A keystroke copier might have been installed on your computer.

'Clean' your communications equipment. Delete anything 'dodgy' from your phone and laptop, including online instant messaging. Delete messages and 'last calls dialled' daily.

Give contacts different names in your phone. Labels such as 'Home', 'Mum' or 'Dad' should not be real. Place the number of your security guard under those labels, or the number of a friend whom you have briefed to know you are in trouble if someone strange calls.

Leith Mushtaq has a warning for anyone who is working with both sides in a conflict: 'Potential enemies have intelligence-gathering abilities beyond your wildest imagination. Assume you are being watched and be cautious who you talk to about your mission. Avoid government or local contacts unless absolutely necessary. Retain your independence. Any mistake, any contact with the wrong person, and no one will trust you.'

Mohammad Tahir Luddin is one of a handful of eminent Afghan journalists working in Kabul. Or at least he was until he fled after being held for seven months in captivity by the Taliban with a *New York Times* reporter, David Rohde. When it comes to being observed, he has some clear advice for anyone visiting Afghanistan:

'Be careful with your words. Stay independent. That is the only way to protect yourself from being kidnapped, killed or tortured. People working in war zones should not repeat the words of their government – "terrorist", "dictator", "terrorism" – as some US media do. These are government judgements. People attack journalists because they are biased. You can call the Taliban what you like if it is properly sourced to someone else. They won't mind and they won't pin it on you.'

Sebastian Junger's work has inspired a generation of storytellers. His reporting of the Afghan War in particular hit me hard, with its vivid illustration of the well-equipped, professional US soldier's struggle in the face of guerrilla-style warfare against an invisible army. He has some advice on how to avoid unnecessary suspicion in countries where paranoia and conspiracy theory are rife:

'In Liberia I was accused of being a spy. The US embassy got me out. It's easy to be accused of being a spy. Be very, very careful with all your e-mail…there's no reason why the security won't ask you open your accounts. Take care to clear your phone of texts too. A friend in Lebanon got into serious trouble over a racy SMS text. Be aware that the government may be monitoring your e-mail or phones. Delete all signs of military or intelligence contacts before you arrive.

'Also, be careful what you carry in a war zone. Take no detailed maps, no compass and no binoculars.

'And when it comes to questions, keep away from anything the enemy might find useful. Back in 1993 in Sarajevo, when I asked a commander on the front about troop strength, he accused me of being a spy and I got into a lot of trouble. Stick to human questions, stuff about what they and the civilian population around them are going through, stuff that will be relevant back home. Specifics about the military machine will get you in trouble.'

/PASSING UNDER THE RADAR

Spies are supposed to be people who can pass through a room, meeting and chatting with everyone, but no one remembers their name or even what they look like the following day. I am not suggesting you put on your tuxedo or slinky cocktail dress and make like a James Bond character, but if you want to pass under the radar, you need to find a way to become invisible. And if you can't manage that, you must become so harmless and boring that you would never be considered a threat.

The Nepal-based journalist Subina Shrestha offers the following advice about going under cover: 'The best thing to do is perfect the art of looking innocent. This is a lot easier if you are a brown girl! Never look directly at soldiers, look down if you have to, smile a lot and cook up stories as you go along. In Myanmar I smiled a lot, but I was very reliant on my fixer's local knowledge. He was amazing, a real pro at making up stories, so we had plenty to tell people as we went along.'

Subina also told me that she and her husband have perfected the art of looking lost and pretending not to understand: 'When we were doing a story in Uttar Pradesh in India, the cops and the politicians were threatening to kill us. They had goons with sticks, so we played simple, lost tourists. That helped, I think, or maybe we were just lucky.'

Shadi Alkasim worked on some highly sensitive stories with the *Baghdad Bulletin* and other media outlets in Iraq. Lives were at risk, so he learnt to hold onto the most important stories until he was in a place where he could shout about them. 'If you cover any important news – a corruption case, issues related to violations of the laws of war, or crimes against humanity – think very carefully before you publish the story. Publication can put your life at risk. My advice is to be patient until you leave the conflict zone, and then to publish what you want.'

/WHERE TO SIT IN A DODGY PLANE

While writing this book, there have been some questions people keep asking me again and again. The best place to be sitting in a plane in the event of a crash is one of them. I hadn't even thought about it. I think I have been avoiding it. I get scared when I fly in big planes these days. Like a lot of frequent flyers, I've had my share of what felt like close calls. The Aeroflot wing clipping the water as it landed at Odessa after a five-second freefall earlier in the flight was probably the worst. But some confidence was restored by the hot South African pilots flying the Amman–Baghdad route. To avoid mortar attacks when landing, they have to let the plane spiral down to the ground. It takes about three minutes from top to bottom, or one appropriately anthemic Coldplay song on my iPod. You shift slightly forward in your seat and, compared to a normal landing, it feels like a nosedive. But these pilots manage it every time, and then they turn around and flash you a smile just to make sure you will recognize your hero if you see him later in the bar.

What scares most people about flying is their lack of control over the situation. But it turns out that we all have some power about the choices we make when we fly, and they get greater as the plane gets smaller. As a skydiver, I am tempted to tell you that if you find yourself in a plummeting aircraft, simply open the door, chuck yourself out and hope for the best. But that's not the most sensible advice, so I turned to a man I know whose day job is to fly some of the scariest routes around – across parts of Africa where runways fear to tread, in planes that look like they were put together with superglue. Meet Mike Sawatzky. He has worked commercial, cargo and NGO flights across the Democratic Republic of Congo (DRC) for years, flying in and out of Kivu while battles rage below. Here's his advice about the best place to sit:

'I prefer two places: either next to the emergency exit or straight behind the pilot – even beside him if I can. Post 9/11 this is no longer possible in most places, but where I live in DRC the cockpit door is left open for you to meet and greet the crew and get to know them.

'The emergency exit gives you the chance to be the first out of the plane before the fuel reaches flashpoint. But sitting at the back of the plane also has some advantages: it gives you the chance to be the last one to hit the deck. Plus, if you are crashing nose-down, you avoid everyone's carry-on duty free hitting you on the back of the head.

'As a pilot, I know that things go wrong and that I have remedied them in the past before the passengers realized what was happening. If a pilot can show me he's cool as his world is falling apart, I can snooze and let him handle the questions after. Maybe that's why I prefer sitting in the cockpit.

'One time I flew with a Russian pilot to a bush strip in eastern DRC. He was a tough ex-military guy; he knew his stuff. I sat right behind this captain with his beer bottle beside his foot. As long as he didn't go for it right before take-off or landing, I knew I was OK. And if anything went wrong, I could at least get in there and get my hands dirty. The gauges might have been in Cyrillic, but I could wrap my head around that – an airplane is an airplane.

'When it comes to small planes, I never understand why people are so paranoid. We all appreciate the buzz of the plane as it passes overhead to land and get us outta there. No one frets as much about jumping onto a 50-ton jumbo jet to go hurtling through subspace for 12 hours – at least not to the extent that they will cancel a $3000 ticket.

'You need to give your pilot the benefit of the doubt. He's paid his dues to get where he is. Check him out: does he look you in the eyes without brushing off your concerns? Does he command the ground crew and cabin crew affirmatively and respectfully? Does he occasionally throw off the extra baggage because it's just too much? Does he have an air of respect for his aircraft even if it's old and lacking paint in certain places? These are all questions you and I have to ask ourselves before we get on board.

'If you don't like the look of the pilot, think hard and weigh your options. In many cases you might not have a choice. This is where the emergency exit seat comes in handy!'

A final, but important, tip on moving around small airports on foot comes from Tom Coghlan: 'Do not walk in front of propeller-driven planes when they have one or more engines turning over. Even at 20 metres, stuff gets sucked into the blades.'

Do not crash your car into a dictator president's security entourage (especially when the entourage is stationary).
Mary O'Shea

4/COPING WITH GUNFIRE, BOMBINGS AND MISSILES

You can't take just anyone from the street and send them into a battle zone. They have to understand the basics – how to discern between a missile, artillery, bullets, sniper or tank fire. I can distinguish these and then react. I can predict when the battle is starting from the people moving into position. I put myself in the position of the soldier. I look for their hiding places. I know the angles. **Leith Mushtaq**

ON A HOSTILE-ENVIRONMENT course a few years ago, I thought I knew everything already, but I couldn't have been more wrong. I and a truly experienced and war-weary cameraman from Jerusalem dozed through most of the classes. Then we were taken on a day trip to an underground bunker for shooting practice. They showed us a bulletproof car and several different types of wall, and asked where we would hide if someone began to shoot at us. Most of us pointed to the bulletproof car. We then watched in astonishment as our teacher shot through the car in seven bullets, followed by a breezeblock wall in three and a redbrick wall in four. Bulletproof, my arse! A lesson was learnt and never forgotten: nowhere is safe.

I should have known that from my time on exercise in Canada with the artillery. We were firing big missiles over dozens of kilometres, then going forward to check on the site for unexploded ordinance. One evening, with the sun going down, we decided to set up camp near a crater made by one of our missiles. We started 'digging in' – no mean feat when you have to bury a giant tank-size gun out of sight from an imaginary enemy. As we dug down, we found a network of chipmunk or some other local critter's burrows. There were dozens of dead creatures, all killed by the force of one artillery shell 50 metres away and 3 metres of mud above them. A near miss can still kill.

I spent plenty of time dodging what felt like targeted fire in Iraq, but in reality I have never been directly shot at. In that situation you need expert advice on where to be if all hell breaks loose – and who better to supply it than Chris Cobb-Smith, a man whose job it is to prepare people before they are plunged into dangerous places, and then bring them out again in one piece. The following information is largely his.

/EMERGENCY PROCEDURES

These are my recommended actions for dealing with shooting, guns, bombs and missiles. They can strike at any time and usually when you least expect it. Where do you want to be when they hit? What can you hide behind or should you just run?

To avoid becoming a target

- Don't wear military-style clothing. Wear bland colours that don't attract attention, but differing shades top and bottom so it doesn't look like uniform.
- Try not to have anything shiny that might attract attention.
- Be careful if filming as a video camera can be mistaken for a weapon: the sun glinting off the lens could be taken for that off a weapon sight, or even for the

flash of a weapon firing. It could attract attack on the ground and also from artillery or aircraft.
- For similar reasons, be careful of using flash photography.
- Consider the implications of the markings on your vehicles – 'Press,' 'Media', the name of your charity or organization. Will it provide immunity or attract targeting? This changes according to the environment.

Monique Nagelkerke has worked for Médecins Sans Frontières for 20 years, and says that over time people living inside a war zone fail to remain alert and prepared for any eventuality. 'The first time we were bombed by Khartoum forces in south Sudan it was Christmas morning. I was awake, but many were sleeping. A plane flew over, lower than usual. I put on my clothes and my contact lenses and got outside in time to see a plane fly back and bombs start raining down. I went straight to look for a team member who was still sleeping in her hut, grabbed her arm and yelled, "We're being bombed." She took out her earplugs and only then realized the danger. As we ran away – too late, the bombs had already landed – the earplug girl looked at me, and said in a lovely French accent, "I am not wearing my bra!" She clutched her rather large bosom in her hands and we continued running away from the stone buildings.

'Lessons learnt: 1) When in a war zone, do not sleep with earplugs in. 2) Wear a bra when sleeping if you have a large bosom, in case you need to run. 3) Never continue looking at a returning plane when in an area that has already been bombed by similar-looking planes. Run!'

If shots are fired near your house or office...

Study and rehearse the following procedures:

- Remain in the building.
- Keep communications equipment to hand.
- Stay together as a group.
- Take cover.
- Lock doors.
- Stay away from the windows.
- Raise the alarm using prearranged telephone numbers.
- Assess whether it is safe to exit the building or better to stay put.

Mary O'Shea recalls: 'In Lebanon I was told to sleep in the bath when there was gunfire or shelling.'

If firing comes closer and there might be a raid on the building...

- Move into the safe room (see page 35) or bomb shelter. Failing that, go under the stairs or into a room with no outside walls.
- Wait for the all-clear before venturing out.
- If there is time as the situation deteriorates, remove glass from the windows and any clutter from the room as it will fly around and cause injury in the event of a blast. Wet mattresses placed up against the walls will absorb fragments and possibly bullets.
- As a last resort, go onto the roof, if accessible. Once everyone is out there, lock the access door, stay away from the edge and signal for help with a torch, mini-flares or a phone.

If you are caught outside...

Your first priority should be to take cover:

- Don't look for the person firing – use your ears and move away from the sound.
- Don't take cover in a place that someone was recently using as a firing position.
- If caught in the open, go immediately for the most obvious cover, such as a dip in the ground, then assess the situation.
- If you have a car, avoid hiding near the petrol tank, and remember that the door will be useless protection. Try to get behind the engine block, by one of the front wheels.
- If you need to observe to assess the situation, look around but never over whatever you are using as cover.
- If in a group and trying to escape the danger, move individually and at intervals, as unpredictably as possible.
- Leave any equipment behind if it is going to hinder your escape.

Monique Nagelkerke agrees totally with this advice, and says: 'Keep your head down. So many times people stand up, look around or look out of the window when there is shooting and shelling going on. The best reaction is literally to keep your head down. Dig down behind a wall, behind a copy machine, behind a coffee table – anything as long as you do not stand up and look around.'

If there is a bomb warning...

- If the bomb threat comes over the phone, ask the caller as many questions as possible and take down the details, e.g. where the bomb is planted, when it will

be detonated and why. Also note whether the caller is male or female, the accent, attitude, any background noise, etc.
- Evacuate the target area.
- Inform the authorities, military, etc.

If there is an explosion...

- Take cover immediately. Lie down under whatever cover is available, even a table or bed. As soon as it's practical to do so, move to a bomb shelter or safe room.
- Assess the situation and bomb direction, then, when safe to do so or under orders, move to the emergency exit in the opposite direction from the sound of the bomb. There might be a secondary device or a gunman picking off targets at the main exit.
- Use prearranged escape routes (see page 31).
- Do not stand in any gathering or crowd. The threat of a secondary bomb or bomber remains.

> The Holy Koran says that whatever happens to us is our destiny, and we trust in the Holy Koran. The date for our death is written; we cannot change it.
> **Sayed Hashim**, captain, Afghan National Army

5/KEEPING SAFE IN A CROWD, PROTEST OR RIOT

In a war zone you have to be thinking all the time 'What if...?' Don't get isolated within a crowd or within a war zone... physically or emotionally. **Dr Carl Hallam**

THE PEOPLE I LOVE are those who tend to follow the path least travelled. They're the opposite of me: I have always felt the magnetic pull of a crowd. If I hear a party, I'll knock on the door. I see a queue and I wonder whether it's worth joining. If I am on the edge of something, I want to be in the middle. It's a weakness that nearly saw me killed several times in Iraq.

Curiosity has driven me into all sorts of dangerous situations. I am often more interested in what I am going to find out, or what I can be a part of, than assessing whether it is safe to go ahead. It was only when I started putting other people's lives in danger that I began to stop and think.

Between Basra city and its airport, where the UK-led forces were based, there was a large crossroads. As the only safe route in and out of the city in that direction, it became a popular protest hotspot in the summer of 2003. They were always sure to grab the attention of passing troops.

I was a freelance reporter with a licence to poke my nose in where it wasn't wanted. A few of my best stories had come from walking up to small, sensible demos and asking what they were complaining about. In the lawless world that was post-invasion Iraq it was one of the few ways for people to vent their anger and make their point known. There were no trusted police, soldiers or politicians to turn to. The only options were to demonstrate or pick up a gun. But those smaller, controlled gatherings were like an entry drug into the world of riots. I was quickly addicted.

So when, one day, my trip to the airport was interrupted by a group of angry young men blocking the crossroads, I was surprised when the Iraqi friend I was with stopped around half a kilometre away from them and said we should turn back. In fact, I was a little annoyed. I was going to be late for an important meeting with a top British Army general.

From a distance, we could see there were about 250 people waving flags and burning tyres. It looked familiar to me – I had even seen one car pass through the raging group already, and I wanted to follow. What I had failed to notice was that all the other cars were stopping and turning back. One of the two friends I had in the car was a British freelancer on a visit from Baghdad. I wanted him to meet the army chief before he left for the capital again. 'Onward,' I said. And we began a stuttered crawl towards the crowd.

We passed a man wandering away from the crossroads, and on the insistence of my friends, we stopped to ask if it was safe for us to pass through. He looked at us through glazed eyes and curled his fingers over the top of the open window of my door, as if to wrench it open. We tried to stay calm as he shouted 'English? English?' at us. In sync, we three shouted back 'Iraqi', 'French' and 'Swedish' – well practised by now. He shook his head and shouted 'English, English' again, turning towards the protest. It was then we saw that he had two grenades in his other grubby hand, now resting next to the one on my door, inches from my face. He looked back at us and my British friend reached across and opened my door, kicking it open to push grenade boy back. We then roared into reverse and he came running towards us. We drove away from the crowd as fast as we could.

That was no riot, but it was a group of relatively well-organized men, dangerous, armed and angry, and looking for a target. No one spoke much on the way back to my Iraqi friend's home with his wife and four children. But every now and then I bleated 'Sorry'.

DO I STAY OR DO I GO?

/ Do I have a valid reason for going?

/ Does anyone know I am here? And do I have someone waiting to hear I am safe?

/ Do I know what the risks are?

/ Does the crowd feel familiar? Have I got an ally within it?

/ Do I know who is running the riot? Do I trust them?

/ Can I get to an airport or embassy if it turns nasty?

/ Do I have an escape route mapped out that will remain open?

/ As your fairy godmother might say, if you can answer yes to these questions, you may go to the riot.

The Al Jazeera correspondent Hoda Abdel-Hamid told me: 'Crowds in general are not good. Crowds in a war zone are worse. There was a huge bomb in Iskandaryia and 55 people were killed. It was at a time when we could still move around, so we found a spot for the satellite. We went to the police station where the car bomb had hit. I remember a kid was there, waving a severed hand around in our faces. While we were there a car went past spraying bullets. I ran with the crowd. In all the confusion, a man shoved his hands down my pants. At the end of the road there was barbed wire. The man was pushing me and I was stuck in the barbed wire. Our security guard pulled me out. But you can't rely on that. You should always make sure you know your escape routes.'

The best advice is to avoid street protests at all costs. Of course, that's not always possible; sometimes they run into you. And sometimes you might join a small peaceful protest that turns into a riot. You might be in an ambulance waiting to deal with the fallout nearby. You might be involved as a protester when it all goes wrong.

If there is one piece of advice that stays with you from this chapter, it has to be 'Stop and think before you go'. Even if you are alone, it's not just yourself that is heading into the line of danger. There are people at home waiting for you to come back, your dog, your colleagues – they all need you to stay safe.

Marc Laban, co-founder of AsiaWorks Television, recalls a violent episode in Thailand: 'In May 1992 all hell broke loose on the streets of Bangkok. A massive anti-government rally exploded into several nights of extreme violence. Unable to disperse the crowds with a show of strength, soldiers opened fire on protesters, killing dozens. The stand-off continued for several nights. I was struck by the protesters' resolve to stand firm: at one point they even drove a hijacked city bus directly at the soldiers. It was the first time I had ever seen anything like this, and I learnt pretty quickly that it is important to put yourself on the sidelines when bullets are flying, and rely on a long lens to record the moment.

'Before I moved to Thailand a colleague had joked, "Going to Asia, eh? You're gonna see a lot of dead bodies." I had laughed nervously at the time. I wasn't laughing now. No journalists were killed but plenty were hurt, mostly by flying debris. An AP journalist nearly lost her eye when she was hit with a ball-bearing.'

There is no safety in numbers when it comes to a riot. You might feel invisible in the crowd, but that mass is a powerful force and it can quickly turn, especially

RIOT PRECAUTIONS

If you know you're going to encounter a riotous crowd, it's a good idea to go prepared for the worst. Subina Shrestha offers the first lot of tips:

/ Take toothpaste to protect against tear gas if you have nothing else to protect you. Smear it under your eyes, not right around, or it will drip into them.

/ Carry a motorcycle helmet. Once bricks start being chucked, you will feel much safer with it on.

/ Figure out ways to escape before you plant yourself in a difficult position. It is always easier if you are at a crossroads when the rioters or the cops start charging.

/ Look for homes that you can use as a safe house if need be. Talk to the owners beforehand.

Basic behaviour

Stick to the following, and you will be much safer:

/ Keep your head down and avoid confrontation.

/ Avoid bottle-necks, where the crowd might be squashed into a tight space, e.g. tunnels, pillars, walls.

/ Walk rather than run to avoid attracting attention.

/ Don't wear military-style clothing, or anything that looks like a uniform.

/ Know where your exits are if you are inside, but stay inside, away from the protest.

/ Remain inside your car unless it has become a focus for the protest. If you must drive, avoid main routes.

Personal protection and first aid

Try to carry the following:

/ As much water as you can manage, both to drink and to use for first aid.

/ Vinyl or latex gloves for dealing with wounds and to protect from pepper spray, which will make the nerve-endings on your hands scream with pain if it gets on your skin.

/ Basic medical kit, including several days of any personal medication (asthma inhaler, etc.) and a doctor's note in case you are arrested.

/ Some kind of sugar hit in case you are drained by adrenalin.

/ Bulletproof vest – if you have assessed the risk and decide it's necessary.

/ ID and emergency contact information – in an obvious place.

/ Two telephones if possible – one in a pocket, one in a bag.

/ Money – hidden both on your person and in your bag.

/ Sanitary towels rather than tampons if you have your period. You might not be able to change a tampon either in a riot or if you are arrested, and a tampon left for more than eight hours increases your chances of toxic shock syndrome.

against a stranger. You cannot predict the whims of a crowd, but when it moves it will move together.

Journalist Tim Albone escaped by the skin of his teeth in Afghanistan: 'My translator and driver saved my life one day in Kabul. We were driving to the scene of an accident involving an American truck – the brakes had failed and it had run over and killed some Afghans, and an angry mob had gathered. As we got close to the scene, we could hear gunshots and I sensed trouble. Tahir, my translator, told us to lock the car doors. Only moments later our car was surrounded by a group of men shouting and trying to open the doors and pull us out. Tahir ordered Azad, the driver, to floor it, which he did. As soon as we broke free from the crowd, Tahir started laughing. When I asked him what was so funny, he said: "You should have heard what they were saying. They wanted to skin you alive." Tahir's quick thinking might have been a life-saver, but he had a terrible sense of humour.'

/ANTI-RIOT WEAPONS

When assessing the risks ahead, you need to think about anti-riot weapons and the possibility of being hit by them. Understanding what you are up against should help you to stay calm and decisive if you ever find yourself face to face with armed riot police.

Water-cannons will knock you off your feet if they hit you directly, and can cause serious injury. Get out of their way, steadily and without drawing unnecessary attention to yourself. If you cannot avoid being hit, stay low and roll into a ball with your back to the weapon.

Rubber bullets come in many shapes and sizes. Some of the smaller ones can cause major injury and even death if fired at close quarters (less than 40 metres). Well-trained riot police should aim for your legs, but if they miss and hit your eye, the bullet will blind you. If you have ever played paintball you will know how much it can hurt to be hit with a non-lethal weapon, and these ain't no paintballs – many of them are actually rubber-coated steel bullets. You should be able to tell if the troops are firing rubber bullets because there will be a small, bucket-like container attached to their weapons instead of a normal magazine of bullets. There may also be a large structure attached to the end of their gun. But don't wait around to see what type of ammunition they're using. Just get away from them as quickly and calmly as you can.

Chemical weapons, such as tear gas, are often used to disperse riots. In fact, exposure to tear gas is also part of British army training – to help you learn how to put on your nuclear/biological/chemical weapons kit under stress within 10 seconds – and also to familiarize you with the effects of tear gas and learn how to cope with them. So there you are, standing in a dark hut listening to the short, nervous breaths of the soldier beside you, and suddenly the gas comes on. A sergeant wearing his gas mask shouts at each of us to sing the nursery rhyme 'Mary Had a Little Lamb' before we can put ours on. By then it's too late. The gas is in your now-weeping eyes, your sour-tasting mouth, making your skin itch and breathing difficult. But soon it's over. We are outside breathing fresh air. A minute later we are shoved back inside for another round of spluttered singing, until no one in that tiny little room shows any sign of panic. We are all resigned to our painful fate. The training worked. What I learnt first of all is that contact lenses are evil after exposure to tear gas.

TEAR GAS AND PEPPER SPRAY TIPS

/ Avoid wearing oil-based moisturizer or sunscreen – the chemicals will cling to it. Wash your hands and face in a detergent-free soap to remove them beforehand. Use water or alcohol-based sunscreen if you need it.

/ Wear glasses instead of contact lenses. The pain of tear gas trapped behind a contact lens is horrendous.

/ Make your own decontamination spray. Dilute antacid – the stuff used for indigestion – with water to spray into eyes and mouth and over your skin. Alka-Seltzer, Milk of Magnesia, Pepto-Bismol, Tums, Eno's or Gaviscon would all work, as would mixing bicarbonate of soda with water.

/ Carry spare clothes in a plastic bag in case you need to change out of contaminated ones, or if you are hit by a water-cannon on a cold day.

/ Wear swimming goggles or a gas mask to protect your eyes.

/ Carry several bandanas soaked in water and put them in plastic bags. Use them to wrap around your mouth. You will need to keep replacing them as the bandana soaks up the gas.

/ Do not touch a tear-gas canister with bare hands. It will be very hot.

/ Do not rub the chemicals into your eyes or skin. Try to stay calm.

Even worse, you have to put a contaminated finger in your eye to take out the piece of plastic that now feels like a shard of glass. Your nose will run, your mouth will water. You will cough and you might feel dizzy.

For the rest of my year in the army I was still able to feel a burn in my eyes every time I put on my gas mask for training. Tear gas and pepper spray will stick to everything exposed, and also to anything you touch, before you manage to wash it all off. You might find yourself feeling the effects for days afterwards if you don't decontaminate before entering your home. These weapons are toxic, but the immediate effects of tear gas will wear off after half an hour in fresh air.

I am told that the pain from pepper spray is more instant and intense, and that you might also feel a strong sense of anger. Pepper spray is much harder to remove from the skin. In a high concentration, it can also cause first-degree burns if left on the skin. In a normal concentration, most of the painful effects should disappear within two hours of moving away from direct exposure.

/CROWD CONTROL

It is worth remembering that crowds are not always going to be hostile. Some come in peace. If you are in a position of authority, they might be more afraid of you than you are of the thousands of them.

Samantha Bolton remembers: 'Refugee crowds without leaders can be organized, especially when in shock. We were the first to see over a million refugees come over the border in Goma after the massacre in Rwanda in 1994. They streamed over in silence in just two hours. They were like dumbstruck cattle and went just where I told them as I was the only figure of authority around. The key is not to be afraid, and to pick out a possible leader if you need someone to negotiate with.'

/BODY ARMOUR OR FLAK JACKETS

You put on your underwear, you put on your trousers and a shirt, then on goes the body armour. The longer you wear it, the heavier it gets. If you are running around, it gets sweaty and dirty. If it doesn't fit very well, it will start to rub and bruise, and then – ouch! – it really hurts.

I wore a flak jacket for 21 days in a row while on exercise with the army. We were told we had to sleep in it, so we did. My arms and hips were bruised for another three weeks afterwards. By the time I emerged from my armoured cocoon, what little need I had for a bra had disappeared and instead I found a washboard stomach.

There is a big debate over whether civilians should wear body armour at all. People working for NGOs often don't as they say the logo on their cars and shirts is protection enough.

Some people, like my colleague Zeina Khodr, are fatalistic: 'I don't believe in armour. If it is your day to die, it is your day. And also it's important not to look different from the people around you.' Others reinforce at least part of this view. Qais Azimy says: 'I don't wear expensive clothes any more – it just draws attention. I try to look more like a local. Body armour too just puts you more in danger.'

THE CORRECT WAY TO WEAR A FLAK JACKET

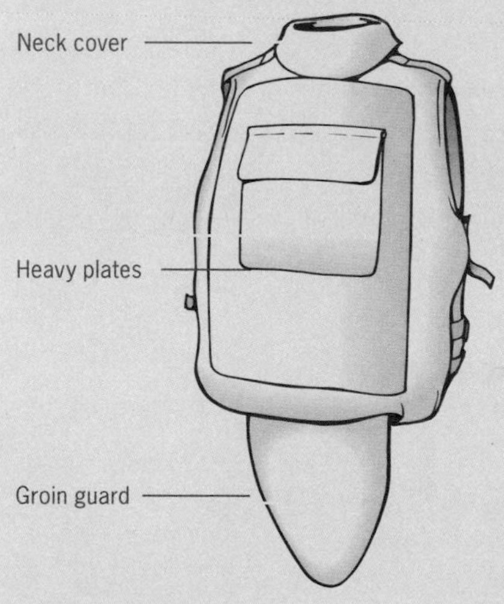

/ The jacket fits if it sits just on your hips and doesn't ride up above your shoulders. It should cover your stomach.

/ It should be done up tightly but be loose enough to enable you to lift up your arms and bend over.

/ Do not remove any components. Keep the heavy extra plates inside the jacket, not outside 'ready to be put in during an emergency'. Keep the neck cover and groin cover attached. Even if they are annoying, they are there for a reason.

/ Most body armour has a removable cover, so when it starts to stink – which it will – wash it and hang it up to dry overnight.

Many even question whether it will save them if they are shot. It is a pain to wear, but feels pretty flimsy when you know it is supposed to defend you from bullets and shrapnel. Captain Sayed Hashim said: 'The Afghan National Army did not used to have helmets and body armour, but now we are getting more – almost all of us have armour. We wear it, but I know it doesn't make any difference to whether we survive or not. That is Allah's will.'

Some people, such as Nick Toksvig, feel the advantages of wearing flak jackets far outweigh the negative aspects: 'The jacket isn't difficult to wear. I have seen it save someone's life when they were shot directly in the chest. At the very least it will hold you together if you are hit. A cameraman I know was working with his flak under a shirt. He was looking straight down the camera and someone came up and stabbed him from behind. The attacker hit the jacket, his hand slid down the knife and he actually ended up cutting himself. My friend ran for his life.'

Shelley Thakral is pragmatic about wearing body armour: 'It's just a necessary part of my kit. Not just for me, but for everyone around me. Of course, you have to know when to wear it, when you don't stand out. But wherever you are, it is another layer of security. As a journalist, I am exposed, so I need to take extra precautions. The risks of not wearing it are not worth taking.'

Leith Mushtaq says: 'It seems pointless to wear the body armour, but wear it anyway so that no one can accuse you of not taking care of yourself if you are hurt. However, don't wear the body armour if you are going to be a target as a result of it.'

If you are lucky, your body armour will be like a jacket, something to put on when you are leaving the house. But you might find yourself wearing it for hours and days and weeks on end.

Sherine Tadros told me: 'I've had big problems with flak jackets. I've tried different sizes with different plates, but they all have one thing in common – they are damned heavy. I found wearing one for a day or two, as I did in Lebanon, just about bearable, but in Gaza, for 23 days, it felt like I was carrying the kitchen sink on my back.'

Sherine offers the following ideas to reduce post-flak back pain:

- When you are taking the jacket off or putting it on, lie it down on something and slip in and out of it rather than trying to lift it over your head.
- Sitting down while wearing your flak feels better than standing, but it is still putting a lot of pressure on your back and shoulders. To avoid this, manoeuvre yourself into a sitting position that takes the bulk of the weight off – perhaps by resting most of the weight of the flak on a table, or holding it up using your chair.
- In the absence of anyone around you willing and able to do so, give yourself back and shoulder massages when you take the flak off, and stretch your muscles.

Body armour is not exactly high fashion, and Laura Tyson points out: 'Women rarely look good in a flak jacket. If you have to wear one, make sure your clothes are dark-coloured and fairly tight-fitting, or else you look like you're going to an embassy fancy dress party.'

Then there's the helmet – a bad hair day for everyone, but pretty essential. Marc Laban advises: 'In an urban riot situation, wear a helmet. One of my photographer friends improvised, tying the ubiquitous Thai street cooking pot on his head.

'These days it is standard practice for broadcasters to send their teams out with helmets and flak jackets, but there are still a lot of freelancers who can't afford proper protection. In that case, buy a motorcycle helmet – or a cooking pot. They're not going to stop a round from an M-16, but they might save you from serious injury.'

If you do decide to wear a flak jacket, make sure it's up to the correct specifications. Look inside for a label with the level of protection specified. The plates should be at least level IV, which will protect against a standard high-velocity bullet.

Ensure your jacket is checked regularly; they do not last forever, and the plates can fracture if dropped or mistreated. The same goes for your helmet and goggles, which again should meet certain specified standards.

When it comes to IEDs, car bombs, random shootings and mortar attacks, I believe that everyone should take every precaution they can to stay alive, even if that means staying at home for years on end or getting the hell out of the country like I did. I want to die for a good reason if I can't die from natural causes. **Imad Shihab**

6/FIRST AID AND EMERGENCY MEDICINE

It is difficult to keep a reality check, to stay sane in a place with so many uncertainties. You get a headache in London and it's just a headache. But get one in Africa and you start to think it's dengue fever or malaria. You have to learn to manage that fear. The fear and worry are often far worse than the headache itself. **Marc DuBois**

READERS OF THIS BOOK have probably been through some sort of basic medical training, but might not realize it. Whether it was putting a bandage on a teddy bear's broken arm or watching hours of *Grey's Anatomy* because you fancied one of the doctors, some sense of first aid has rubbed off. The problem is working out which bits are fact and which are fiction.

The good news is that common sense almost always prevails. It's just a little more complicated in a war zone or during a disaster. Time and limited resources mean that you will be forced to prioritize. Say, for example, you don't have a stretcher or neck brace – do you move the person with a potentially broken back out of the line of fire or not? Or say you're in open ground when snipers start firing – do you run and save your life, leaving someone bleeding to death behind you? Who do you help when you have to choose between one starving child and another? Often the choices have to be made in seconds. There is almost never a correct answer.

I was in the British Army for a year before I went to university, and during that time I was given about a week's worth of Red Cross training. In the army they limit your choices. There is a strict battlefield order of who gets attention and who doesn't. It's brutal. If an injured person isn't breathing, you leave them and move onto the next one. You don't even try to help. You are issued with one giant bandage – though people carry as many as possible – and it should be used carefully. When in battle, you'll get morphine too. And that should be guarded for the most acute moments of pain.

Soldiers are prepared for the worst – in fact, taught to expect it. And if you are working anywhere near them, you should be too.

Journalist Tim Albone took this advice and told me all about it:

'Before I left England for Afghanistan I went on a "Surviving Hostile Environments" course run by ex-special forces operatives near Hereford. It turned out to be one of the smartest things I did.

'On 13 December 2005 I was travelling with Canadian troops on the border of Kandahar and Helmand province when the armoured jeep I was in was hit by a roadside bomb. When the dust settled, it turned out that I was the only one who could move. The driver and the front-seat passenger were both trapped and had broken legs. The gunner, who had been standing half out of the top with an armoured turret for protection, had simply disappeared.

'I remembered my security training: they had told me on the course that it is always safer to stay in an armoured car, but I soon had to reassess this idea. The guys in front started cursing at me and telling me to hurry up and get them out – they were in a lot of pain. I remember the moment I pushed open the armoured door: I was convinced I was going to get shot. Luckily, there was no follow-up ambush, but what I saw was shocking enough. The gunner had been flung out of the vehicle and was lying a few feet away with the armoured gun turret on top of his chest. I was convinced he was dead. Then he started shouting. I pulled the turret off him and was amazed to find he was totally unharmed.

'We both set about getting the two men out of the front of the jeep. It was a complete mess; the engine block had been thrown a few feet away, one tyre had been completely destroyed, and the other lay some distance away. I was surprised that no one was coming to help us. I later found out that they were sweeping the area for mines, but as we were in a dip by a dry riverbed, we couldn't see them working their way slowly towards us, their mine detectors at the ready. I felt we were completely alone.

'Once we had got the driver and passenger out of the front seat, I remembered some of my first-aid training and set about putting it into practice. I cut off the soldiers' boots and, using the medical kit I had been given, splinted their legs. They were a bit of a mess: the bones were sticking out and I'm pretty sure without the training I would have had no idea what to do. When the medic finally got to us, about 20 minutes later, he was pretty quick to undo one of my splints and redo it. I hadn't done it up tightly enough. It was clear that a one-week course was no replacement for years of training, but what it meant was that while we had the wait, I didn't panic and I set about doing something. Without the training, I'm pretty sure I would have been more nervous and less certain of what to do. The incident taught me the importance of preparing for the worst and not going into a war zone without some kind of training.'

BBC correspondent Caroline Hawley agrees in principle, but warns that doing a course is no guarantee of doing the right thing in a medical emergency: 'When violence strikes unexpectedly you're caught off guard. In November 2005 I was in Amman, on a break from Baghdad, enjoying the kind of meal out that you could only fantasize about in Iraq, where many of the city's restaurants had shut down. When the suicide bomber blew himself up in the lobby of the Hyatt Hotel, we had just ordered a beer in the Asian restaurant on the lower ground floor. The sound, of course, was deafening. I snapped my head around to see a column of fire and smoke on the stairway in the middle of the hotel. Then I saw the bloodied bodies – or were they still just about alive? I'll never know. One man had vomited and defecated. I ran to get the ambulances to come round to our part of the hotel. It was a relief to get away from all the blood. But why didn't I think to put the injured in the recovery position first? In the shock of it all, I seemed to have forgotten the elementary rules of first aid.'

This same thing might happen to you, so the first lesson is to trust your instincts. So many people I know are nervous of using the medical knowledge they learn. Nervous they will get it wrong. Nervous they won't remember how to do anything.

Inside hot classrooms after long cold runs in the rain I nodded sleepily through most of my Red Cross training in the British Army. I had regular updates throughout the year, and thought little had gone in. But two months later, when I was in a car accident in Botswana, I managed to whimper Red Cross instructions to my 12 injured friends while passing in and out of consciousness myself. They hopped into the next car that would take them, and I was left with two friends to wait for an ambulance. I couldn't move my legs, so we refused several offers of a lift from passing farmers. Dehydrated, concussed and sick with pain from my crushed back, I wanted a doctor with a proper stretcher. It was like holding out for a London ambulance on the edge of the Okavango Delta. Silly. The ambulance did come eventually and four nurses each grabbed one of my limbs and threw me into the back of their dirty van. I thought I would never walk again, but I did...the next day.

The point is that, even in the direst of circumstances, these few pages of medical advice *will* come back to you. And even if you recall just one paragraph, you could help save someone from worse injury or even death.

I have tried to keep the information brief. Where common sense seems too obvious to mention, I have left it out altogether. I am no doctor, but I have had a few of them look over this text for me.

Warning: You might go out alone, but you are likely to find yourself working or at least living with others if you are in a dangerous place. It is essential that you tell those around you how to deal with any health problems you have: diabetes, asthma, allergies, heart and blood-clotting problems are some obvious ones. As the leader of a team, it is a good idea to start any trip by asking about any health problems amongst your group (see also page 21). You need to know how to use your own medical kit and any special medical treatment or equipment belonging to the people around you.

/YOUR MEDICAL KIT

This is a contentious subject. Everyone has a different opinion about what is important. But a medical kit, however small, can help you survive. Keep it packed at the bottom of a grab bag (see page 41), full of other essentials, such as your phone and ID, and check it before each trip.

Your medical kit should contain:

- **Pain relief** – aspirin in case someone has a heart attack and non-aspirin for other forms of pain, as some people are allergic and aspirin should not be given to people under 18.
- **Water sterilization tablets** – to be used when boiling suspect water is impossible (see page 201).
- **Antibiotics** – enough for a week's full course. These can be difficult to get in some places, so they're worth hoarding when you find a country that sells them without a prescription. Check the expiry date. If giving them to someone else, always ask about allergies, e.g. to penicillin. It's worth knowing that the names of penicillin-type drugs usually end with 'cillin' (for example, amoxicillin, flucloxacillin) so if you can buy something that sounds different, it might be useful for those who are allergic. But check any packaging information first.
- **Antihistamine** – in cream and pill form, for rashes or insect bites.
- **Antiseptic** – cream, liquid or spray, or iodine or alcohol wipes. If you choose something like TCP, it can double up as a throat gargle.
- **Diarrhoea pills** – useful for desperate moments, especially when on the move.
- **Salt tablets** – to replace all you lose in an injury, or after a long active day when you have perspired freely.
- **Butterfly stitches** – to hold large wounds in place.
- **Plasters and bandages** – of all shapes and sizes, plus some sterile gauze pads. Tampons and sanitary towels can also be used to cover wounds: you need enough plaster or sticky tape to hold them in place.
- **Vinyl or latex gloves** – to avoid introducing infection while you are dressing wounds and to protect you from blood-borne infection, such as hepatitis B. Could also be used short term to keep dressings on fingers and feet dry.
- **Condoms** – can be used to keep fingers and feet sterile and waterproof for a short period of time. Also useful as portable water carriers or party balloons.
- **Small scissors** – people never seem to have them when you need to cut plaster or clothing.
- **Malaria tablets** – I have often skipped these and been lucky enough to avoid getting ill. I have always argued that the side effects outweigh the danger. Here, however, I defer to the advice of Dr Carl Hallam, who has worked in some of the most festering malarial bogs: 'Take anti-malaria tablets. Europeans do not do well with *Malaria falciparum* (severe malaria). They can die in 24 hours because they have no resistance. It adds hugely to the workload of doctors already burdened with dealing with other problems locally. If you really feel you can't take

anti-malarials, then take the malaria cure with you [see page 138]. But you need to learn how to take it and be confident in your diagnosis.'

This view is reinforced by Leith Mushtaq, who told me: 'It's not just bullets that can kill you – a mosquito can too.'

To the list opposite you can add all the extras you might need: asthma inhalers, pills and potions for the relief of cystitis and thrush, an extra pair of reading glasses, blister treatments... These are all things that some people cannot live without.

There are, of course, other medical preparations you need to make too, as outlined in Chapter 1 (see page 20).

/FIRST AID

Step 1: Call for help

In a medical emergency you should always call for help, but don't hesitate to treat the patient if the injury is serious. If you are alone, carry out the first few checks (see page 106) and any necessary immediate treatment, such as stopping the flow of blood, then call for help. If the heart has stopped, do CPR (cardiopulmonary resuscitation, see page 108) for one minute, then pause to call for help.

Normal vital signs

	Adults (14 plus)	**Children** (3–14 years)	**Infants** (1–3 years)	**Newborns** (0–12 months)
Pulse (beats per min)	60–100	80–120 (till 5 years) 70–110 (till 14 years)	80–130	100–160
Respiration (breaths per min)	12–20	20–30 (till 5 years) 15–30 (till 14 years)	20–30	30–50
Temperature (°C)	37	37	37	37

Remember that in serious medical emergencies you are really an assistant to the doctors who are on their way. You need to take a mental or even written note of any changes in your patient. If you administer drugs, note how much and when.

Step 2: Work out if it's safe for you to help

Consider the following before you start giving help:

- Are you in the middle of a motorway with cars streaming by?
- Is there a battle going on around you?
- Is the vehicle the injured person is in stable? Is the engine off?
- Is what just happened to your patient likely to happen to you?
- Is there a chance any fire might spread?
- Is there someone nearby who can help make it safe for you to work with the casualty?

Always be aware that what has happened to your patient could happen to you.

ABC – the first checks

ABC stands for airway, breathing, circulation. Always check these things if the casualty is unconscious, otherwise it's not necessary: the casualty will be talking to you and it will be obvious what is wrong.

Airway – is the airway open and clear? Is something obstructing the breathing? If so, you need to try to remove it. The casualty can choke on their own tongue if you are not careful. You need to tip their head backwards before you start to check inside the mouth for obstructions. If the mouth is clear, then clearing the airway means putting one hand on their forehead to gently tilt the head back and raising their chin using two fingertips.

Breathing – is their breathing normal? Put your cheek down to their face and listen and feel for breathing. Look to see if their chest is moving. If there are no signs of breathing after 10 seconds, start CPR immediately (see page 108).

Circulation – is the patient bleeding? Do a head-to-toe check (see opposite) for bleeding and other problems. Bleeding needs to be treated immediately (see page 116). It might lead to shock – and that can be deadly.

If all three ABC are fine, place the casualty in the recovery position (see page 112) and focus on getting some emergency help again before carrying on with second checks (see page 112).

HEAD-TO-TOE CHECK

/ Check breathing and pulse – the rate and strength of both. (The normal rates are on page 105.)

/ Start at the head, carefully checking the scalp for signs of a fracture – swelling or depression.

/ Check the casualty's hearing. If they have any clear fluid or watery blood coming out of either ear, it could be a serious head injury.

/ Look at the pupils (the black area) in both eyes. If they are different sizes, it could indicate a serious head injury.

/ Look for A discharge from the nose: it could be a sign of a serious head injury.

/ Look inside the mouth. Are the teeth intact? Does the person have dentures or anything else in their mouth that might obstruct breathing?

/ Check skin colour. If there is a blue tinge on their lips, it could mean a lack of oxygen. Cold, pale, sweaty skin indicates shock. Flushed or hot skin could be heatstroke or a fever.

/ Check along the limbs, looking for swelling or deformity. This could indicate a fracture.

/ Look for blue fingers and toes. Ask about any abnormal sensation in their legs and arms.

/ Check clothing for any sign of incontinence, which might suggest spinal or bladder problems.

/ Feel the stomach – are both sides the same? Is there any sign of rigidity, which could indicate internal bleeding?

/ If you think the casualty has no broken bones (neck or limbs), run your fingers down the spine, looking for anything that feels abnormal, such as swelling or bones sticking out.

CPR for adults

Cardiopulmonary resuscitation (CPR) is an essential part of your first-aid armoury. While the chances of bringing someone back to life with CPR are very slim, it *can* happen, sometimes even immediately. The shock of the pressure on their chest might be enough to kickstart their body again, but probably not. 'Oh,' I can hear you thinking, 'what's the point then?'

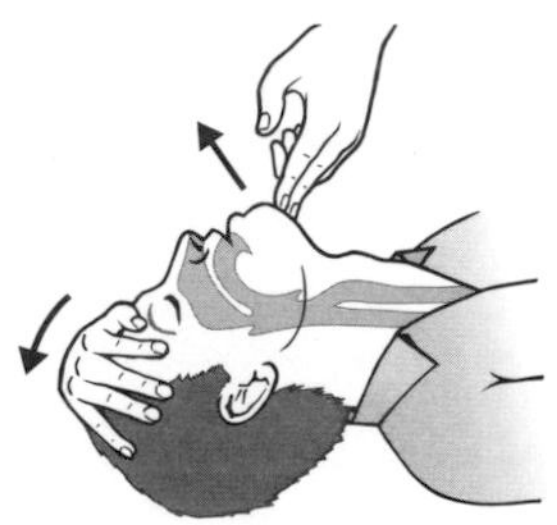

Lift the chin and tilt the head to open the airway.

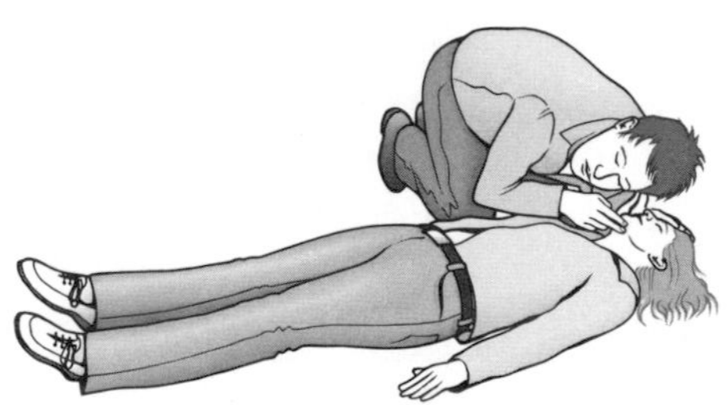

Listen for breathing, feel for breath on your cheek, and look for the rising and falling of the chest.

The point is to keep the casualty's blood moving around their body, pushing the oxygen you have blown into their lungs to their brain and limbs until the professionals arrive with some decent drugs and machinery. You are a replacement for the casualty's own heart and lungs.

There are two elements to CPR: chest compressions and 'mouth-to-mouth' or the 'kiss of life'. You carry out 30 chest compressions for every two breaths.

If you get confused which way round it is, just think about how many times your heart beats in a minute compared to your breathing rate. We breathe only about 15 times a minute, but our heart needs to beat about 70 times a minute on average.

Chest compressions for adults

Kneeling next to the casualty, find the right place for your hands. You are looking for about two fingers up from the bottom of the breastbone. You place the heel of your hand right in the middle of the chest avoiding the ribs and stomach (see illustrations opposite, at top).

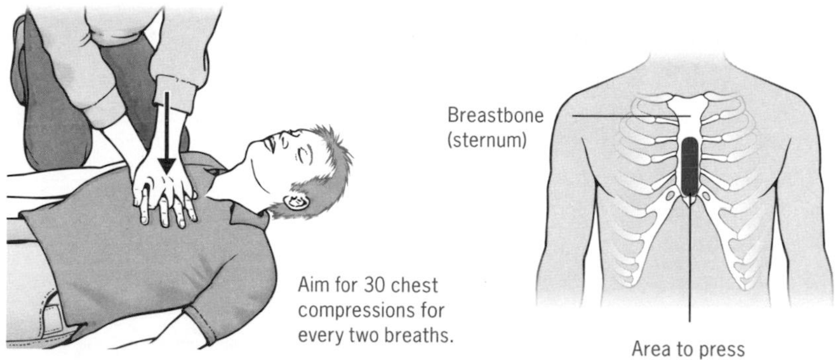

Aim for 30 chest compressions for every two breaths.

Wrap one hand through the other and, leaning directly over the casualty so you have your full weight on your hands, push hard down, but not hard enough to break their ribs (a depth of around 5 cm). Let the chest rise again and continue with your next compression. You need to do a total of 30 compressions at a rate of around 100 a minute – quite fast – and then give two long breaths (as described below). You will get tired quickly, so it is good to work in a team to ensure you can keep going as long as possible.

Mouth-to-mouth resuscitation

After 30 compressions you need to administer two long breaths. Make sure the airway is still open after all the up and down movements, then put one hand on the forehead and two fingers on the chin to lift it up. Move the hand on the forehead down to pinch the soft part of the nose and gently open the casualty's mouth.

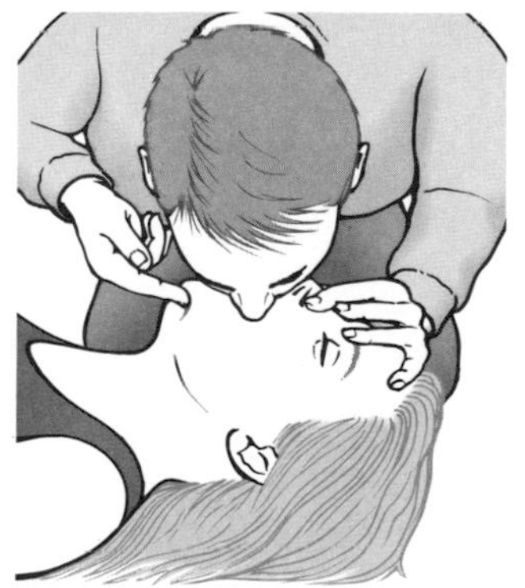
Place your mouth over the casualty's mouth and exhale. Withdraw and listen and feel for breathing.

Still tilting their neck back and holding their nose, breathe deeply into their mouth. Turn your head and check the chest is rising. If it isn't, then it's not working...you need to adjust the head in order to make it work. In total you need to give two of these deep breaths, however many times that means adjusting the head and starting again. The idea is to give the casualty essential oxygen.

Now move back to the chest compressions: another 30 before you give two more breaths. If you are working in a team, you must stop the chest compressions while the breaths are given in order to check that the lungs are rising.

Mouth-to-nose resuscitation

This technique can be used when there are injuries to the mouth, poison or other dangerous substances around it, and in drowning incidents. Create a seal with your mouth over the person's nose, hold the mouth shut and breathe into the casualty. Then open the mouth to allow the person to breathe out. If they have just been dragged out of water, this will allow them to choke water up without interference from you.

Where toxic substances are involved, you can still do mouth-to-mouth by using a face shield – a piece of plastic with a hole in the middle – which fits over the casualty's mouth and thus avoids you having to touch the area directly. They are often found in shop-bought medical kits, but you can make one on the spot if necessary: a thin T-shirt will work as a barrier if stretched across the mouth.

Continue CPR for how long?

Most people will tell you to continue for between 45 minutes and an hour. But in reality you will carry on as long as you can if there is a possibility of rescue. This will be a lot easier, of course, if there is a team of you. But if there has been no sign of life after the first five minutes, you are unlikely to see any result until the real doctors arrive. That's not because you're doing anything wrong; it's because the doctors have the right kit, such as drugs, defibrillators and oxygen, and they might even have heart-lung machines back in the hospital.

CPR for babies

By 'baby' I mean a child up to the age of three. Carry out all the basic ABC checks (see page 106) with extra care as the signs may not be as obvious. If the baby is not breathing, start CPR, as follows.

Emergency breaths first

You need to start by giving the baby a big intake of oxygen as their body does not absorb oxygen as well as an adult's. Tilt their head back, with one finger this time rather than two. Keep one hand on their forehead. With a baby you need to create a seal over their mouth and nose with your mouth. Give them five initial slow breaths. Remember a baby's lungs are smaller than yours so the breaths should not be as deep and full as with an adult or older child. Check to see if their chest is rising and falling each time. Then move onto compressions.

Chest compressions for babies

Find the bottom of the baby's breastbone and move one finger-width up towards the middle of the chest. Take two fingers and use minimal pressure to press the chest down to around a third of its height. Allow the chest to return to normal, then continue with the next compression. Do 30 before you stop to give the baby two breaths. The rate is the same as that for adults – around 100 compressions a minute.

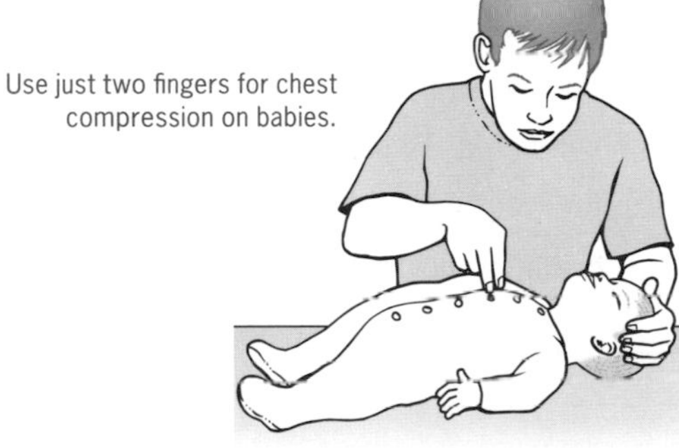
Use just two fingers for chest compression on babies.

CPR for children

Here I mean children aged between three and 14. Carry out all the ABC checks (see page 106) with extra care. As with infants, start by giving five initial breaths (see opposite), this time covering just their mouth with yours. Now move onto chest compressions, following the method of adult CPR, but using just one hand, not two (see page 107).

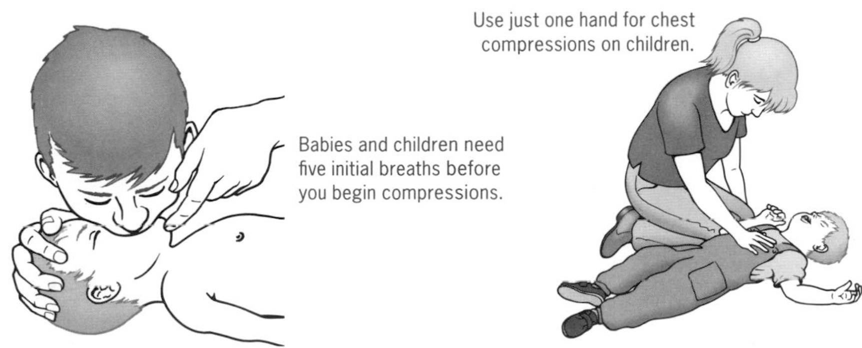
Babies and children need five initial breaths before you begin compressions.

Use just one hand for chest compressions on children.

The second checks

Find out what happened and look for signs of injury head to toe whether the person is conscious or not (see page 108). Ask the following questions, if possible, about the patient's recent and longer medical history:

- What medication they are taking (e.g. asthma inhaler, blood pressure pills)?
- When did they last eat or drink?
- Do they have a condition such as epilepsy, diabetes or anaphylaxis? Such conditions will affect the way you approach treatment. If the casualty is unable to answer, look for a medical warning bracelet or pendant. These items can look very fancy, so check and double-check.

- Where is their usual medication, such as their insulin injector pen? Take a look at it.
- Do they have any allergies?
- What is their recent medical history, e.g. illnesses, operations and treatment they are already receiving, and what drugs have they taken that day? Write it down.

Recovery position for adults and children

This applies to an unconscious but otherwise unhurt person (not a baby) and should be done only after you have established the following:

- The casualty's airway, breathing and circulation are stable.
- The head-to-toe check (see page 107) has not revealed a back or neck injury.

The recovery position is designed to keep the airway open if the casualty is having trouble breathing, and will prevent them choking if they vomit.

With the casualty lying on the floor, kneel at their side. Place their nearest arm out to the side. If they are wearing glasses, remove them.

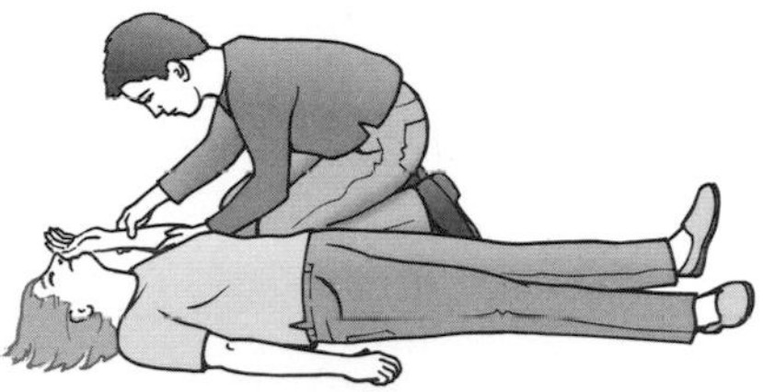

Take the arm furthest away from you over to their nearest cheek, palm out.

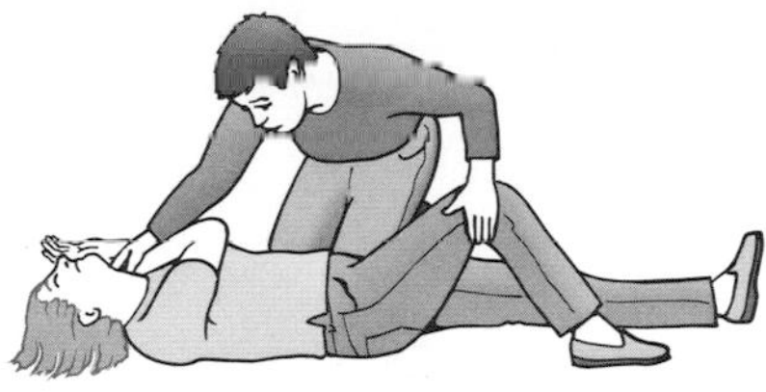

Lift up the furthest knee to a bend. Hold that with one hand and their head and palm with the other, and gently roll them over into a foetal position. Their head should now be resting on their hand.

Make sure the airway is open by tilting the head back slightly. And for stable support, ensure the straight thigh and bent knee are at right angles to each other.

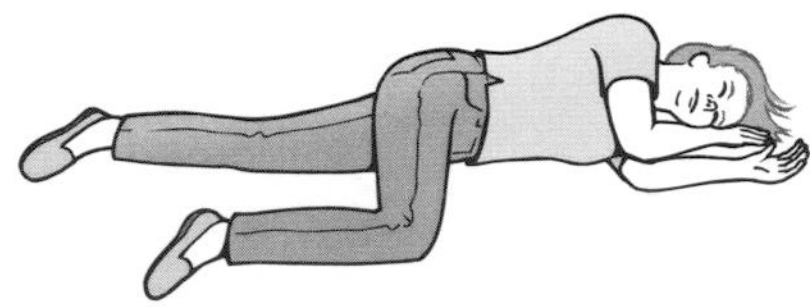

Recovery position for babies

Hold the baby in your arms as shown in the diagram below. Their head should be tilted slightly downwards to stop them choking on their tongue or vomit.

Recovery position for a suspected spinal injury

As it can be very dangerous to move someone with a suspected spinal injury, approach with extreme caution, as follows.

If the casualty is stable, leave them as they are on the ground. One person should be assigned to make sure they do not move their head. That person needs to get comfortable as they could be there for some time. Extra support, such as towels or clothing, can be put around their hands to relieve the strain.

If the casualty is having trouble breathing, you might be forced to move them into a recovery position. This should be done as a last resort. It is the same process as the normal recovery position (see page 113), except that somebody holds the head while the turning process happens. They must continue to hold the head stable after the turn has happened, so, as before, they need to get comfortable.

The Heimlich manoeuvre

With adults and children over the age of around seven, stand behind your choking patient, who should be leaning forward. Wrap your arms tight around them, creating a fist with your closed hands between their stomach and the bottom of the breastbone. It is where you hiccup from – the diaphragm. Give yourself plenty of room to move your hands, then pull sharply back and up, lifting them if necessary with the force. Carry that out five times. Stop, give five more hits between the shoulder blades, then repeat the Heimlich manoeuvre. Continue alternating the procedures until the obstruction is coughed up. Do not give up – keep trying.

With young children under the age of around seven, the Heimlich manoeuvre is very different. Lay them on their back and use the force of just two fingers in an upward thrust movement.

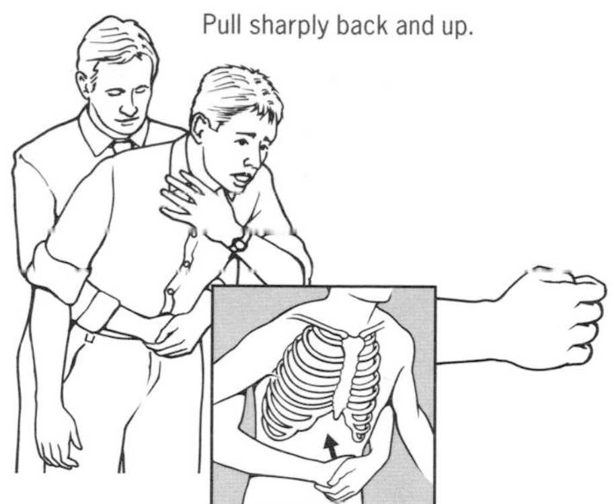
Pull sharply back and up.

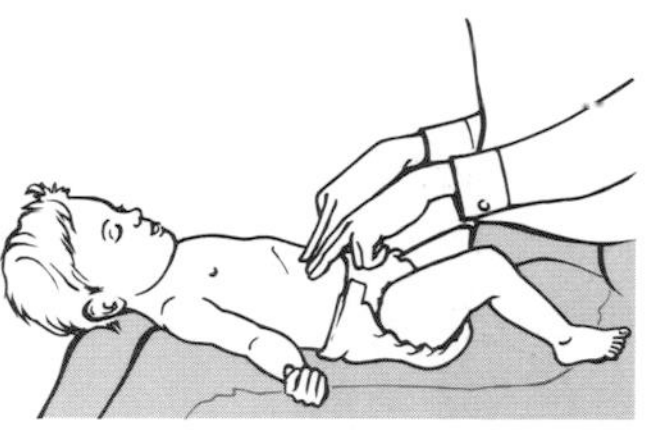
Use just two fingers for the Heimlich manoeuvre on children under seven.

Immobilizing fractures

The best way to stop a broken limb moving is to splint it. You can use anything – a fence post, a ski pole, a walking stick, a windscreen wiper, a roll of newspaper... even a magazine wrapped around a break works well. Splinting is a matter of logic and listening to the patient.

If a limb is broken, you need to make sure that the areas above and below the injured area are immobilized. For example, if you're dealing with a broken shin bone, you would immobilize the knee and the ankle. Use splints either side of the limb if possible, and put padding between them and the body to avoid bruising. Tie any knots on the uninjured side.

If there is nothing you can use as a splint, tie the injured limb to the body: one leg to another, for example. Put padding in any natural gaps and tie with wide pieces of cloth above and below the injury. Tie any knots on the uninjured side.

Be prepared to adapt. If you cannot move the broken limb straight, or if the break is at a joint such as the knee or elbow, splint as they are – bent. You can splint one bent leg to another, or put a bent arm inside a sling.

If the neck is broken, wrap a large scarf around it as tightly as you can without affecting the person's ability to breathe. Alternatively, wrap a folded newspaper around it. If the person is lying down, put something heavy at either side of the head.

If the back is broken, minimize all movement. Put something heavy at either side of the head and all around the body to prevent movement.

If a sling is needed, use material that isn't too stretchy. Fold it into a triangle and slide it under the broken arm, keeping the shorter pointed end towards the elbow. Tie the long ends behind the neck. There are in fact several ways to put on a sling, so experiment with folds and knots until the patient is comfortable.

If this traditional sling is not comfortable, use any method that works for the patient.

A full sling should be used for any injury to the lower part of the arm, or to immobilize a limb if the collarbone has been broken or a shoulder dislocated.

If there is a splint on the upper arm or elbow, it might only be necessary to tie the sling around the wrist.

Pressure points to control bleeding

There are several places on the body where arteries flow near the surface and pressure can be applied to stop bleeding elsewhere. The idea is to press on a point between the casualty's heart and their wound to stem the flow. You will need to move your finger around a bit to find the right spot.

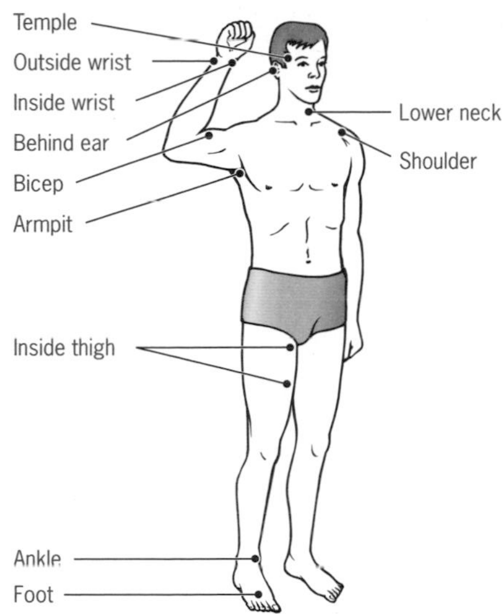

Tourniquets

The subject of tourniquets is very controversial in the medical community because people have lost limbs when they have been applied too tightly or left on for too long. Note the following rules:

- They should be used only when trying to tie the end of an artery.
- They can be applied in only two places – around the upper thigh near the crotch, or on the upper arm near the armpit. They cannot and should not be applied to other parts of the body.
- The tourniquet should be made of a cloth around 3 cm wide so that it does not cut into the limb or damage any nerves.
- Wrap it around the limb at least three times and tie a loose knot (A). Put a stick or pen on top of the knot (B) and tie another knot over the top (C). Twist the stick until the blood stops flowing, then tie a piece of string around the top of the stick to stop it unwinding (D).

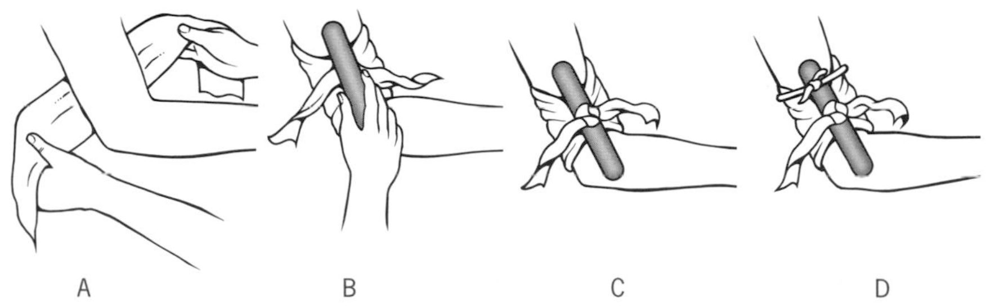

- Check that fingers, toes and nails are not turning blue as this is a sign that the tourniquet is too tight and needs to be released immediately.
- Release the tourniquet frequently to allow blood to flow back into the limb.
- When the flow has stopped try to locate the severed artery so that you can tie the end with some string or fishing line sterilized in alcohol or by boiling. Then release the tourniquet slowly to see if it has worked.
- Never leave a tourniquet on long-term or unattended.

Treating wounds

- Preferably wearing latex or vinyl gloves, apply pressure with your fingers or a dressing of some sort until the bleeding stops. Be careful to avoid pressing down on anything stuck in the wound, such as gravel or glass.
- Raise the limb if you can while carrying out subsequent treatment.
- Clean the wound – with cooled, boiled cloths if you have nothing else – but do not remove any foreign objects and dead flesh unless there is no hope of professional help any time soon. If you must do so, use a pair of sterile tweezers.
- Gently apply antiseptic from the inside out to avoid passing infection inwards from unclean skin.
- Apply a dressing. If blood shows through, put another one on top, and reapply as often as necessary. The dressing will need to be changed if it smells or gets wet, or if the wound becomes infected.
- A deep, clean cut might need stitches. For this you need a sterilized needle and sterilized thread, and should start in the middle of the wound, working towards either end. You need to make individual stitches, pulling the two sides together and knotting the ends of the thread for each stitch.

Use individual stitches to close the wound.

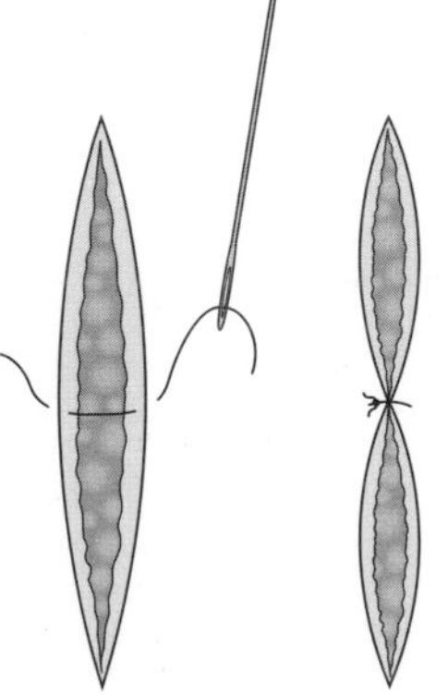

- Butterfly stitches, which are actually plasters, require even more deftness to apply. One clean hand, preferably the casualty's, should hold the cut tight while you open and apply the sticky butterfly stitches.

Warning: Try to get a tetanus shot as soon as possible after cutting yourself. This nasty infection is not caused by rust, as so often believed, but rather by bacteria found everywhere in the wild. If left too long, tetanus will cause painful lockjaw. Make sure your tetanus jabs are up to date before you travel.

When your help is unwanted

There are all sorts of reasons why someone might refuse your help. Hypothermic patients, for example, will be disorientated and unable to listen to your advice about what they should be doing to help themselves. People with a head injury also often have the illusion that they know what is best. And someone in a lot of pain might think it would be better for them to die right there than to go through the added pain of your trying to move them somewhere safe. Refusal could also be a cultural thing. A woman might not accept treatment from a man, or her family might refuse on her behalf even if she agrees.

The only advice here is to go in slowly. Approach with open hands and face and don't rush a patient into doing something that might feel awkward for them. They might have a panic attack or go into shock if they are taken by surprise. Sometimes it would be better to instruct people they trust to do the work for you. The best approach always depends on the particular circumstances.

Following your instincts can get you into trouble. By the time I got to Iraq in 2003, I was better prepared than previously, having reminded myself of Red Cross basics. After a bomb at the UN shattered a hot Baghdad afternoon, my colleagues and I hurried to the scene. We were there for a story, not to help, but we spent the first 20 minutes ferrying people to the local hospital in our two cars. I stood still for a minute in all the mayhem. The man next to me looked into my eyes and then collapsed, a pool of his blood rushing out on the grass. I could see a piece of shrapnel, like a huge deformed salad bowl, stuck in his side. Ambulances were nowhere near and I knew it would be better if he were lying on his other side, off the shrapnel, so I rushed in without thinking and was trying to roll him over. Suddenly, I was surrounded by a crowd of men and aware that I had run out wearing only a small T-shirt, not my usual billowing Iraq-friendly 'Dad shirt'. In their eyes I was a practically naked girl groping a man. I stepped back and left the scene altogether to murmurs of 'whore' in Arabic. The man died, but there was little I could do.

/A–Z OF MEDICAL EMERGENCIES

Abdominal injuries

Basic cuts to the abdomen can be treated like any other wound – simply cleaned and dressed. But if some of the guts are exposed or even falling out, different treatment is required.

Action: Do not dress the wound. Do not attempt to put anything back inside. Doing the latter could cause further damage and will make the surgeon's job more difficult. Keep the extruding organs damp and covered until you can get proper medical attention.

Warning: Do not give the patient food or water. They will need an operation, and it could be dangerous for them to ingest anything if there is injury to their intestines. Just wet their lips instead.

Allergies

Bee stings, milk, latex (gloves or condoms), anaesthetic, pollen, dust, nuts, shellfish and many other things can be deadly to some people. If you are working in a team, you need to find out about any health issues your colleagues have and how to deal with the symptoms when they present themselves. If any of you suffer from a serious allergy, the details should be written on the individual's body armour and helmet. It's also advisable to wear a medical warning bracelet (see page 112).

First signs: Mild reactions may include struggle for breath; rash or swelling of lips, tongue, face, feet or hands; itchy eyes; tender stomach; if an allergen (the cause of the allergy) has been ingested, it may lead to diarrhoea or vomiting. More serious reactions may show as more extreme forms of these symptoms. The throat may swell, making it hard to breathe. This could sound like hyperventilation or an asthma attack. The allergy may also present as shock (see page 141), which might eventually lead to loss of consciousness.

Action: If anti-allergy medication is carried, use it. This is likely to be epinephrine (previously called adrenaline in Europe) which may be in a container that looks like a pen. The commonest brand is EpiPen®.

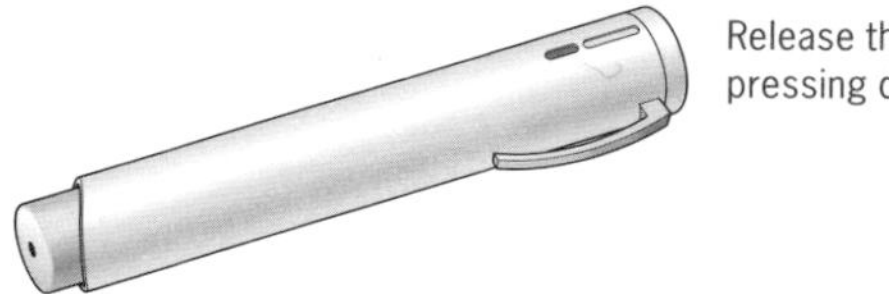

Release the injection by pressing down at this end.

Press this end against the leg or tummy.

You take off the lid and the safety release, place the needle firmly against the thigh (it can go through clothing) and it should automatically inject the patient. You can give a dose of epinephrine every five minutes if it doesn't work initially.

Carry on treating the symptoms of the allergic reaction. If you see the signs of shock, raise the person's legs and calm their breathing.

If the allergic reaction is not something you have come across before, look help amongst the locals. They are probably used to it.

> Some weird insect took a liking to my neck in Kosovo. It bit me and it hurt. We were in a small village and my medical kit had almost too much in it. I sought local advice, and a woman applied the leaves of a plant to the affected area for immediate relief. **Nick Toksvig**

Amputation

You will need a saw. Some survival kits come with a sort of bendy saw. If not, a large penknife saw will do if you are desperate. Desperation is when the choice is between losing limb or life – trapped under a concrete pillar in a burning building, that kind of thing.

Action: Make a tourniquet (see page 117) with the aim of seeking out the main arteries after the amputation is done and tying them closed. The tourniquet is only temporary and should not be left on long.

Take a deep breath and steady your hand. Cut through the skin; it will retract. Cut through the muscle; it will retract. Cut through the bone. Immediately begin the search for the arteries (the big blood vessels that are gushing blood) and tie them closed with sterile thread (boil it if necessary, except if it is plastic, in which case you should soak it in a mild bleach or sterilizing solution).

Release the tourniquet and place a light bandage over the end of the stump. Begin treatment for shock (see page 141). Breathe again.

Asthma attack

The victim of an asthma attack will usually know what to do if they are a regular sufferer, but it is good to know how to support them.

First signs: You will hear the person struggling to get breath into their narrowed air passages, which go into spasm during an attack.

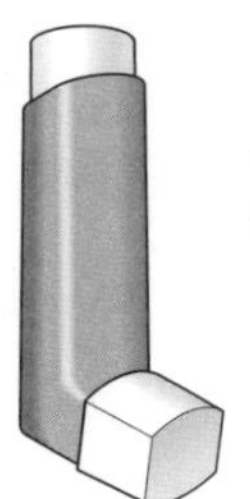

The asthma pump to use during an attack will be blue.

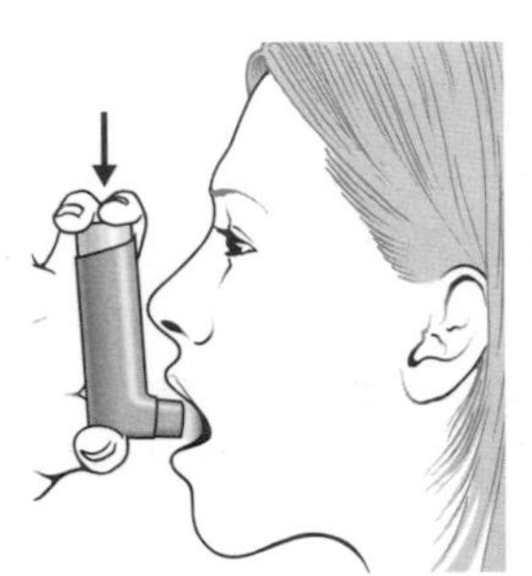

Action: If they are a regular asthma sufferer, immediately seek out their 'reliever' inhaler (in the UK and many other countries these are colour-coded blue, rather than brown which is a preventative; but this coding is not universal so ask the patient). Sit them in a position they find most comfortable. Do not lie them down. Take the lid off the inhaler and place the hollow mouthpiece in their mouth. Ask the patient to breathe in as slowly as they can and then try to hold their breath as you press down the top of the cartridge. It should be one fluid movement. If they have difficulty co-ordinating this, then push the end of the inhaler into a plastic or polystyrene coffee cup and use it as a mask.

A mild attack should ease within minutes. However, seek further treatment before it happens again or gets any worse.

If the attack is more serious, it will not ease. The person will become exhausted, managing only to whisper as they become more breathless. If necessary, you can give 1 puff of their inhaler every minute up to 20 puffs. If they fall unconscious, begin the ABC checks (see page 106). Most importantly, you must open the airway. Call for urgent help as soon as possible and continue ABC until it arrives or the sufferer is stabilized.

Bites (see page 197)

Bleeding

Minor wounds will stop bleeding when pressure is applied, with or without a bandage. After a short time the blood will begin to clot naturally and stop the wound from bleeding. If the wound is in an arm or a leg, you can raise the limb at the same time as applying pressure in order to slow the blood pumping on the wound. Once the bleeding has stopped or eased, apply a dressing or stitches (see page 118).

Large wounds are treated in a similar way, but you need to apply pressure for longer. First pack the wound with a large dressing, as clean as possible, then put pressure on top of that for 5–10 minutes. This should stop or significantly slow the bleeding. After that, wrap a bandage around the dressing to keep the pressure up. Once the bleeding has completely stopped, put on a new dressing if possible or apply stitches (see page 118).

If you see blood frothing from the chest, this is serious as it can lead to a collapsed lung (see page 128).

Arterial wounds are evident when blood pumps out fast and at high pressure. There is too much gushing for the blood to clot, but it must be stopped. You can try putting pressure at the point where the blood is spurting from, or you can try cutting off the flow to that artery further up the limb or body (see pages 116 and 117).

Internal bleeding is difficult to diagnose and there is nothing you can do about it, but you should look out for the signs: pain; external bruises; hardness if it is in the abdomen; bloody discharge from the ear, mouth, nose, anus, vagina or urethra. If any of these signs are present, get the casualty to hospital as fast as possible. While waiting for expert help, you can prepare the patient for shock (see page 141).

Burns

The treatment of a burn depends upon its severity or depth.

First-degree burns are superficial, like sunburn, affecting only the epidermis or outermost layer of skin and causing no blisters.

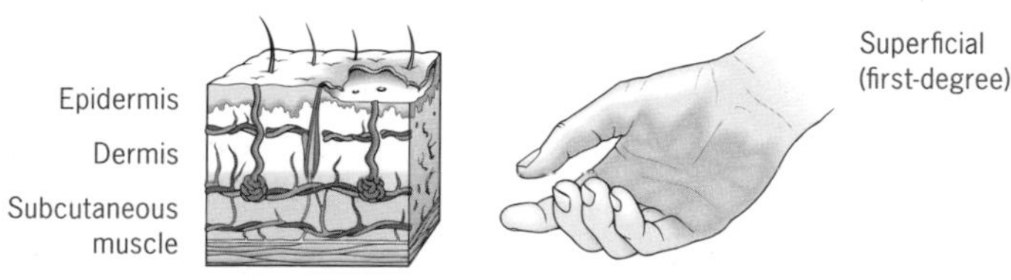

Second-degree burns are slightly deeper, reaching below the outer layers of skin and blistering up. The blisters contain fluid released from the tissues below. These burns usually heal well, but can be dangerous if across more than 20 per cent of the body (10 per cent in a child). In that case, the massive loss of fluid from all those blisters can kill through shock (see page 141). You can judge the extent with the palm of your hand, which has an area of about 1 per cent.

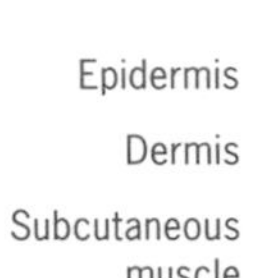

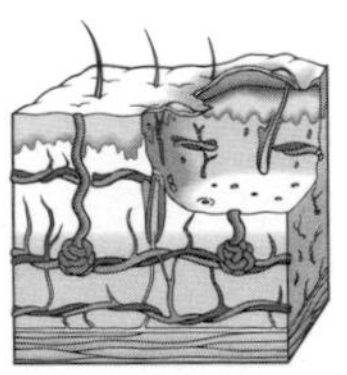

Partial thickness (second-degree) burn

Third-degree burns are deep, affecting all the layers of skin, and may reach down as far as the nerves and muscles. In this case the casualty can't feel pain because the nerve endings have been burnt. However, it is important to keep the burn protected and clean as even a small third-degree burn left untreated could become septic and therefore deadly.

Epidermis
Dermis
Subcutaneous muscle

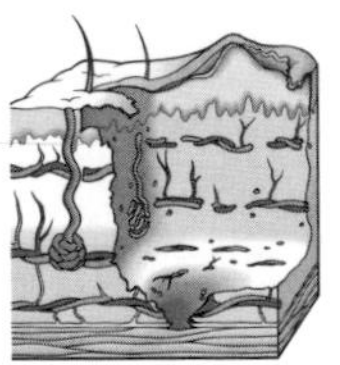

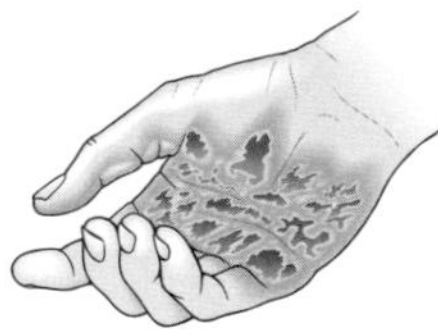

Full thickness (third-degree) burn

Minor burns

In this category are first- and second-degree burns. These should be treated in the same way as severe burns (see below).

For information about sunburn, see page 194.

Severe burns

In this category are third-degree burns, electrical burns and chemical burns. With the last two, you need to make sure the casualty is moved away from the source of the burn before you begin treatment. And be aware that chemicals can still burn even when watered down, so take care to avoid the water wash-off from your treatment.

Action: Cool the burn to stop the burning process. Flood the burn with water for at least 10 minutes, but watch the casualty's body temperature. If they start to shiver, it will make the inevitable shock worse.

Remove clothing and jewellery around the burn. If anything is stuck to the burn, cut it down as small as possible and leave it there.

Do not burst any blisters. Do not use any type of cream, lotion or potion, even if it says 'for burns' on the packaging.

Take clean plastic, preferably something like cling film as that is sterile on the interior of the roll, and attach it to the burn to prevent infection. Use tape to stick it in place, but make sure it's stuck to the plastic, not to the skin, as the burn may be bigger than it first appears. If the burn is on a foot or hand, you can encase it in a plastic bag, or even a condom if it is comfortable and doesn't cut off blood circulation. If there is nothing you can use as a plastic dressing, take something non-sticky, such as a sterile dressing, and use that instead.

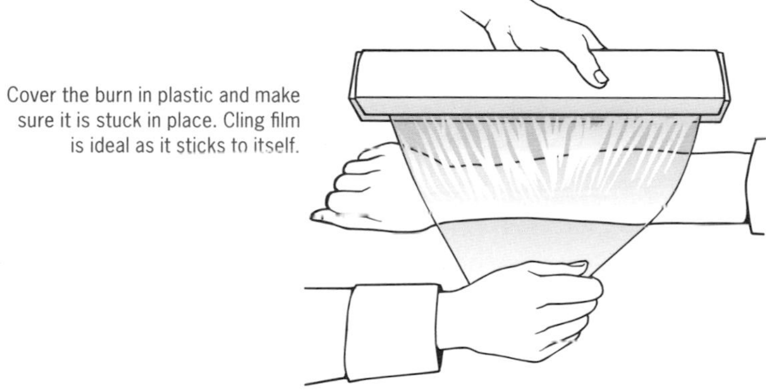

Cover the burn in plastic and make sure it is stuck in place. Cling film is ideal as it sticks to itself.

The casualty will need to replace lost liquid and salt, so dissolve about half a non-heaped teaspoonful of salt (and a tablespoonful of sugar too, if possible) per pint (500 ml) of water and keep giving it in small doses. However, if there is any chance they could be on an operating table in the next few hours, give them nothing but sips of this liquid.

Warning: A casualty with severe burns will almost definitely go into shock before long because of the fluid loss (see page 141). You need to get them to hospital as soon as possible.

See also Fire (page 134).

White phosphorus burns

During Israel's war against Hamas in Gaza in 2009, dozens of civilians were hit with white phosphorus. This chemical is meant to be used for creating a smokescreen during an attack and it is not supposed to be used directly as a weapon. It burns on contact with air and can be used to set areas on fire, but if it comes into contact with skin, it will set the skin on fire. Even if it doesn't hurt anyone at first, it lies on the street and around homes, where children can play with it, and causes a lot of damage after the daily battles are done. There are very few doctors who have had to deal with the effects of white phosphorus on a daily basis. As the head of the burns unit in Al-Shifa hospital in Gaza, Dr Nafez Abo Shaban has the dubious honour of being an expert on it. He recommends the following treatment:

'Cover the affected area with a piece of cloth soaked in water to cut off the supply of oxygen. The phosphorus will burn as long as it is exposed to the air, and the burn will go deep down to the bone. In an ideal situation, the patient should be taken into an operating theatre to remove all the phosphorus. This will stop the burning and also enable the medics to remove the dead tissue.

'Some with massive burns develop systemic complications, such as an imbalance of salts in the blood. This can be fatal, so they should be admitted to an intensive care unit.

'If there is no hospital nearby, scrape off the phosphorus with a piece of wood, *not* metal. This will be very painful as the chemical will be stuck to the patient. In some cases it will rip the flesh away. The patient needs to be aware and supported through the painful process. Once this is done, treat it as a normal burn.'

Chest wound

A penetrating injury to the chest can pierce the lung, which then starts dragging air inside (for this reason it's called a sucking chest wound). This causes the lung to shrink and the cavity around it to fill with liquid. The result is known as a collapsed lung, and it can endanger the other lung as it gets worse.

First signs: Blood frothing out of the wound. Breathing shallow and laboured. Blood may be coughed up. If conscious, the patient will be panicky, and their skin will become grey-blue.

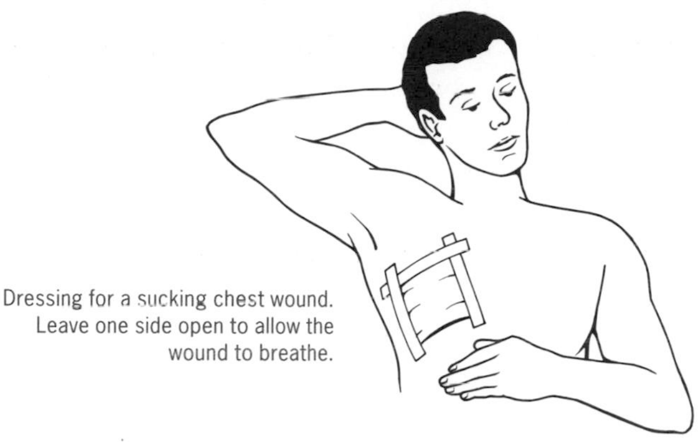

Dressing for a sucking chest wound. Leave one side open to allow the wound to breathe.

Action: Calm the patient and ask them to hold their hand over the wound to seal it. Place a sterile dressing over the wound and tape it on two sides. Next take a square of airtight material – a piece of foil or a plastic bag would work – and place over the dressing, taping it tightly on three sides of the square so that it doesn't get sucked inside the wound. This will not allow air in through the wound, but it will allow air out.

Cholera (see Fever and Dehydration, pages 133 and 191)

> People who smoke need to be particularly careful around infectious diseases. Smokers always catch cholera far more quickly than others because they are constantly bringing their hand to their mouth. **Samantha Bolton**

Choking

First signs: Inability to speak, noisy breathing, persistent cough, blue tinge to lips and nails because oxygen is depleted.

Action: If breathing is not obstructed just encourage them to keep coughing. If it is, first check the mouth for any obvious obstruction, such as vomit. Then, supporting the chest of the casualty with one hand and leaning them slightly forwards, give up to five hard hits between the shoulder blades with your other hand.

With children up to the age of about seven, tilt them downwards and pat rather than hit on the back, their head tipped down so they don't choke again.

If the hitting or patting doesn't work, move onto the Heimlich manoeuvre (see page 114).

Collapsed lung (see Chest wound, page 126)

Concussion

A bang to the head can lead to a mild brain injury.

First signs: Headache; balance problems; looking at the light is painful; vision may be affected; possible ringing noise in the ears; seizures may occur; confusion, forgetfulness and speech problems are common. The casualty might show an altered mood, particularly slowness and lack of energy.

Action: Seek urgent medical attention if you or anyone else experiences any of the symptoms above. Meanwhile, rest and monitor vital signs. Symptoms can last for weeks and lead to other brain problems if left untreated.

Dehydration (see page 191)

Delivering a baby

I used to help with the lambing at a farm near my granny's place every year. It always amazed me how easily the sheep seemed to get up and carry on with their day immediately after giving birth, and how simple the process was in most cases. I have neither given birth nor helped any human give birth, but the following information, though basic, has been checked and double-checked by experts.

First signs: Lower back pain, regular muscle contractions, bloody discharge from the vagina are all signs of impending childbirth. When a woman's waters break, it might look like she has wet herself, but the fluid comes from the amniotic sac inside the womb. Despite what you see in the movies, the waters breaking before labour begins happens in only 13 per cent of cases. It can also be just a tiny bit of unexpected fluid rather than a dramatic gush. By then the expectant mother is likely to know what is happening, and she will make sure that you do too.

Action: I am told that if the birth is sudden and unexpected, it is likely to happen naturally. You just need to offer support as the burden is all on the mother-to-be at this stage. The only things you have to do are to find a clean space, clean towels or clothing, a sterilized blade and a piece of sterile string (boil it if necessary, except if it is plastic, in which case you will have to soak it in a mild bleach or sterilizing solution).

Let's break it down...

Stage 1: Early labour

The initial contractions are getting the baby into the right position for birth. They will become stronger and more frequent as time passes. It might take hours for the baby's head to work its way down to the right place. There are many ways to help the labouring woman:

- Find the position in which she is most comfortable during her contractions – sitting, kneeling, lying, surrounded by cushions or in a bath of clean water.
- Calm her in any way you can – with words, music or touch.
- Make sure she is breathing deeply during her contractions or she might pass out.
- You can massage her back if it helps. Use ice cubes to cool her down if you have them, or just wipe perspiration away with a cool towel.
- Do not give the mother anything to eat. Tiny sips of water are best.

Stage 2: Labour and birth

The pushing begins naturally, when the body prompts it. Help the mother to find a comfortable position: she can sit as upright as possible with her legs apart, or lie on her side with her knees drawn up, or crouch as if she is squatting to pee. Whichever way she chooses, she will need something clean underneath her – plastic sheeting will do if that's all you have – and, if she would feel more comfortable to be partially covered, something to go over her knees.

- At this stage the mother needs to pant – short open-mouthed breaths. She needs to keep breathing.
- She should not push during contractions.
- Do not pull the baby's head or shoulders during delivery. Support the head and shoulders as they emerge, and be prepared for the baby to be very slippery. There is a reason why rookie doctors talk about 'catching babies'.
- If the umbilical cord is around the baby's neck, gently unwind it. If it gets broken, the baby risks losing vital blood.
- If the baby emerges feet first and the head is stuck in the birth canal for more than three minutes after the shoulders have come out, you can pull very gently, never with any force, by placing your thumbs over the baby's hips. As you do this, rotate the baby first clockwise then anti-clockwise a few degrees to free the arms.
- If the mother poos during the birth, which sometimes happens, you should wipe it away, front to back.

Stage 3: Immediately after the birth

- Take the baby and hold it upside-down while supporting its head. This allows the fluid to drain from its mouth.
- When it cries, wrap it in something warm and put it on the mother's chest. If it is not crying or does not seem to be breathing, you need to begin CPR after two minutes (see page 110).
- About 10 minutes after the baby is born the afterbirth is expelled – your work is not done until that is out. Retain this for later so that the doctor can assess if everything has come out.
- If you are expecting help, do *not* cut the umbilical cord yourself: wait for the professionals. If not, you need to take your sterile string and tie it tightly around the cord 15 cm from the baby's tummy. It needs to be tight or the baby will lose blood. Tie another knot 5 cm from the tummy, then use your sharp, sterilized blade to cut between the knots. Put a dressing on the cord until it stops bleeding. Tie another piece of string about 10 cm away from the baby's tummy.

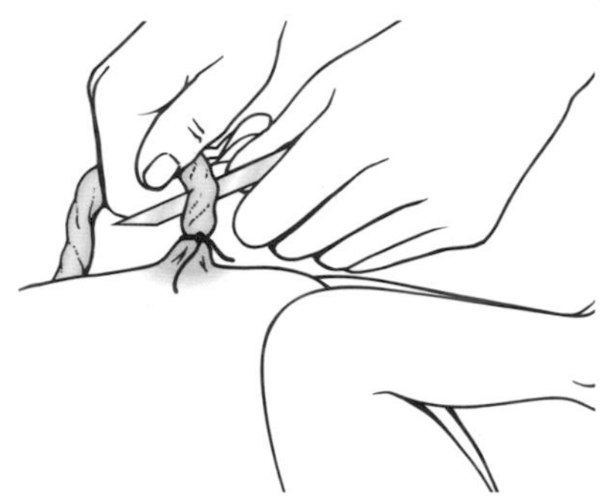

- Now you need to look after the mother. She will need water, sugar and rest. If the bleeding or pain is severe, you need to treat her for shock (see page 141).

Warning: If you are a pregnant woman travelling somewhere dangerous or remote, make sure you have everything you need to give birth – string to tie the umbilical cord, a fresh blade to cut it, and something warm to wrap the baby in.

Diabetes

If someone in the group you are working with has diabetes, you need to know about it. Not telling you is irresponsible; at the very least, it may explain the person's occasional grumpy mood and needle marks on their body. They should also brief you on how to treat them if anything goes wrong.

If you are in a war zone or a dangerous place, you might get separated, so they should have the fact that they are diabetic clearly written on their helmet and body armour. They should also be wearing a medical warning bracelet (see page 112).

Diabetes is all about blood sugar levels, either too much (hyperglycaemia) or too little (hypoglycaemia). You need to know the signs in case they have their first-ever experience of either when you're together. Because it can be difficult to decide which they have, the safest immediate treatment is sugar. Strangely, it has little effect on a hyperglycaemic person, but will get a hypoglycaemic individual back on the road to recovery. That's why diabetics often travel with sweets in their pockets. If they have type 2 diabetes (i.e. they have some control over their sugar levels but not much), sweets might be all they carry, so don't always expect to find an insulin pen.

First signs of hyperglycaemia (high blood sugar): Quickened pulse; *no* sweating; rapid breathing and thirst. Their breath may smell like nail varnish or pear drops. As it gets worse, they will become sleepy and eventually fall unconscious.

Action: Use an insulin pen – place it against their thigh or into the fat of their stomach and press down on the end like a ballpoint pen. Insulin is the chemical normally produced by the body to regulate blood sugar, so it should help to bring them round. Hurry them to a hospital.

First signs of hypoglycaemia (low blood sugar): Sweating; rapid pulse; short temper; weakness and hunger. They may appear drunk and will get less and less responsive before eventually falling unconscious.

Action: Sit them down and feed them sugar and liquid – orange juice or a fizzy drink is ideal. Once they have recovered they can decide when they should have a dose of insulin, usually when it was next due in any case.

Find their glucose-testing kit and help them to use it so you can check you are not giving them too much sugar.

If they fall unconscious before you can get enough sugar inside them, take them to a hospital as soon as possible.

Diarrhoea

I don't know how many times I have gone to a place off the trodden pathway secretly hoping for a touch of diarrhoea. It seems like a good way of getting rid of that last bit of tummy. But try as I might – drinking tap water in Delhi, eating meat on a week-long boat trip in Vietnam, consuming fish in Ladakh – it never seems to come when you want it.

I have since learnt my lesson. It started with salmonella on a boat holiday in Turkey – the loos flushed only once every night, so I had to fling myself into the water in the dark to avoid embarrassment. On another occasion I had terrible tummy problems on a 16-hour journey from Basra to Amman that could have got me killed. I was supposed to be invisible in case our presence at a petrol station or food stop alerted hijackers further up the road. But I kept having to run out to use the loo at each place we passed. It was usually a fetid, stinking hole in the ground, with no door and a grinning audience. But the most painful couple of days I ever spent was two hours north of Timbuktu, running to and from a tent in the Sahara. I woke up naked on a sand dune after passing out on a dash to a private corner of the desert to find a Tuareg guard smiling down at me, offering me his hand.

Poo stories are brilliant, but I wouldn't encourage you to go after them.

Action: Find any way you can to make the person comfortable and give plenty of liquid. Avoid all dairy produce, as that will aggravate the stomach. When they can start eating again, try simple foods – pasta, bread, biscuits and potatoes – before moving onto a normal diet. If the condition is very serious, the loss of fluid could lead to shock (see page 141). Seek medical assistance. A doctor will be able to prescribe drugs to help relieve the pain.

Look out for bloody diarrhoea – the chances are that it's dysentery, which requires antibiotics. Seek urgent medical assistance. In the meantime, keep well hydrated with whatever liquid you can keep down. Water with a tablespoon of sugar and half a teaspoon (non-heaped) of salt per pint (500 ml) will work.

Monique Nagelkerke advises: 'Do not take the usual anti-diarrhoea remedies to stop bloody diarrhoea as this could result in bowel damage.'

Dislocated shoulder or finger

First signs: Obvious deformity, with the bone protruding under the skin where it shouldn't be. The muscles will spasm and hold it there unless it is put back.

Action: Immobilize the shoulder or finger (see page 115) until you can get proper medical help. It is dangerous mending a dislocation as nerves or muscle can get stuck in the joint. It is also incredibly painful.

If you *must* tackle the dislocation yourself, this is how you do it. Put your foot in the person's armpit and pull on the arm until the shoulder clicks back into place. For a hand, pull on the finger until it clicks back into place. Once the dislocated part is back in place, immobilize it (see page 115) and let it rest for some time.

Drowning

Action: Carry out ABC (see page 106) until the casualty's vital signs are normal again. Put them in the recovery position (see page 112) and start to warm them up. Even if they appear to be fine, they will need proper medical treatment because any residual liquid in the lungs will cause irritation and lead to the airways becoming narrowed a few hours later.

Warning: Drowning can also lead to hypothermia (see page 187).

Dysentery (see Diarrhoea, page 131)

Electrocution

If someone has been electrocuted, don't touch them. You need to turn off the power first – at the mains – not the dangerous plug. If that is not possible, you need to move the source of the power away from them, or them away from it, before you can start treatment. Use a non-conducting tool to help you: a rope to pull the patient away, or a piece of wood, a plastic box or even a book to push them. Once they are safely away from the source of their injury, begin ABC and all other necessary treatment.

If someone has been struck by lightning, you can touch them. But if the injuries allow it, you need to move them away from the site of the incident as quickly as possible before you start treatment. Despite the well-known saying, lightning *does* actually like to strike the same place twice. Continue with treatment from ABC to secondary checks and deal with their symptoms while waiting for help.

Fever

Usually a sign of other illnesses, fever can arise from infection in the ear, throat or teeth, measles, chickenpox, cholera, flu or meningitis (see page 140), but the basic symptoms are the same.

First signs: Temperature above 37°C; cold and shivering, but sweating; headache and pains all over the body.

Action: Put the casualty to bed and give lots of cool liquid to replace that lost by sweating. Painkillers may help to bring down the temperature.

Fire

• Switch off all electricity in the room, pulling out the plugs if necessary. Turn off the mains. If you are not sure what the source of the fire is, use a heavy blanket rather than water to put it out. Water on an electrical fire or a flaming pan of fat will make the problem worse.

• If the room is filled with smoke, stay low. Air will be clearest at floor level. Shut the door of the room you are in and put a blanket along the bottom of it. Now open a window.

• If someone's clothes are on fire, move them to the floor so they aren't standing up any longer – that way the flames won't rise up to their face. Wrap them in a heavy blanket and roll them on the ground until the flames are out.

• If someone has suffered burns, see page 123.

Fractures

In the field, particularly if you're a long way from the nearest hospital, you might need to reset broken bones, so it's a good idea to learn how to hold them in place until you can get some professional help.

Closed fracture

This type of fracture is described as 'closed' because the skin is not broken.

First signs: Pain and tenderness, even to the lightest touch. Swelling will start almost immediately. The limb may look distorted or appear shorter than the other limb. If the patient moves, they might feel the bones grating together. Do not try to do this as a test.

Action: If you are expecting medical help to arrive soon, do not attempt to put the bone back in its correct placement. Simply immobilize it (see page 115) and wait for the expert.

If you are not expecting medical help any time soon, you can try using traction, which involves slowly pulling the limb until the ends of the bone fall into place. If you have a helper, keep the traction up while you apply the splint and immobilize the limb (see page 115).

Open fracture

First signs: The bone pierces the skin. It will be very painful and will need professional attention as soon as possible.

Action: Clean and dress the wound, as there is a risk that both the wound and the bone will get infected.

If the limb is too bent by the fracture to splint, you will need to straighten it. You are not trying to put it back in the correct place – you simply want to move it so that you can immobilize it (see page 115) and thus prevent further damage. It is best to do this as soon as possible, before swelling starts, and preferably when the patient is already unconscious. After that, seek medical attention.

Frostbite (see page 188)

Head injury

My most recent experience of a head injury was when a friend slipped after several hours of drinking and dancing and hit his head on a table. The blood rushed out – a metre-wide pool about 5 mm thick. We spent five hours in hospital with him, where he was checked and double-checked, but he was fine. In fact, the cut turned out to be tiny – just enough for a 2-cm disco scar and a dramatic tale to tell.

It was a typical head injury. Tons of blood and lots of panic, but ultimately nothing much to worry about. I hope that is the worst you ever see. But the reason the doctors paid so much attention to my friend was the risk of brain damage.

First signs of significant brain injury: A fall in the level of consciousness so that the casualty does not open his eyes, except possibly very briefly; does not reply to you, or makes just an incoherent noise; and makes only a generalized withdrawal of a limb to a painful stimulus rather than a purposeful movement. Very dangerous signs of bleeding in the brain are if one pupil (the black centre of the eye) is bigger than the other, or if blood or clear liquid discharges from the eyes, ears or nose. If these signs are present, the casualty needs urgent medical attention.

Action: When signs of brain injury are present, or the casualty is unconscious, dress the wound (see overleaf) and leave the person in the recovery position (see page 112) with their airway open. Make regular checks of their breathing, circulation and responses to touch or sound till help arrives.

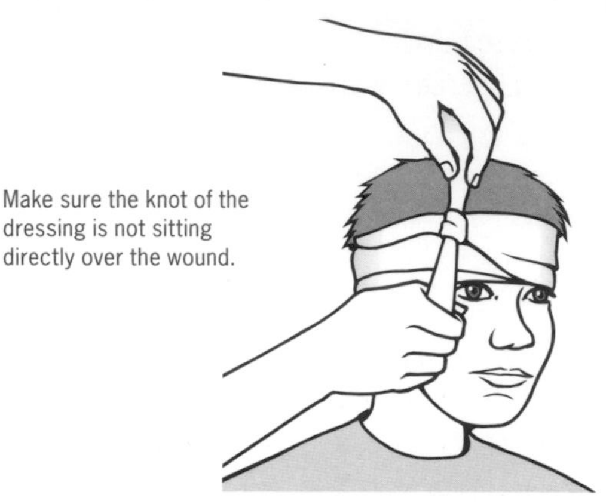

If the casualty is conscious and has no signs of brain injury, sit them upright against a wall. Cover the wound with a clean dressing and apply pressure with your hand until the bleeding slows. Clean the wound, then put another dressing on the injury and keep it in place with a bandage or strip of material. (See page 104 for information about dressings.)

Heart attack

The usual cause of a heart attack is a blockage or clot that cuts off the blood supply to a part of the heart muscle. This condition always needs medical attention.

First signs: Chest pain that does not ease with rest; the pain can shoot up to the jaw and down both arms. Difficulty breathing; collapse, suddenly or after a spell of dizziness; blue lips and ashen skin; irregular pulse; great fear.

Action: You need to take the strain off the heart, so sit the casualty down and place support around them so they can rest.

If the casualty is conscious, get them to take an aspirin – 300 mg. It will thin the blood and help to take the strain off the heart. If they have their own medication, help them take it.

Keep checking their breathing, pulse and responses to sound or touch. If they stop breathing, begin CPR (see page 108).

Heatstroke (see page 193)

Hyperventilation (see Panic attack, page 140)

Hypothermia (see page 187)

Infection

If a wound has not begun to heal within 48 hours, it is infected. In fact, it is hard to avoid infection occurring if you are not in a totally sterile environment.

First signs: Increasing redness around the wound; swelling and heat in the injury and surrounding area. The more dangerous stage is when a red line trails off from the wound to a nearby gland. That means the infection is spreading. Then there will be fever – hot head, sweating and shivering (see page 133).

Action: Change the dressing as often as possible. If the wound is stitched, remove the stitches and drain any pus. You can do this by using heat to draw it out. Soak a cloth in hot water, let it cool a little, then place it on the wound. Take a rock heated in the fire, wrap it in a towel and apply that to the wound on top of its dressing.

If there is a red line leading away from the infected area, you need to seek medical attention as soon as possible and start on a course of antibiotics.

In desperate straits urine can act as an antiseptic. During my British Army training, I remember there were a lot of boys who offered to pee on my badly blistered feet after we'd run 10 kilometres carrying a large log between the six of us. I can only think it was something to do with marking their territory. I opted to wait until I could see the army nurse back at base, but all he offered was antiseptic. Boring.

Inhalation of smoke/fumes

Anyone who has inhaled smoke or fumes is likely to have a low concentration of oxygen in their blood, so getting them into fresh air is a priority.

First signs: In the case of smoke, the nose or mouth will be blackened with soot; there may also be mouth blisters or swelling; redness and swelling of the tongue; difficulty breathing or talking. With fumes there will be headache; breathlessness; confusion; impaired consciousness.

Action: The inhalation of smoke, carbon monoxide, carbon dioxide or solvents and fuels are all treated in the same way. Before attempting rescue, open the door or window to let fumes escape, but only if you can avoid exposing yourself to the fumes. You can prevent some inhalation of smoke by placing a mask over your nose and mouth, but gases are impossible to filter.

Sit with the casualty in fresh air, either at an open window or outside, and help them to normalize their breathing. Check their vital signs – pulse, breathing and level of consciousness (see page 105) – until help arrives. Note that after smoke inhalation, the airways can swell even hours after the patient seems fine. While you are on the way to hospital, keep the neck and chest free of clothing and feed the casualty sips of cool water and ice to relieve the pain.

Warning: Make sure your gas oven, heating system or indoor fires are all well ventilated to guard against poisoning. If you are not sure, leave a window open at night.

Lightning strike (see Electrocution, page 133)

Malaria

Early diagnosis and treatment of malaria is key. If you are in a malarial area, you need to keep a close eye on yourself and your team. This illness should not be taken lightly – it can be deadly.

Malaria incubates for some time, usually developing three weeks after the infected bite, but it can take up to 10 months to appear.

First signs: Flu-like symptoms; perhaps also vomiting, diarrhoea, coughing and yellowing of the eyes (because it targets the liver); can develop into bleeding problems, shock, kidney failure and coma. Cerebral malaria can lead to seizures and a temporary sort of mental illness.

Action: Treat what you can, such as the diarrhoea and fever, but you need to get the person to a hospital as soon as possible. Meanwhile, keep them as quiet and cool as you can. Stress is not good for malaria.

The best approach to malaria is to avoid getting it in the first place. Areas where the skin is thin are the most vulnerable – wrists, inner arm, neck and ankles – so long sleeves and socks are essential. Cover yourself in whatever repellent works for you, and soak your socks in the stuff too. Get yourself a mosquito net that is soaked in repellent and learn how to use it properly – there should be no gaps and it should not touch your skin. Ask advice from others as to what natural repellents work for them. Vitamin B12 and Marmite are two that I know of.

Then there are the pills. Ask your doctor for advice about anti-malarial drugs, such as Artesunate, Fansidar, Amodiaquine and Malarone. Locals might not take them, but that does not mean you should follow their lead. They might have built up a resistance to the parasite. It is important to choose the right drug for your circumstances and different ones are advisable depending on where you are, so expert help is essential. Note that Artesunate must be used in combination with another drug – Coartem is probably the best brand name.

Malnutrition

Journalists working in war zones often come upon terrible hardship, and it's really difficult not to help when starving children are involved. However, Laura Tyson, who has worked in many humanitarian disasters, advises caution: 'In the aftermath of the tsunami a Sky TV News crew found a seven-year-old boy called Martunis, who had been stranded up a tree for 17 days in a flooded area, having been separated from his parents. He survived on noodles and other stuff floating by. The Sky team, who saved his life, fed him army ration packs as he was so malnourished, but this was a bad mistake. If someone is malnourished, high-calorie ration packs can make them very sick indeed. And he was, but he recovered later. The correct response is, ideally, to seek medical help before giving them any food of your own that they may not be used to digesting.'

With either adults or children, don't be tempted to meet starvation with a doughnut. The recovery from malnutrition should be gentle and strictly confined to certain foods in certain quantities or it can lead to further complications.

GARLIC: A FRIEND INDEED

According to Mary O'Shea, garlic tablets work a treat as a mosquito repellent: 'I volunteered as a butterfly catcher in a rainforest in Costa Rica during a college summer and was massacred by mosquitoes. I tried everything to stop being bitten, including percentages of DEET [a chemical repellent] that made my watch melt. Then I started taking one garlic tablet a day and discovered it really does work. Now I never travel without them.'

This is backed up by friend and film-maker Laura McNaught, who has spent a large chunk of her working life filming strange sicknesses in malaria-infested bogs. 'Once you've seen DEET melt the soles of your shoes, smothering it over your skin seems even less sensible. I've found that taking extra-strength garlic pills is a good mozzie deterrent once the garlic starts to seep through your pores. Unfortunately, the rest of the crew also keep their distance.'

Meningitis

First signs: Some or all of the following may appear: flu-like symptoms, commonly with severe headache; pain in the limbs; eyes sensitive to light; stiff neck; in an infant the soft spot on the top of the head may be tense or bulging; in the related but much more serious condition septicaemia, a distinctive rash with purple spots develops, sometimes in minutes; if you press a glass over them, the spots do not fade.

Action: Treat like a normal fever (see page 133), but if the symptoms worsen or a rash appears, rush to hospital for treatment. If you are more than two hours from a hospital, give an antibiotic at four times the usual dose. Repeat every two hours if there is still no chance of medical attention.

Nosebleed

People always seem to think there is a secret trick to stopping a nosebleed, but there ain't. The key is to avoid sniffing, as that will start the bleeding again. You need the blood to clot. The patient will naturally want to avoid having blood running down their throat, so lean them forward, hold the soft part of the nose and wait for the bleeding to stop. They need to continue breathing through the mouth for some time after it has stopped to avoid the urge to sniff.

Panic attack

Seeing awful or strange things for the first time, or experiencing dramatic events, can lead to symptoms that might puzzle or frighten you. I once woke up from a nightmare breathing very heavily and with my heart beating at a hundred miles an hour. I was hyperventilating (over-breathing), and passed out several times from the effects of it, but I thought I was having a heart attack. Eventually, I managed to get help and go to a hospital. There I learnt that hyperventilating can last hours, whereas a heart attack usually lasts only minutes. I also learnt that hyperventilating is just one of the symptoms of a panic attack.

First signs: Racing pulse; dizziness; sweating and cramps in the hands and feet; difficulty getting air out of the lungs (hyperventilation).

Action: Deal with the hyperventilation because relieving that will alleviate the other symptoms. Breathing in and out of a paper bag is no longer recommended as a way of calming hyperventilation. Instead, move the person to a quiet place, away from crowds, and get them to focus on their breathing, encouraging them to take slow, regular breaths. Hold them firmly, reassuring them that you are there to help.

Septicaemia (see Meningitis, opposite)

Shock

This is not the kind of shock you might feel after experiencing a robbery or receiving bad news. That's emotional shock, which can be cured by drinking a large mug of sugary tea. The type of shock arising from injury is a lot more serious. It means there is inadequate blood circulating and this may cause the heart, kidneys, brain or other vital organs to be deprived of oxygen. This type of shock can kill you.

Common causes of shock

- Massive fluid loss – usually blood from internal or external bleeding, but it can also be caused by diarrhoea, vomiting, serious burns or severe constipation that leads to colon problems.
- Heart problems – these can stop the blood moving fast enough around the body to carry oxygen to your most vital organs
- Spinal cord injury
- Hypothermia – when the body's core temperature drops below 35°C
- Low blood sugar
- Severe allergic reaction
- Drug overdose
- Major infection

First signs: Racing pulse; pale, clammy skin; sweating. As it gets worse, the pulse may fade away altogether at the wrist. The casualty will start to pant with shallow breaths. Their skin will go grey, they will feel dizzy and sick, and be screaming for water. In the final stages they will become aggressive. They will gasp and yawn for air, then fall unconscious before their heart stops.

Action: Treat the cause of the shock as best you can until the professionals arrive. You need to get as much blood as possible to the person's heart and brain. Raise their feet or lay them on a slope with their head pointing downhill.

Poor circulation will make them cold, so keep them warm with a blanket or with your own body heat. Avoid applying anything very hot, such as a close radiator or a hot-water bottle, as it might disturb the flow of blood, which shrinks away from the heated area to try to cool the body down.

The symptoms of shock can be worsened by pain and fear, so give reassurance. Although the patient will be very thirsty, just wet their lips or give sips of water, no food. They need an empty stomach in case emergency surgery is required later.

Spinal injury

You won't need me to tell you how dangerous it is to move someone with a spinal injury. The spine and brain are the two most fragile parts of the body, and two of the most difficult to assess in terms of injury. If there is any suspicion of a spinal injury, particularly to the neck, you must be extremely cautious (see pages 114 and 116).

Sprains

A sprain involves the tearing of muscles or ligaments around a joint, but it can feel as painful as a break and should be treated like one initially.

First signs: Swelling and bruising; pain increases when the joint is moved.

Action: Immobilize the part as early as possible (see page 115). Loose crêpe bandaging will work. It should not be too tight in case of further swelling.

Pack ice onto the affected area or soak in cool water as often as possible, and raise the limb to reduce swelling at night.

If your boot is already on when you sprain your ankle and you still have some walking to do, leave it there. The moment you take it off, it will swell up like a balloon, and then you are stuck carrying your boot and hopping along on one leg.

Stroke

A stroke is a collapse in part of the brain after a disruption to the blood supply. It can affect people in any number of ways, from a vague sloping of the eyes to death. As a result, strokes are notoriously difficult to recognize. Even the victim might not recognize the effects.

First signs: Facial weakness, arm weakness and speech problems. There are various tests for these:

- Face – are the features unusually uneven? Is the person able to smile? Is their mouth or eye droopy?
- Arms – can they lift both arms to the same level?
- Speech – can they speak clearly? Can they recall words easily?

Other areas may also be affected. The legs may go numb. One side of the body may appear paralysed or slumped. The vision may be affected. They may fall suddenly, or be affected by a severe sudden headache.

Action: Speed is of the essence. The earlier the patient gets medical care and rehabilitation, the better their chances of recovery. You can do very little, only support them, calm them and hold their hand while waiting for expert help. If they stop breathing, begin CPR immediately (see page 108).

Sunburn (see page 194)

Trench foot (see page 190)

Vomiting

Vomiting can be caused by any number of different problems, from food poisoning and fever to altitude and car sickness. But if it is caused by an infection, it can be passed easily from person to person if the conditions are not kept as hygienic as possible.

First signs: Gagging reflex; extra saliva in the mouth; nausea.

Action: Move the casualty away from the cause of the problem if it is physical, such as an allergy or sea sickness. Your aim is to calm them and make sure they are drinking enough fluids and salts. If the vomiting continues over a day, or is particularly severe or blood filled, you need to get medical assistance as soon as possible.

When the casualty is well again make sure they eat only simple foods, such as pasta, bread or potatoes, for the first 24 hours.

> *Fortuna fortis favet* (Fortune favours the brave). I never really understood this until I found myself in various dangerous situations where, invariably, the most dangerous thing was indecision. *Fortuna fortis favet* should not be mistaken for recklessness or aggression. Often the brave call is restraint, decisively turning back or breaking an engagement rather than pursuing it. But invariably the unlucky men who were injured in a contact, or the unfortunate teams that got stuck in difficult situations, were those who didn't commit wholeheartedly.
> **Patrick Hennessey**

7/ FEEDING YOURSELF UNDER FIRE

You can eat anything… When I was teaching Royal Marines what they could eat *in extremis*, I would buy maggots from a fishing tackle shop, add some beetroot and they would turn pink, like prawns. The class would gobble them up quite happily, and only felt squeamish when I told them afterwards what they had eaten. The lesson is: don't die or get sick for the sake of being fussy. Food is fuel. It is amazing what people can survive on. **Dr Carl Hallam**

SURVIVING ON A DIET of monotonous food is hell for me. Faced with limited options – say, falafel seasoned with sand every evening for four months, or 'Menu F' army ration box for 21 days, or Baghdad hotel spaghetti bolognese for a month's worth of lunch and dinners – I often choose not to eat at all after a while. I get lazy and I get hungry.

But tell me that there is no food for the next three days and I will transform into an über-efficient hunter-gatherer, a jungle chef par excellence, whose sole mission is to present anyone within plate-pushing distance with gourmet grubs, boiled potato scraps, strangled hen or whatever I can get my hands on.

I discovered I had these abilities while on a tour through the rainforests of northern Bolivia. We were 10 hours' boat-chug away from the nearest town when we heard that the river had been blocked off by a local strike. We were supposed to return that day, but we decided to stay in camp and wait for it to end as these strikes can get violent.

When the drinking water grew dangerously low and the petrol for powering the boat almost ran out, our wise guide decided we needed to take control of our own welfare. He began to delegate tasks amongst us plump, dirty-looking Westerners. We didn't know where our strengths would lie. I was chosen to be the piranha-catcher, but it wasn't meant to be. Six hours hunched over our dugout canoe and I had managed to get through all the bait – potential food for the evening – and failed to catch anything at all.

The trick with piranhas is speed. They will always go for the bait, but if you hesitate for a second, they will bite off the hook with their tiny, sharp teeth before you can reel them in. I'm sure there are many ways to catch them, but our guide told us to keep the line short – around half a metre long – and tied to one finger. The moment you feel even the slightest tug, you simply flick your finger up, bringing the greedy fish and hook to a bounce on the boat floor.

I had lost three hooks by the time I conceded defeat and handed over to my vegetarian friend Kathy. With her extraordinary patience and future doctor's digits, she began to pluck piranhas from the water with all the ease and rhythm of a metronome.

One group returned to camp with grins as wide as their captured snake was long, while another group was covered in cuts and bruises sustained in bringing home a huge juicy palm heart. I made fire, boiled water and listened to their tales of how man took on nature and won. That night we feasted. But hunting and gathering is exhausting work. Relentless too. People grew bored with the long treks to find dangerous beasties, and the even longer ones dragging back palms through the mosquito- and leech-infested jungle. By the time a passing boat told us that the strikers were willing to let us through, we were hungry and tired of the adventure. We wanted a can of baked beans and a cold beer. We headed home, most of us having used our penknives properly for the first and last time.

We had been in a fertile area where, despite our difficulties, it was relatively easy to find food. Outside the jungle, of course, food is cheap and very easy to come by in many parts of the world. That makes it even harder for most of us to cope when that quick bite to eat is snatched away.

Laura McNaught remembers getting by on a very limited diet in the Congo: 'You can survive on beer and bananas for longer than you might think – in my case, three days. In fact, anything deep-fried or fruit with skin should be OK, especially if it's washed down with some bug-killing alcohol. Boiled eggs and a Dioralyte [rehydration powder] are a good breakfast option, and you can never pack too many cereal bars.'

/EAT LOCAL

This book is not about extreme survival. It is about survival in unfamiliar and difficult surroundings. Survival against the odds, but mainly against man rather than nature. And when nature wins – in an earthquake, flood or tsunami – you need to be prepared (see page 183). In this chapter I am largely assuming you are not intending to be too far from local people and therefore some kind of food. But I have included some basics about hunting, gathering, fishing and fire, which should keep you going if, for instance, your car breaks down in the middle of nowhere and your original plans are thrown out the window.

Danger and war don't have to mean deprivation, particularly if you are on the 'winning' side. In fact, if you are on an embed with the US military, you will probably get fat on their rations. Back at their base, where you can choose from one of multiple fast-food outlets, you will begin to wonder why you ever had a craving for a Big Mac with double cheese and curly fries.

Each culture you meet will have its own extremes. I have been living in the Arab world for the last few years, so I know the people there adore sugar, especially in their tea and coffee – enough to stand a spoon up in your cup in some cases. In my humble experience, Iraqis have the sweetest tooth. When it comes to food choices, I recommend playing to your host nation's strengths. The sticky pastries, the delicious pistachio ice cream, the cardamom coffee... These can fire your engine for hours every day. The people really know what they're doing. And this food is safe. If you push for the less familiar, that is when you are going to get into trouble. For example, opting for sushi on Lake Titicaca can land you in Lima with a drip in your arm after 15 painful hours on a bus to get there. I've seen it. But go for ceviche, the local version of sushi, and you will probably be fine. The most important thing to know about the food you are eating in out-of-the-way places is whether it is safe... because you are a long way from a hospital.

For some that means excluding foods their guts don't trust. Kamal Hyder told me: 'I am quite fussy about food. I've been in situations when a goat has been alive one minute and is served up to you on a plate 15 minutes later. I don't trust it. I make excuses, say I am too sick to eat meat. I always carry a tin or two of Cheddar and some olives. You can always find warm Afghan bread, warm tea. Stuff like that is always safe. But be careful with water...it can kill.'

My best advice is to stick to what the locals are eating. Ask around and learn what you can and can't eat. Gather knowledge rather than trying to gather your own food. It will serve you well when there is no one around to help.

Also, work with your surroundings. If you are in Outer Mongolia and you are not a fan of fermented yak's milk, you need to find a way of politely saying no. If you are a vegetarian and a village kills their last goat in celebration of your arrival, it is going to be tough to find a way out.

Samantha Bolton told me: 'I gave up being vegetarian after two weeks of boiled and roasted goat and no vegetables in the refugee camps in Tanzania. There's no point in being precious about diet. It's a waste of time. Just eat what you are given.' Leith Mushtaq, however, has a different approach: 'Normally, I am vegetarian, so I always take a supply of tinned food. I don't eat meat for politeness' sake. I pretend I am sick.'

Having worked and travelled with a few vegetarians and fussy eaters, I implore you, do not bother to explain your moral reasoning for saying no. Just do as Leith does and pretend to be ill. It is a lot less painful, and it works...although they may then rustle up a special local potion to make you better instead.

A good diet is a varied one. In the long term you need to make sure you are getting a balance of protein, carbohydrate and fats. You need vitamins and minerals too. Sticking to one kind of food will limit your nutrients.

/FOOD IS NOT JUST FUEL

When you're far from home and a long way from anything familiar, food can be incredibly comforting. My colleague and friend Hoda Abdel-Hamid has spent most of her adult life flying in and out of war zones or dangerous places. Until recently,

Baghdad was like a second home for her. It was there that she got engaged over the phone to the man who is now her husband. I was there too, and afterwards we celebrated with all sorts of goodies from the bottom of her bag. She has learnt how to keep herself happy when times are tough out in the field: 'If I am going for a long stint, I take treats – mainly food like Parmigiano, foie gras and good chewing gum. On a day you finish work early you go to your room, pull out a treat and it turns into a party.'

Food is important in so many ways, not least in keeping up energy and morale. Nick Toksvig recalls: 'In 1985 we were working on a Lebanese hostage crisis story. It meant 18- to 20-hour days of endless live interviews with the studio back in London. I commandeered the hotel kitchen and made sure the troops were fed. Even journalists march on their stomachs.'

Chris Helgren was Reuters' chief photographer in Baghdad for almost two years after the war. He spent most of his time training a team of young Iraqi photographers, who had done mainly weddings until 2003. He looked after them as if they were family, and that involved the occasional family feast – usually a barbecue in the back garden. There was always a lot of food. Returning to the Reuters bureau from Basra, where the shelves were still pretty bare and my translator was on a permanent diet, I always looked forward to these parties. Now editor-in-charge at the Reuters UK pictures bureau, Chris has been all over the world with his job, and knows the importance of a good meal when home is far away:

'I didn't eat chicken for a year after I left Iraq. Every day for the two years that I was based in Baghdad, lunch and dinner came from polystyrene boxes loaded with chicken and rice. Or rice and chicken. Or rice and rice. Or rice, chicken and rice... Our bureau was outside the American Green Zone, which offered greasy comfort food, and even Chinese take-away. While at a US air base north of the city, I even spied a taco bar in the gymnasium-sized food hall. But for us, there wasn't much choice when it came to take-away.

'What to eat while on assignment is a perpetual issue. When I was based in Sarajevo during the Bosnian war, we had a cook who used what seemed to be half a kilo of salt in every dish. In other places, such as Jerusalem and Kuwait City, or anywhere for that matter, extended stays in hotels lay bare the problem of never-changing menus. If you're sick of what's on offer after a week, a month later it's unbearable.

'My advice is learn to cook. In Baghdad my salvation came when I discovered an international supermarket, where, for a premium, you could buy British-brand mayonnaise, Italian pasta, Japanese soy sauce, even pancake mix from the USA. Soon our local staffers were watching me in the kitchen as I prepared spaghetti with a ragu of chorizo sausage, although they wouldn't touch it themselves. They considered all pasta, whether it was Japanese noodles or ravioli, to be "macaroni".

'Food is also a big logistical concern on the road. After American and British tanks stormed across the Kuwaiti frontier into Iraq, we gave chase and lived in the desert for about three weeks. Other journalists were embedded, while we were unilateral. This meant we had to fend for ourselves in procuring food, water, fuel and finding safe places to pitch camp for the night. So, on a rather irregular basis, we would receive huge duffel bags sent from colleagues in Kuwait, loaded with canned meat or beans, noodles, dried fruit, chocolate and cigars. We found that we could easily trade a Snickers bar for a bottle of water from a British Royal Marine, but a cigar could fill a 20-litre jerrycan with precious diesel for "Brenda the Defender", our armoured Land Rover.'

/FENDING FOR YOURSELF

When you are out of options and forced to turn to nature it can be scary for a mainly urban generation. Survival is hugely reliant on instincts, but sometimes you need to know which bit of wood goes where to make a snare or a fire. The information that follows is all about that. But it is in no way a survival manual to live off for months. I hope the tips here will get you through till a rescue team arrives.

CHRIS HELGREN'S FANTASTIC FOOD TIPS

/ Use word of mouth to find local markets, but be aware of hygiene. Even soft drinks can be contaminated on the outside with bacteria, so don't just crack one open and drink from the can or bottle. Wash everything – that's all food packaging, including cans – before you open it.

/ Barter an item of food that the armed forces can't get (such as Snickers bars) or use local souvenirs to make trades. In most cases the soldiers can't leave their base to shop, so in return for your stuff, you'll get a good supply of water, fuel or ready meals.

Continued overleaf

/ Cigars are great for trading: they don't go rotten and (unlike chocolate) they don't melt. Small (8-oz) bottles of alcohol are generally good as well, but absolutely not if you're in a Muslim country. Cigarettes are not usually useful for barter because they're so easily obtainable.

/ If you have the luxury of ground transport, pack a cookstove – gas, or whatever they recommend locally – and enough fuel for a couple of weeks, together with instant coffee and/or tea and sugar. The cookstove means you can heat soup or anything, so you're never stuck for a hot meal. You'll also need some cooking pots – one small, one medium.

/ Learn how to make cowboy coffee (aka Bosnian or Turkish coffee). In most places you'll be able to find ground coffee, but not necessarily any fancy coffee-making equipment. Simply put the coffee in a pot, bring to the boil, then leave to stand so that the grounds sink to the bottom.

/ Dried pasta is light, easy to pack and takes only a short time to cook. It requires even less cooking time than rice, and when you don't have much cooking fuel that's important.

/ Try to eat vegetables and fruit where and when you find them, taking the usual precaution of thoroughly washing and/or peeling/cooking them, otherwise you risk ending up with the very opposite of Montezuma's Revenge – constipation.

/ Be very wary of fresh or frozen meat or fish in any area that suffers electricity shortages, as these mean failures of refrigeration. Canned stuff is safer in these areas.

/ Don't eat ice cream in dodgy places. Milk can easily go bad or be contaminated, but the flavourings used will disguise the taste. The same applies to sherbet/sorbet/ice-based foods: the ice itself may be made with contaminated water.

/ A condiment such as hot mango pickle, which keeps for a while without refrigeration, can make otherwise inedible rations edible.

/ Carry a small vial of dishwashing liquid – it's to your detriment to let kitchen hygiene go. A war zone is not the place to give yourself an avoidable case of food poisoning. If you run out of soap, an old fisherman's trick is to use sand to wash your plates, utensils, etc.

SAFE TO EAT

Icy regions

Arctic willows are surprisingly nutritious: the leaf contains seven times more vitamin C than an orange. The flowers, which look a bit like elderflowers, and the bark are both edible once boiled.

Lichens are plant organisms that grow on rocks, trees and walls. Often grey, green or yellow, they are safe to eat, but need to be boiled first.

Spruce trees have some edible parts, namely their young shoots and inner bark. They must be boiled before being eaten.

Temperate regions

Dandelions can be eaten, leaves, stems, flowers and all, but they are diuretic (make you pee), so eat them only if you have a plentiful source of water.

Dock leaves are best known for relieving the itchiness of nettle stings, but are also nourishing either raw or cooked.

Nettles can be eaten raw, but tough old leaves might sting the mouth; take the sting away by boiling in water or heating them over a fire.

Tropical regions

Bamboo is edible from the root down.

Palm has a soft, edible central core.

Plantains are green bananas, very easy to recognize. They need to be cooked, unless very ripe, in which case they turn black. Bake them in a fire.

Wild figs look the same as normal figs, but are smaller.

Desert regions

Boabab fruits look a bit like melons and can be eaten straight from the tree. The tree they grow on is large and hollow, so can also provide shelter.

Mescal is the heart of the agave plant, and no relation to the hallucinogenic mezcal cactus. It looks like an overgrown artichoke about 50 cm high and needs to be baked.

Prickly pears are oval fruits that grow on a type of cactus. They have very fine prickles, so wrap up your hands to pick and peel them.

Maritime regions

Kelp is a type of seaweed that looks like green linguine pasta. Cook in boiling water.

Laver or sea lettuce is a purple seaweed with frilly-edged, ribbon-like leaves about 3 cm wide. Boil until jelly-like before eating. (Dried laver is the stuff wrapped around sushi.)

UNSAFE TO EAT

Unless you have a guarantee that it is safe, *do not eat*:

/ Anything red
/ Anything with a milky-looking sap
/ Fruit composed of five segments
/ Decomposing or old leaves
/ Mature fern plants
/ Anything with furry barbs or tiny thorns
/ Anything that tastes or smells of peaches or bitter almonds – it probably contains one of the most dangerous plant poisons

/GATHERING FOOD

I am not going to list all the possible plants and fruits you can eat in the wild. For that you need to find someone local to help you. If they don't know if a plant is safe to eat, avoid it.

If you're on your own, the best advice is to approach everything with caution – even if it looks friendly and familiar. Try a tiny bit, rub it on your skin and wait for an hour. If there's no reaction, chew a tiny bit in all areas of your mouth, then spit it out and wait a couple of hours for a reaction. If nothing happens, swallow a small quantity and wait five hours without eating or drinking anything else to see if your tummy likes it. If it does, try a bit more, but always be ready to make yourself throw up if you suspect it may be poisonous.

/FISHING

Believe it or not, fishing and hunting are a lot simpler than gathering, and what you catch can be a lot more rewarding and less dangerous than plants and fruits. Here I'm going to pass on some techniques that you might find useful one day.

How to catch a fish

The best times to catch fish are early in the morning and late at night. You will need a hook and (if you don't have a fishing line) a length of thin string. It needs to be strong enough not to snap from the weight of the fish and should be tied tightly to your hook. If you don't have a hook, you can improvise and make one out of a tin can, a hairpin, a piece of barbed wire, a strong barb from a bush, or the loop of a dangly earring.

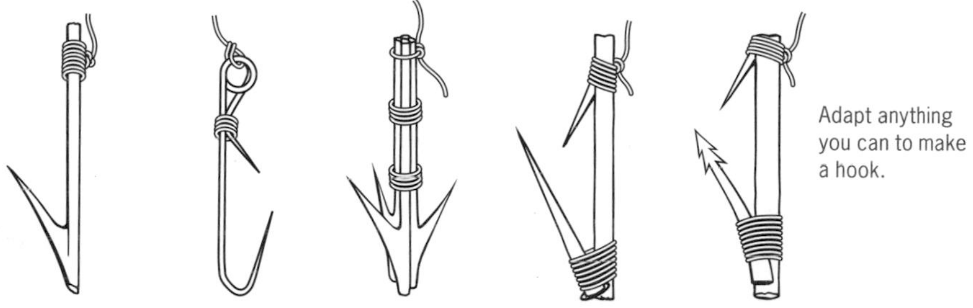

Adapt anything you can to make a hook.

Failing any of the above, you can simply put a sharp straight stick, like half a toothpick, through a piece of bait and hang it like a T-junction at the end of the string.

A makeshift hook made from a sharp stick or toothpick.

It depends where you are fishing, but you might need to use a combination of floats and weights along the line in order to dangle your bait in the right place. If not, the bait might fall flat on the bottom if it's in a lake with no movement, or the current might push your line back against the bank. You can use corks, polystyrene or empty plastic bottles with the top done up as floats, and stones for weights.

If you like, you can leave a line like this overnight so that breakfast will be waiting first thing in the morning.

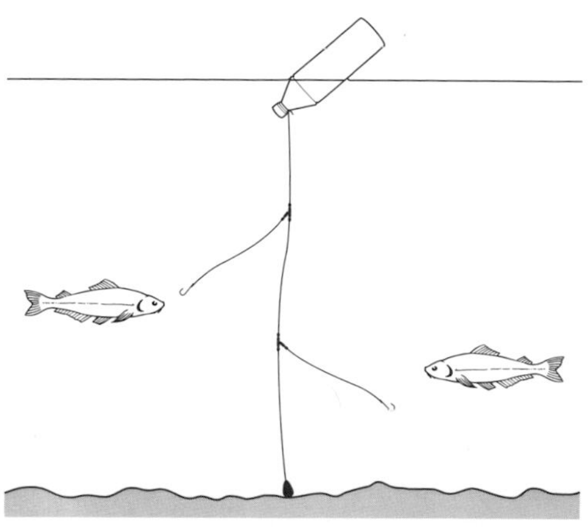

For live bait you can use anything that wriggles, but it needs to look attractive. For fake bait try feathers, small bits of cloth, or even a fish shape whittled out of wood. Keep trying until you find something that works.

If using an improvised hook and line is beyond you, there are all sorts of traps you can invent to catch fish, provided you have a little imagination and a lot of time. Here are some examples of fish traps where the bait inside is accessible by a narrow funnel. The fish can squeeze in but they will find it much more difficult to get out again.

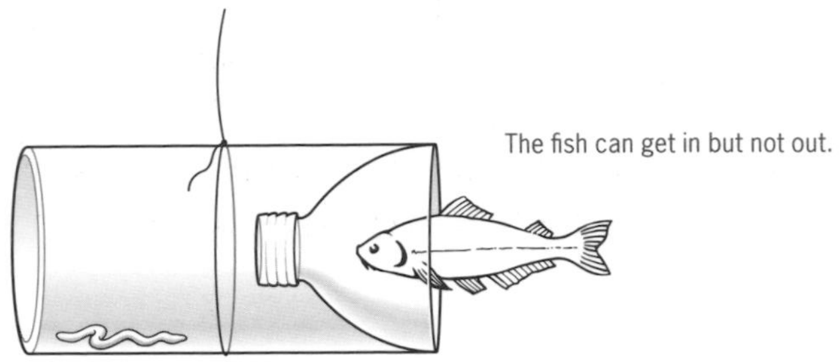
The fish can get in but not out.

If you are dealing with shallow fertile water, you could also try spear-fishing. Make sure your shadow is not over the potential catch or you will never succeed.

Warning: You can shoot fish with a gun, but never do so with the gun barrel in the water. It will explode, causing the bullet to fire backwards and might kill you.

And another warning: Don't eat fish you find floating on top of the water – you are likely to explode with hideous food poisoning or worse.

How to gut a fish

Any fish over 5 cm long will need preparation before eating. Cut its throat and let it bleed until it stops. Then make a cut from the top of the throat to the bottom of itsbelly and pull out everything inside (you can save it to use as bait).

Clean the fish with water. Provided it is fresh, you can eat it raw. If you prefer to cook it, see opposite.

Cut from the throat to the belly and remove the guts, which can be saved to use as bait.

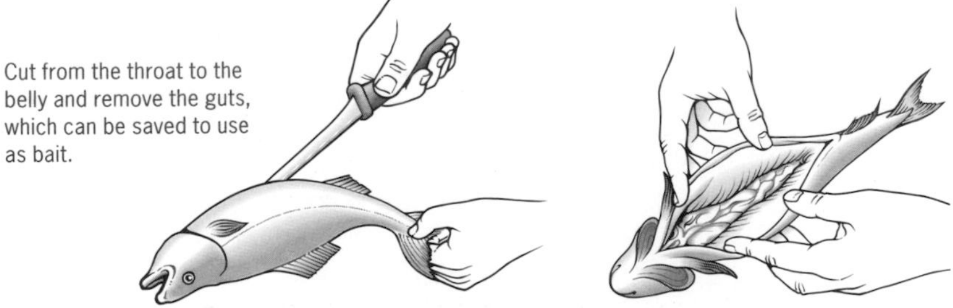

How to cook a fish

Once your fire is going, pop the fish in a pan (if you have one) or on a stick and balance it above the fire with rocks. If you have some foil, you can wrap the fish in that and put it straight on the fire as long as you have a safe way of retrieving it. When fully cooked, fish should lose any jellylike consistency and become opaque. Poke a knife into the centre and check that the flesh is cooked all the way through. Beware of bones when eating it.

How to collect and cook shellfish

Shellfish are found all around the ocean. If you are lucky, you might find a lobster in a rock pool. More likely, you will find clams and mussels clustered around the bottom of rocks under water level. Gathering them is easier and safer after the tide has gone out. And don't get trapped plucking shellfish when the tide comes back in. Being thrown against rocks by a wave could cause a nasty infected cut if there is any coral element. Oysters are found near river mouths, mainly in shallow waters. They are also found on the seabed, sometimes buried in sand, which makes them much harder to find.

If cooking clams, mussels or oysters, put them in boiling water or a hot pan with the lid on for a minute or so until the shells open and the flesh is opaque. Throw away any that are still shut when you are done with the cooking.

/HUNTING

There are a hundred different ways of catching your dinner, be it bird or animal. By far the easiest is shooting. But if you don't have a gun or much ammunition, use a bow and arrow. Alternatively, use one of the methods below to capture your quarry without weapons.

Note: Even if you start out as a vegetarian, when it comes to survival, your killer instincts will kick into action.

Making a snare

A snare can be as big or small as you need it to be. For example, use rope for a deer, wire for a rabbit, and string for a rat or bird. In your kit you will need:

- Wire
- String or ripped-up lengths of clothes or rope
- Collection of strong and springy wood

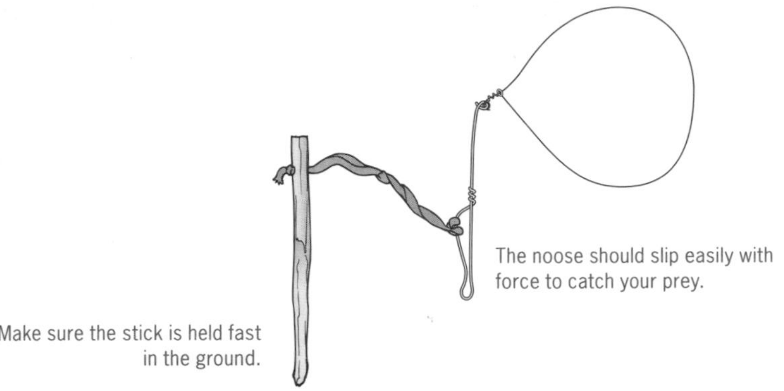
The noose should slip easily with force to catch your prey.

Make sure the stick is held fast in the ground.

Make a small loop at one end of the wire by twisting it back on itself. Feed the other end of the wire through the loop, then make another small loop at the straight end. Tie a length of string to that final loop.

Hammer a stake of wood into the ground using a shoe or some other heavy object and tie the string to it.

Put the snare in a place where the animal is likely to put a limb or its head, and

WHERE AND HOW TO SET TRAPS

/ It is best to set traps along well-trodden animal tracks and routes. Do not set them near where animals live or sleep, as they will recognize the foreign object and avoid it. On less familiar tracks they're more likely to pause for a close look and get caught.

/ Do not leave your scent on the trap or trail as it could make the animal pause for thought. Wear gloves if possible, and make the trap from wood and other materials from the area you are in.

/ Try not to move leaves or earth around when you make the trap. Camouflage it as best you can, covering any new string or freshly cut wood in mud.

/ The trap needs to be strong, as the animal will be fighting for its life.

/ Catching birds can be easy if they have a regular roosting spot that is accessible to you. Try covering one of their favourite branches in tiny snares and you will find several trapped in the morning with little effort and no bait expended.

then drag the snare with it, pulling the lasso tight and trapping it. The snare can be either on the ground or propped up, baited or unbaited (either might work). See illustrations below for ideas.

To avoid the animal pulling your stake out of the ground, or chewing itself out, or other game getting hold of it before you do, try using a spring snare. Tie your snare to a sapling, which is being held to the ground by an easily nudged notch in a stake. When the animal runs through, it will be flung up into the air and away from escape.

The more traps you set, the greater your chance of success. Using bait in them may waste a bit of your own food, but it could win you a bigger prize. If the first bait doesn't work, try another. You will need to be patient. Animals will be suspicious at first about the new addition to their landscape, but they will eventually forget and run into the trap.

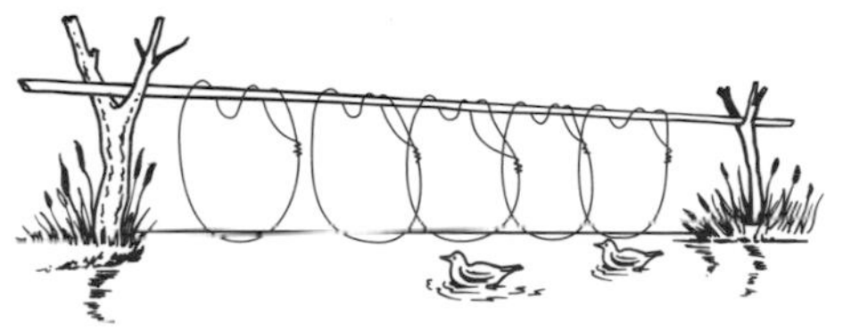

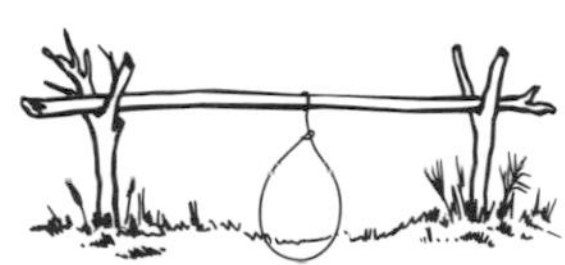

A few different ways to catch your prey

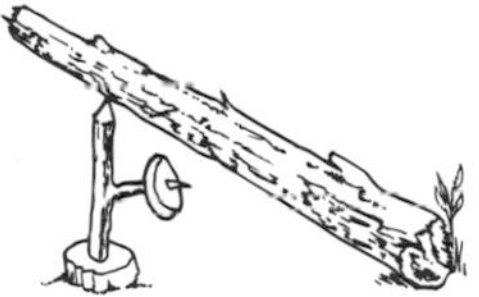

How to make a deadfall trap

If you don't like the idea of using a snare, where an animal could be trapped for hours before you find it, you could make something more humane, like the deadfall trap overleaf. This way the animal should be killed immediately.

A deadfall trap can be made without any sort of kit at all – just the rocks and materials you have around you. Animal sees bait, eats bait, knocks over stick propping up rock or large log; animal is knocked on head and killed or trapped until you can find it. You will need help setting this up, and be careful not to get yourself trapped in it by setting off the trip wire or twig – whatever method you're using.

First, cut a square notch in the upright stick and balance two other sticks on it in the shape of a figure '4'. You'll need to make simple V-shaped notches in the balancing sticks to achieve this. Next, carefully balance a flat rock or a 'cage' made of twigs against your arrangement of sticks. Once perfected, this trap can be made to any size.

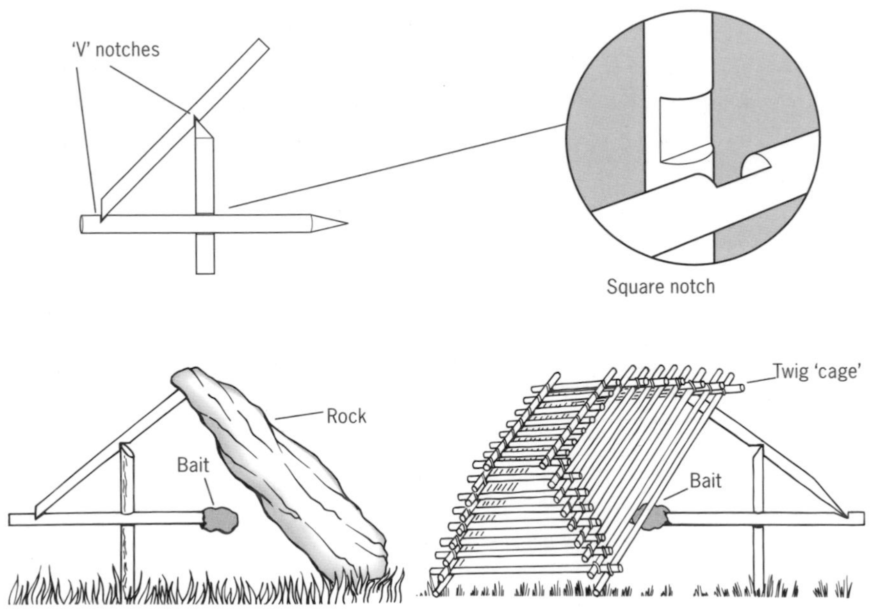

The rock or 'cage' needs to be balanced but easily dislodged.

If these arrangements don't work for you, there are otherways to make deadfall traps, as shown below.

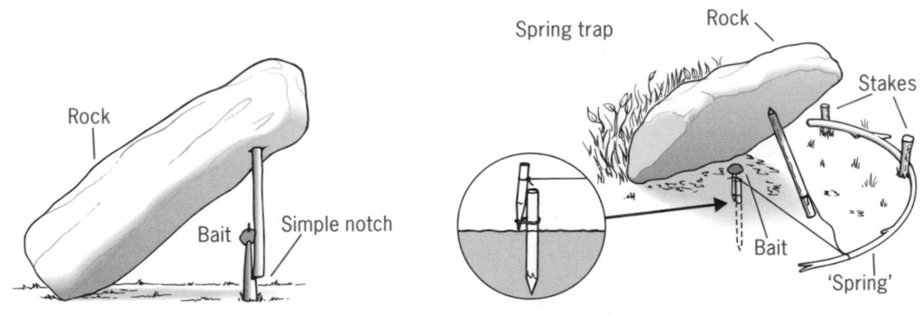

How to catch flying birds

Large birds will go for bait thrown in the air. Tie a stone to the end of a string, wrap some bait around it and throw it up. One of the birds will go for it and then drop to the ground with the weight. Grab the bird while it is still stunned and break its neck by pulling hard.

/HOW TO PREPARE ANIMALS AND BIRDS FOR EATING

Before you do anything else, check the animal for signs of disease, such as a misshapen or discoloured head. If you see anything odd, do not eat it. Also, be careful not to expose any of your own open wounds to the animal's body fluids, whether it is diseased or healthy.

The next step is to bleed the animal. Hang it up by its feet, cut the main arteries running through the throat and leave to hang until the bleeding stops. This applies to animals large and small, and to birds.

Skinning furry animals

- Remove the testicles and scent glands. These are around the bum on cats and dogs and most small wild animals. Deer have them on their rear legs.
- With the animal on its back, cut along the lines illustrated in the picture below, being careful not to cut into the gut. You'll need to be extra careful if working on a small animal.

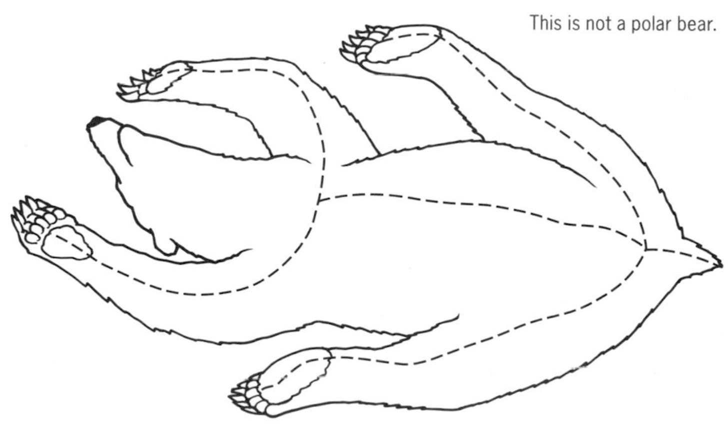

This is not a polar bear.

- Insert your knife under the central cut between the fur and the skin, then use your fingers to pull the skin away, lifting outwards from the stomach. Do the same along the legs.
- Turn the animal onto its stomach and cut around the tail and throat. Push your hand up from the tail along the spine and pull away the hide as a whole. Cut through any areas that are stuck.

Note: There is no need to skin a pig. Gut it first (see page below), then burn the hairs off and wash with warm water. Check that you have removed all ticks and parasites attached to the skin before cooking.

Preparing birds

While it's possible to skin a bird, they will keep for longer if simply plucked, and you will not lose the calorie value of the skin. Chop off the head and feet. Start plucking at the stomach and move outwards.

Gutting

- Suspend the animal by its front feet. Pinch and lift some skin away from the stomach near the ribs and make an incision about 5 cm long. (You pinch it to ensure you don't pierce the organs by mistake and cause a spill.)
- Cut carefully down towards the rear of the animal and up to the breastbone. The guts will spill out. Cut out the kidneys and liver. If any of the guts or organs look discoloured or mottled, do not keep them.
- Cut through the membrane over the chest cavity to get to the heart and lungs, then pull them out too. Ensure the bum is clear by pushing through the hole, then wash it with water.

/FIRE

It's hard to think where we'd be without fire. It is a mark of civilization. A sign of warmth and often welcome. It makes your water safe and your food more interesting and edible. So let me tell you about how to make it.

It needs a spark and some highly flammable fuel and oxygen to keep going. If you want a big fire, you need to give it lots of oxygen and lots of fuel. If you want a small fire, don't fan the flames and you will have a sort of barbecue effect that requires less fuel. Smouldering is good, smoking is bad. Smoking means you are wasting fuel. Chemistry lesson over, let's move on to how you actually get that spark.

How to make fire

Take a box of matches or a lighter...now wouldn't that be nice? For this exercise you are going to make your own spark, so you will need lots of dry fuel in various sizes:

Tinder – such as wood shavings, pages ripped from books (I have left you a couple spare at the end of this one), newspaper, pine needles, feathers or cotton.

Kindling – dry sticks and small logs.

Your main fuel – whether it be wood and coal, or a mix of sand with oil or petrol in a deep hole, dried animal droppings, or peat logs dried out over a fire.

Pick a spot. It needs to be on dry ground, or on a raised area made of rocks or wood above wet ground if that is all you can find. Clear away all the leaves and general muck around the area where you want the fire. You will need ventilation, or at least a chimney, but not too much wind. If it is very windy, dig a little hole for the fire.

Put dry rocks around the fire. This will stop it from spreading if it is very windy. The rocks can also be used as stands for pots, and later can be wrapped in clothing and used to warm your sleeping bag.

Warning: Do not use wet or flaky rocks as the change in temperature and pressure could lead them to explode.

KNOW YOUR WOODS

Softwoods: cedar, fir, giant redwood, larch, pine and spruce

Hardwoods: ash, beech, birch, chestnut, elm, lime, oak, sycamore and walnut

If you can't tell one tree from another, do the following test: make a mark in the wood with your fingernail. The bigger the mark, the softer the wood. In fact, you can't make a mark on hardwood with your nail. Also, hardwoods burn hotter and longer.

There are many ways to produce a spark. I will start with the easiest method and head back to cave-man times.

Battery method: Take a car battery or a large torch battery and attach two wires or jump-leads to the positive and negative outlets. Be very careful not to let them touch while you do this. Bring the opposite ends almost together close to your tinder and a spark will fly across. Catch it on your tinder, blow the flame and you have the beginnings of a fire.

Be careful not to shock yourself by touching the two ends together.

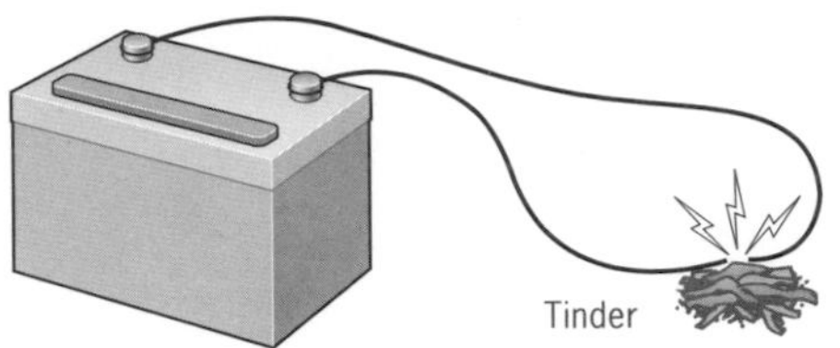

Lens method: Take a strong pair of glasses or a magnifying glass, or use a broken light bulb or the end of a bottle – many things work, so experiment. Fiddle with the angle from the sun till you create a laser of light and direct it at your tinder. Blow gently as the spark takes and you have the makings of a fire.

Focus the magnifying glass onto the leaves.

Flint method: Flint is a stone found everywhere around the world. If you strike it with a steel knife (most pocket knives are made of stainless steel), it will spark very effectively.

Magnesium method: If you are very efficient, you might have a tinderbox complete with fluff, steel and flint. It may even have a block of magnesium as part of the kit. This is to be shaved off onto your tinder before you begin trying to make the spark.

Magnesium flakes in fluff or tinder will help make it highly flammable – if you can make a spark.

Wooden drill method: Otherwise known as the hard-work method, this is used only by those caught totally unprepared. For this you need to add muscle and perseverance to the standard ingredients above – tinder, kindling, oxygen, fuel – plus a piece of flattish softwood and a hardwood stick.

Cut the hardwood stick into a point at one end.

Cut a v-shaped chunk out of one side of your softwood. Put your tinder in that nook or cranny and gouge a hole next to it with your knife.

Stand the stick in the hole and start turning it vigorously, rolling it between your hands, until the heat produced lights the hole and you can blow that gently onto the tinder.

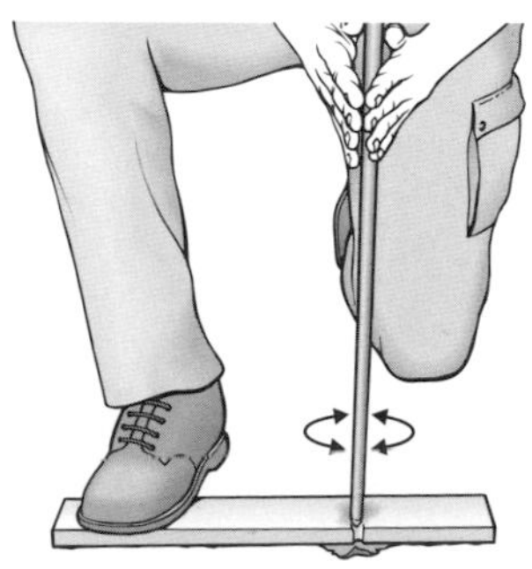

Bow and wooden drill method: This makes the previous process faster, but you must have some string handy. Put a rock on top of your hardwood stick and you can add pressure to make the whole thing work better (see below).

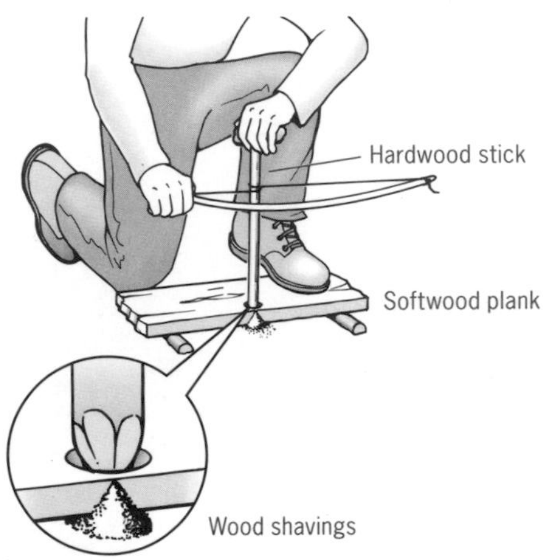

Plough method: This uses the same implements as the drill method. Create a furrow in your softwood base (as shown below) and keep 'ploughing' the furrow with your hardwood stick until the smoking pieces of softwood fall down into a tiny fire and you can work it up to something larger.

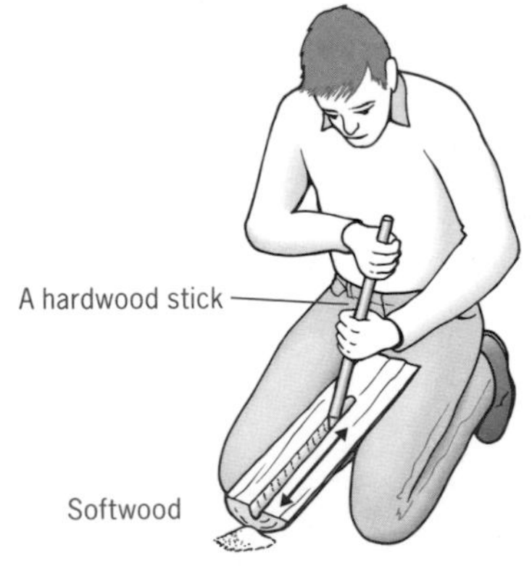

For safety, eat local. Do not eat crudités or salads in the Sahara. **Mary O'Shea**

8/AVOIDING TROUBLE IN SEX, LOVE AND WAR

Joking and laughing is very important. Don't take your work too seriously. It doesn't pay to panic. **Zeina Khodr**

I DON'T KNOW WHAT it is about danger, but it seems to make everyone horny. Beautiful sunsets, oysters and booze are aphrodisiacs for some. But put someone's life on the line, surround them with others under the same pressure and bang – you have a recipe for a sexual explosion.

It might be 55° Celsius and the air con's not working. You might not have washed for a week. You ran out of toothpaste a month ago. But none of that matters. And just like that, you are suddenly in a lot more trouble than you were before the cravings kicked in.

Sometimes, of course, craving has nothing to do with it – at least for female journalists. Jane Dutton told me: 'It is amazing how many men will try to make a move on you – even politicians and bigwigs. When I first started out, people I grew up watching on television, 40 years older than me, were suddenly groping my leg. It made their colleagues resent me. It is hard learning how to put these men in their place and retain relationships on a professional level.'

HOMOSEXUALITY

The usual situation in war zones is, sadly, one rule for straight people and another if you are gay. Breaking the rules in regard to sex is always dodgy, but homosexuals who are caught doing so can get badly hurt or even killed.

/ Think carefully about where you choose to live and where you work if you want to be openly gay.

/ With *great* caution about who you ask, take advice on attitudes towards homosexuality in the local area.

/ If there is a thriving underground gay culture, join it but remember that it's underground and you should keep within its boundaries.

/ The smaller and more secret the gay community, the higher the chances of sexually transmitted diseases. Be prepared.

In many of the dangerous places mentioned in this book, men and women are far more hands on with their friends of the same sex than we are in the West. It doesn't mean they are gay, but you never know. You might feel more comfortable with a same-sex partner in these places than at home, but don't flaunt it. Keep it private.

In Baghdad after the war people were hopping from bed to bed like rabbits in springtime. There were no rules, and even less judgement at play. The place was lawless, and for a small but hardcore minority, so was the bedroom. One neighbour of mine was managing to juggle two girls on the same floor of our (very small) hotel. I thought that was quite impressive until we went to a party at a nearby hotel and another girl sat on his lap while he talked about his girlfriend back home. I met good wives and husbands who kept their wedding rings hidden away. And men and women who threw long-held sexual identities out of the nearest hotel window. They were gay for a day or a month... Offers you wouldn't give a thought to at home can seem suddenly sexy when dressed in danger.

The obvious reasons for having sex in the wider world are amplified in a dangerous place. Popular science might explain it as your adrenalin-pumped body wanting a last chance to procreate. But having carried out a highly unscientific study amongst my friends, I would say that comfort and boredom are the principal factors motivating sex. Life anywhere away from home can be lonely, and the desire to be included, to be a part of something, draws many into bed. You might be under a lot of stress, finding it hard to sleep. Sex, and just plain human touch, will help some people deal with those pressures. Then there are the sexual scoundrels who look forward to time away from home to add a little something extra to their otherwise faithful relationships.

Monique Nagelkerke advises: 'Don't screw with the crew. Flirt with the same gender; it's exciting and there's no risk of anyone getting pregnant. And don't worry about being embarrassed: when you leave the country you most likely will never meet up again.'

When time is precious and you are surrounded by danger, disaster and death, very little thought is given to the consequences of having sex. It's awful to think of asking your devout Muslim translator to buy you some condoms, but how much worse would it be to ask him to buy you a pregnancy test? Unfortunately, all too often, casual sex in war zones leads to broken hearts and broken marriages.

My friend Shadi Alkasim has a simple solution: 'It's very hard to have sex in conflict areas, especially in Arab and Islamic countries. Customs and traditions may put your life at risk if you have sex. My advice is to masturbate.'

/BOOZE AND DRUGS

Alcohol and drugs are often freely available – even encouraged – in a war zone. However, too much of either will lead to trouble. I have seen many a girl and boy ruined by one vodka too many. I have been amongst them. At one point my best friend even boycotted looking after me at parties. A killer shot would tip me over into monster mode. I learnt my lesson the hard way – via a few panicky morning-after pills, lost friendships and lost boyfriends – so I am now hyper-cautious about overdoing the booze in professional or dangerous situations.

Where there is danger, though, bravado follows. War zone junkies with years of experience writ on their faces will tell you to have another drink and 'forget the curfew', the underlying message being that you should join in the naughtiness in order to be part of the gang. Me and my gang at the *Baghdad Bulletin* did exactly that one night and were shot at twice on our screaming rush home in the early hours of the morning. We were breaking the law and no one would have been too sympathetic if we'd been killed. 'I would never have done that,' people would say. But the thing is, they would, and do.

Drinking competitions when you're knackered, just returned from the field, see you pitted against burly cameramen and security guards. The competition? To prove you're able to live on the edge and survive to tell the tale. People don't just drink, they inhale. Individuals spend thousands of dollars on illicit alcohol and other mind-enhancing substances 'to help them sleep'. It doesn't work. And no one remembers why you had 30 shots before you threw up and collapsed in the hotel lobby.

You therefore have two choices if you want to remain sane and safe and out of the wrong people's beds. Say no, or find a way to minimize the impact of the booze:

- Make sure the regular barman knows to make every third vodka and tonic without any vodka when the orders go up to the bar.
- Eat a mouthful of food for every unit of alcohol.
- Drink a glass of water between each drink.

/SEXUAL HEALTH

Of course, this is often a taboo subject, or maybe just overlooked. Sexual health is probably the last thing on your mind as you head off to a dangerous place. But if you're there for a while and find yourself running out of contraceptive pills or landing in some sort of sexually related trouble, it will be the only thing on your mind. Finding someone to help you will be more difficult out there than anywhere else in the world. Asking advice from the wrong doctor could put you in front of a judge, facing the harsh local laws before you've had time to say 'condom'.

Helen Asquith is a London-based doctor working towards a career in international public health. She has travelled widely, observing doctors and hospitals around the world. Her streetwise view of medicine led me to ask her to write some advice on sexual health in dangerous places. Some of the advice below is a little unorthodox because it is aimed at solving problems when there are no professional solutions around. If you have access to medical help, though, you should always consult a doctor about any sexual health problems as soon as possible.

/PREVENTING SEXUALLY TRANSMITTED DISEASES (STDs)

High rates of sexually transmitted infections and war zones go hand in hand. There are two main methods to stop infection in the first place:

Abstinence – former US President George W. Bush advocated this for Africa, but it's not always feasible.
Condoms – the only form of contraception that prevents STDs.

A responsible sexually active adult should also have regular STD checks, especially when they change partners. Many STDs do not always cause symptoms, but you might pass infection on to a partner who develops serious complications, including infertility.

Perhaps you feel that you do not have sex often enough to warrant this? Don't kid yourself! If you have sex with one person who has had sex with 20 people, you are effectively taking on that person's risk.

/COMMON STDs

While the list overleaf is not exhaustive, it covers some of the infections most likely to cross your path, describing their symptoms and what course of action to take.

If you have had unprotected sex and develop any of the symptoms listed, you should (if possible) go immediately to a reputable health centre for an STD test.

Sexually acquired infections

If you think you have one of the infections listed below and opposite, you should never have sex without a condom.

STD	WHAT IS IT?	SYMPTOMS	TREATMENT
CHLAMYDIA	Bacterial infection The danger in women is that there are initially no symptoms, so the infection can develop into pelvic inflammatory disease, potentially causing infertility.	MEN: 50% have no symptoms. May have: Pain on peeing; need to pee more often; penile discharge. WOMEN: 80% have no symptoms. May have: Increased vaginal discharge; pain on peeing; abnormal bleeding (after sex or between periods); low abdominal pain.	Antibiotics need to be prescribed by a doctor after appropriate tests.
GENITAL WARTS	Viral infection	Single or multiple lesions or open sores located on any part of the genitals that has come into contact with infected partner; warts have cauliflower-like texture; usually little discomfort.	Does not require urgent treatment. Can be removed by freezing or with a medicated paint.
GONORRHOEA	Bacterial infection The danger in women is that there are initially no symptoms, so the infection can develop into pelvic inflammatory disease, potentially causing infertility.	MEN: Profuse green, yellow or white penile discharge; pain on peeing; need to pee more often. WOMEN: Often no symptoms. May have: Pain on peeing; low abdominal pain; abnormal bleeding (after sex or between periods); possibly yellow discharge.	Antibiotics need to be prescribed by a doctor after appropriate tests.
HERPES	Viral infection	Multiple small genital ulcers, usually preceded by small blisters that burst; may be painful; may have crusted over; initial infection may also cause fever and lethargy.	Needs to be diagnosed by a professional; it cannot be cured, but outbreaks can be controlled with Acyclovir (anti-viral) on prescription; outbreaks generally occur with decreasing frequency and severity over time. For symptomatic relief try: warm salt baths; distilled witch hazel applied to the ulcers.

STD	WHAT IS IT?	SYMPTOMS	TREATMENT
HIV	Viral infection Human immunodeficiency virus attacks the immune system, and in many people this eventually results in the severe complications of Aids (auto-immune deficiency virus).	Some people have an initial flu-like illness around the time of infection; others have no symptoms at all until many years later, when they develop complications of a weakened immune system.	Currently there is no cure, but when immuno-deficiency becomes severe, sufferers are started on anti-retroviral drugs.
NON-SPECIFIC URETHRITIS	Bacterial infection Causes inflammation of the urethra. Affects only men.	Pain on peeing; need to pee more often; possible penile discharge.	Antibiotics need to be prescribed by a doctor after appropriate tests.
SYPHILIS	Bacterial infection Causes short-, medium- and long-term symptoms. Can be completely cured if caught early, but has serious complications if left untreated. More common in the homosexual population.	In early syphilis a small, painless ulcer may develop at the site of infection, healing in 2–6 weeks; later symptoms include headaches, fever and rash; over time, other complications may develop.	Antibiotics need to be prescribed by a doctor after appropriate tests.
TRICHOMONIASIS	Protozoal (parasitic) infection	MEN: 50% have no symptoms. May have: Mild penile discharge; penile itch or redness. WOMEN: Smelly green/yellow vaginal discharge; possibly pain on peeing, or vulval discomfort.	Antibiotics need to be prescribed by a doctor after appropriate tests.
VIRAL HEPATITIS	Viral liver infection Generally, type B hepatitis is sexually acquired, but types A and C may be too. Hep A is usually mild and self-limiting. Hep B and C may get better, but can sometimes cause severe chronic complications.	Acute symptoms may commence several weeks after exposure, when the liver becomes inflamed; jaundice (yellowing of the skin); feeling unwell and/or fatigued; loss of appetite; possibly feverish.	Seek medical attention immediately.

Non-sexually acquired genito-urinary conditions

CONDITION	WHAT IS IT?	SYMPTOMS	TREATMENT
BACTERIAL VAGINOSIS	Overgrowth of normal vaginal bacteria, causing discharge Not sexually acquired. Affects only women.	Watery white/grey discharge (fishy smell); vaginal irritation.	Antibiotics, so you will need a prescription. Avoid perfumed soaps and douching.
CANDIDA	Yeast infection (also known as 'thrush' in women) Rarely sexually acquired. Often results from recent antibiotic treatment altering the normal balance of vaginal flora.	MEN: Penile itch or redness. WOMEN: White curdy vaginal discharge; vaginal itch; vaginal discomfort.	General advice: Keep the genital area clean and dry; avoid tight underwear. Over-the-counter treatments include: Canesten (clotrimazole) cream applied to affected skin; women can also use a pessary; oral anti-fungal available on prescription. If symptoms persist, consult a doctor.
CYSTITIS	Urine infection	Pain when peeing; frequent urge to pee but only a small amount is passed; pain at the bottom of the abdomen, between the hips and lower back; discoloured or cloudy urine.	Drink lots of water (not other soft drinks), up to 3 litres a day; if symptoms continue for more than two days, seek medical attention; if there is blood in the urine, or it is cloudy or brown, seek urgent medical attention; if far from a hospital, try taking a general antibiotic until you reach help, but only if you know you are not allergic.

/URINARY TRACT INFECTIONS

Does it burn when you pee? Are you bursting for the loo, only to find that a pathetic trickle of liquid fire (perhaps laced with blood) is all you can produce? Are you sometimes worried that you won't make it to the loo in time?

These are the symptoms of a urinary tract infection (UTI), such as cystitis, the bane of many women. Hot climates, lack of sufficient drinking water and dehydration make it even more likely to occur. Here are some tips on how to prevent and treat infection.

- Stock up on over-the-counter cystitis remedies before you go abroad. You can even ask your GP to give you an advance prescription of appropriate antibiotics.
- Keep well hydrated, especially in hot climates.
- Always pee after sex. Normal urine is sterile and will wash away bacteria that have managed to work their way up the urethra during sex. This really works.
- If you feel a UTI coming on, start drinking even more water, or cranberry juice if it is to hand. Take a sachet of cystitis relief if you have one.

If you haven't stocked up on antibiotics in advance but think you need them, it's best to consult a doctor. If that's not possible, you might be able to buy them without prescription from street pharmacies. Try to get local advice on which ones are reputable. Antibiotics useful for UTI include:

- Cefalexin – 500 mg twice daily for three days
- Amoxicillin – 500 mg three times a day for three days
- Co-amoxiclav (Augmentin) – 250 mg three times a day for three days

Warning: Do not take these antibiotics if you are allergic to penicillin. Ask a doctor back home what you can and can't take if you are allergic, and ask him to provide some for you. Always read the label and always take the full course of the drug.

If you develop fever, abdominal pain or back pain, or feel unwell, you should seek medical attention immediately as you may be developing a kidney infection.

/CONTRACEPTION

The contraception you use at home might not be the best for your trip. Asking yourself the following questions before you leave might stave off difficulties or disasters down the line.

Are you planning to have sex on your travels?
If so, take a supply of condoms. This is the only form of contraception that can protect you from sexually transmitted infections.

Are you on the pill?
If so, consider switching to a longer-term form of contraception (see chart opposite).

Do you use contraception for medical reasons (e.g. regulating periods or skin conditions)?
In this case, you probably need to stay with the pill, but check that you have enough to last your trip.

Will your GP prescribe enough pills to last the trip?
If not, you need to find out if you can obtain more pills at your destination. If your brand is not available, find out in advance what the equivalents are in other countries.

/WHICH CONTRACEPTIVE METHOD IS BEST FOR YOU?

If using any method other than condoms, you will need to consult a doctor before you start a new one.

For more detailed advice on contraceptive options, please visit the website www.patient.co.uk

/THE CONTRACEPTIVE PILL

The pill works by preventing ovulation. Taking a pill on seven consecutive days is sufficient to prevent ovulation. In addition, omitting more than seven days of the pill (i.e. lengthening the 'withdrawal bleed') allows ovulation to occur.

It is important to note that the 'withdrawal bleed' you get with the pill is not a true period. It occurs because of the hormone-free seven days between packets. Some pill brands require the user to stop taking a pill for a week. Other brands include a week of dummy pills so that the routine of pill-taking is not interrupted.

Types of contraception

METHOD	WHAT IS IT?	ADVANTAGES	DISADVANTAGES
COIL	Small T-shaped device that sits in the cervix, with top 'T-bar' in the uterus. It works by preventing implantation of a fertilized egg. Two types: IUD (intrauterine device or copper coil) Mirena® (hormone-coated coil)	Do not have to remember to take pills; lasts up to five years before requiring change; few or no side effects; possibly heavier periods; Mirena® can reduce menstrual flow.	Has to be inserted by a doctor; small but increased risk of pelvic inflammatory disease resulting from STDs travelling up from vagina into uterus. Therefore not advisable for women regularly changing sexual partners. Some doctors are reluctant to give to women who have not yet had babies as it is thought to be more painful. However, this should not put you off if you think it is right for you.
CONDOM	Latex 'bag' placed over the penis – a physical barrier preventing sperm entering the vagina.	The only method that protects against STDs; does not require a prescription.	The 'bag' can break; man has to agree to wear it.
IMPLANT	Progestogen-filled device placed under the skin. The hormone is slowly released into the body, preventing ovulation.	Lasts three years; very effective; do not have to remember to take pills.	Involves a minor operation using local anaesthetic; periods may become irregular, but are often lighter or stop altogether; some women develop side effects, but these often settle after the first few months. Ask your doctor for details before you start.
INJECTION	A slow-release dose of the hormone progestogen, which prevents ovulation.	Very effective; do not have to remember to take pills.	Injection needed every 8–12 weeks; periods may become irregular, but are often lighter or stop altogether; some women have side effects, so ask your doctor what they are before you start. The injection cannot be undone, so if side effects occur, they may persist for longer than 8–12 weeks. Normal fertility after stopping may be delayed by several months.
PILL	Daily pill taken by mouth that changes the body's hormone balance so that ovulation does not occur.	Several types available, so should be possible to find one that suits; can be used to delay periods if pills are taken without a break (see page 178).	Available only on prescription; you might run out; you might forget to take them; some women have side effects, so ask your doctor what they are before you start.

Why have a hormone-free period at all? There are two reasons:

- To reduce a woman's exposure to the hormones which, over a long period of time, are known to increase the risk of deep-vein thrombosis and certain cancers.
- To mimic the natural menstrual cycle.

It is a common misconception that missed pills towards the end of the packet do not matter as a 'period' will soon follow. In fact, the opposite is the case: during the bleed, hormone levels are at their lowest and ovulation is more likely. If unprotected sex has occurred in that time, pregnancy might result.

Missing a pill

If you forget to take a pill, what you should do depends on the type of pill you are taking. Ideally, you should find out in advance by reading the leaflet that comes with the pills.

Ovulation and pregnancy may occur if you miss pills, especially if the omission occurs at the beginning or end of the packet. In order to prevent pregnancy, you should use condoms for a week after the missed pill.

Running out of pills

If you run out of pills in a foreign country, one option is to switch to condoms. However, you may be able to buy an equivalent to your current pill (i.e. one containing similar hormone levels) but with a different international trade name. A useful website on which to look this up is the IPPF Directory of Hormonal Contraceptives (http://contraceptive.ippf.org).

Kathleen McCaul came out to Iraq with me from Oxford University to work at the *Baghdad Bulletin*. We were both as wide-eyed and naive as each other. She had an amazing ability to use that innocence to win her one exclusive interview after another. That access to the top corridors of power also made her vulnerable. At meetings that were supposed to be professional interviews sex-starved politicians, lawyers and soldiers, buoyed by the excitement of talking to their first girl in months and armed with an illicit bottle of booze, thought she was ripe for the picking. She had to learn how to bat them off with her eyelids:

'I guess the first way to prevent yourself getting pregnant is by not having sex. But in stressful situations with not much other than work to do, an affair is a good way of letting off steam and doesn't give you such a hangover as whisky, although it can have more serious consequences if you aren't careful.

'Not getting pregnant is pretty straightforward. Use a condom. Always carry condoms with you. Many of the countries mentioned in this book are rife with HIV. You want to come back with good stories, not a lethal STD.

'If something does go wrong, the morning-after pill is readily available practically everywhere – even up a mountain. You might get a few odd looks when you ask for it, but don't let that put you off.

'I think a greater danger than getting pregnant is getting trapped in a relationship that is furtive and ultimately unsustainable in conservative countries. It hasn't ever, in my experience, ended happily. How do you avoid it? Don't stay up late talking when there is a power cut. Don't go on trips to remote, romantic places in the countryside. Don't pick apart your personal stories and histories on walks in deserted gardens.

'Avoid married men, especially if they are married to their cousins. Avoid men with girlfriends. Avoid your translator. Above all, avoid your boss, especially if their father happens to be a head mullah or something like that.'

/EMERGENCY CONTRACEPTION

The morning-after-pill is available in the UK and many other countries as an advance prescription. This means that you can hold up to three packets of the emergency pill in anticipation of a burst condom or accidental lapse in contraception. It is available for purchase from certain pharmacies both in store and online, and in the UK is also available free from family planning clinics and GPs at the doctor's discretion.

Warning: Do not use the morning-after pill as a regular method of contraception. It is a heavy dose of hormones that can cause side effects in some women.

/DEALING WITH PERIODS

In most places you can buy anything you need in the way of sanitary towels or tampons from a pharmacy, but if you are in a place with no pharmacy, there are some other options. Ask women locally for advice. My experience has been that people who live with less modern amenities tend to be very open in talking about the mechanics of the body – periods, pee and lots of diarrhoea! It is a good idea to pack your own toilet roll or baby wipes. In many places there will be only water to wash yourself after a trip to the loo, and it can get messy if you are not practised.

Delaying a period

There are bound to be times when it is more inconvenient than usual to have a period, so it's worth knowing how to delay one. There is no failsafe way of doing it, but you could try one of two methods.

1. Running packets of the contraceptive pill together

This method is more effective if you have been established on the pill for a while. Check with your doctor or nurse about the best way to do this with your brand of pill. For most pill types, you can run up to three pill packets together without a break. This is known as tricycling.

Fixed-dose pill (all the active pills in the packet are the same): Simply take up to three packets one after the other without the pill-free interval.

Phasic pill (two or three different types of active pills in one packet): Running packets together can result in breakthrough bleeding, but this will not reduce the efficacy of the contraception. Consult your nurse or doctor for advice.

Packets containing seven dummy pills (in a packet of 28): If you know for sure which the dummy pills are, you can throw them away and start the next packet of real pills. If you are unsure, read the instructions or check with your doctor or a pharmacist.

2. Taking norethisterone

This is a synthetic hormone similar to naturally occurring sex hormones. It is available only on prescription and is not guaranteed 100 per cent effective. If you want to try it, you should consult your doctor before your trip to check that it is suitable for you and to issue a prescription.

The usual dosage is 5 mg of norethisterone three times daily, starting three days before the anticipated onset of a period. Menstruation will occur 2–3 days after you stop taking it.

Note that norethisterone is *not* a form of contraception.

Perhaps inevitably, there are some risks involved in taking norethisterone. The main one is the risk of developing deep-vein thrombosis (DVT). You should not take this medication if you are at high risk or have a strong family history of DVT. Other side effects of norethisterone include migraine. Always read the label and consult a doctor before taking this.

Sanitary protection

What do you do if your bag containing all your spare stuff for periods gets stolen? What if you run out of tampons in the remoter parts of some Muslim countries, where they are as hard to find as hen's teeth?

Since the ancient Egyptians invented the first tampons – made from softened papyrus – life for women has become considerably easier. Hippocrates recorded in the 5th century BC that Greek women were improvising with lint wrapped around bits of wood – sounds scratchy! The modern tampon with handy applicator was actually invented in 1929 by a man, Dr Earle Haas. He called his trademarked device Tampax, but then sold the company to a lady called Gertrude Tendrich, who made all the money.

The great lesson from all this is that women survived for millennia without the modern conveniences we take for granted. Indeed, in many of the wilder places you might be visiting today, women make do with very little. And so can you. The key thing is to do it safely and cleanly, planning in advance if possible.

Sanitary towels are by far the most common period product available globally, although many forms in remote places seem more akin to mattresses than pads. As many a maiden in distress will know, alternatives can easily be fashioned out of toilet paper, cloth or kitchen roll.

Tampons are generally harder to find, but fashioning alternatives to them is not impossible, as the women in ancient Egypt demonstrated. Anecdotes from adventurous ladies caught *in extremis* recommend the temporary use of alternatives such as a rolled-up wad of toilet paper or kitchen roll (verdict: rather dry). Or a rolled-up wad of clean medical dressing.

I lived with a similar ad hoc method to this for four months in Basra. It worked, but I blessed the BBC girl who gave me all her leftover goodies when she was heading back up to Baghdad. I probably could have found tampons if I'd asked locally, but given that my translator was a man…I was a wimp.

However, a few notes of warning are necessary:

- Always use clean materials.
- These improvised items are harder to remove than a normal tampon.
- Keep them in for a shorter time and replace with a proper tampon as soon as possible.
- They are unlikely to be sterile, therefore increasing the risk of toxic shock syndrome (potentially a very serious infection).

Can you use two tampons at once? Officially, the manufacturers of Tampax® advise against this. However, for heavy flow, many women have used this method without mishap.

How long can a tampon stay in? The official answer to this is eight hours. The longer the tampon remains inside, the greater the risk of developing toxic shock or pelvic infection. For legal reasons, we cannot advocate exceeding this limit. However, anyone who has slept longer than eight hours in a night will know that there is some flexibility in terms of time. Use your judgement.

The Mooncup® is a great alternative to tampons and pads, and is endorsed by several seasoned travellers of my acquaintance. This reusable menstrual cup is made of soft, non-latex, medical-grade silicone and is inserted in the vagina a bit lower than a tampon. Once in place, it collects many hours of menstrual fluid, which can simply be emptied into toilets. It is easily disinfected with boiling water.

Proponents of the Mooncup® argue that it is more economical, comfortable and environmentally friendly than any other method. If you're new to it, give it a trial run before departure. It can be bought only online from www.mooncup.co.uk or www.mooncup.com in the USA.

If you are still not sure about anything you have read here, you can find further information in *The Oxford Handbook of Genitourinary Medicine, HIV and AIDS* (OUP, 2005). There are also several useful websites:

GP Notebook: www.gpnotebook.com
NHS Choices: www.nhs.uk
Patient UK: www.patient.co.uk
WHQW: www.womhealth.org.au

/SAFETY FOR GIRLS

Some attention is good. Flirting is fantastic, in all sorts of ways, not least for getting things you might not otherwise have had access to. It might even get you the occasional free drink. Oops! But it can also lead to problems. Where sexual appetites are high or long unsatisfied, or if you are the only girl in a team of men, flirting can be misread as interest. Even worse, it can shout 'I am here for the taking' to the wrong sort of man.

Sometimes there is nothing you can do about unwanted attention. There's no protecting yourself from being sexually harassed by a man who wants to get you into bed, or from a man who does not respect you. But in the highly charged world you currently find yourself in, it's a good idea to stay within the safe, anodyne zones of flirtation.

Samantha Bolton observes: 'Flirtation can be useful for getting onto supposedly full planes, etc. Tell the rebels or whoever you are negotiating with that you are married. Carry a ring that can work as a wedding ring when required.'

Sadly, rape is often a weapon of war, and is not restricted just to the battlefield. It slips onto the streets, into the villages and, for many women, into their homes.

As a visitor, you can try to avoid it by not walking into dodgy areas, by not drawing attention to yourself with your behaviour or jewellery. If you get a bad feeling, run – and remember the self-defence advice on page 227. A surprise, quick and targeted attack on your attacker could well scare him off.

Acting stupid, intentionally or otherwise, can sometimes get you far. **Mary O'Shea**

9/SURVIVING EXTREMES

I got through the stress and the smell of the Indonesian tsunami with a combination of Xanax and Tiger Balm.
Marc Laban

THIS BOOK IS NOT for people who are setting off into the jungle with nothing but a penknife and two sticks to rub together. But all of us have found ourselves out of our comfort zone at one point or another, and this chapter should help you to win the battle against nature.

It is amazing what a little effort in the short term can achieve in the long run. In the army it was drummed into me that it was 'easy to be uncomfortable'. In other words, they taught us how the small effort it took to be comfortable was well worth it. Those lessons, such as how to bunker down in icy conditions and how to conserve water in hot places, later proved really valuable.

It was in the army that I learnt how to make a mobile refrigerator in a desert. Simply, wet a sock, pop your hot can of Coke or bottle of water inside and let the wind blow against it. The evaporation will cool your drink by a couple of degrees. Do it a few times and you have something that is far enough below body temperature to be refreshing. Genius.

/BASIC SURVIVAL

Assuming you have been dropped in the middle of nowhere with little or no kit, your four top priorities will be:

1. Finding a source of water

If there is no stream or lake at hand, head for lowlands, such as a valley.

- Look for pools in rocks. If the water is too shallow to scoop up in your hands, use your clothes to soak up the water, then wring them out into your mouth or a cup, or suck on them to get the water.
- If you have the right tools, dig down until you find water.
- Look for where animals are headed – there will be water nearby. And don't forget to collect rainwater.
- Try plants for water. Test them first and avoid any with milky sap as it could be poisonous. Even in the driest of deserts you can find water in cactus plants, or even come across prickly pears (see page 151).

Warning: Ration whatever water you have. Don't drink urine or salt water, and boil all the water you find to drink: diarrhoea will only dehydrate you further. (See page 161 for making fire and page 201 for sterilizing water.)

2. Finding food

There is a whole chapter devoted to the subject of finding food (see page 144).

3. Finding shelter

Maybe you'll be lucky and find something ideal for sheltering you from the elements, such as a cave. If not, it might be necessary to make a shelter.

- Use a fallen log as the topside of a roof, using long sticks to make the structure – one end on the log, the other on the ground – covered in mud or leaves.
- Make a wigwam by binding saplings or sticks together and covering it with plastic sheeting, if you have some, or branches if you don't.

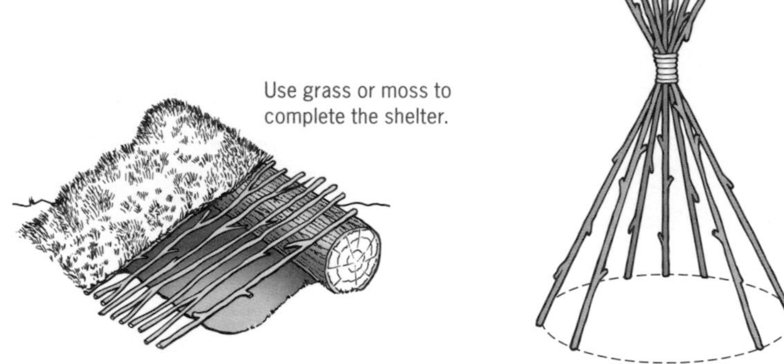

- Dig a hole in the ground and cover it with plastic sheeting weighted at the corners with rocks.
- In snowy conditions, dig a snow hole in packed snow and in open, flat areas to avoid avalanches. Use a snowdrift if there is one big enough (see below).

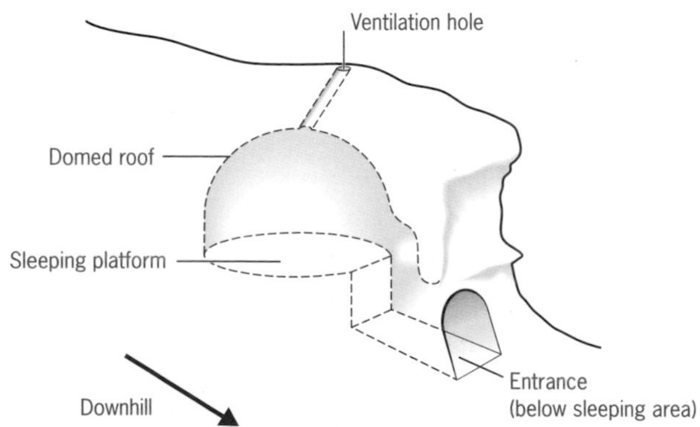

Use every resource you have to hand, plus a little strength and imagination.

Warning: If you light a fire inside your shelter (you can even do this in a snow hole), make sure there is ventilation for the smoke to escape so that you don't suffer carbon monoxide poisoning or breathing problems.

4. Finding rescue or civilization

- If people know where you are, stay put. If you had a car or plane crash, always stay with the wreckage – this makes it easier for rescuers to find you.
- If no one has a clue that you are even missing, let alone where you were going, you need to move yourself towards civilization. Or find a spot where you can signal rescuers using smoky fires or reflection (if you're lucky enough to have a mirror, glass or space blanket).
- If you set off on foot, make sure you're not walking around in circles. Take a bearing on a landmark in the distance and stick to it. If there are no landmarks in sight, you are probably better staying still and conserving your water, unless there is no hope at all of rescue.
- A good tip is to follow rivers downhill as civilization is likely to be found at some point along the way. Also, the river will be a ready source of water.

/COPING WITH COLD

There are a few benefits to living in a desert as I do in Doha. One of them is warmth – I hate being cold. My friends look to me like a canary for a warning of gathering frost. When I start shivering inside my carefully chosen five layers of ultimate manmade materials, they put on their jackets. I don't mind lying under a duvet or in front of a fire with a gale blowing outside, or trekking through the snow to a warm restaurant. But if I am cold and I can see no end to it, I become grumpy and miserable. Not great company.

There are a few tricks I have learnt along the way about coping with cold, and I've discovered many more in writing this book. The first one is to eat – a lot – something that Dr Carl Hallam agrees with:

'I was in north Norway for three months every winter as a British Royal Marine, learning how to cope with cold weather from the bossy staff sergeants, who had a saying – "Any idiot can be cold". You will cool down just like any other object in the environment unless you are prepared for it. We would eat around 5000 calories a day: one big meal in the morning and one in the evening, with a rest after both of

CLOTHING TO KEEP OUT THE COLD

Innermost layers should consist of wool and manmade fabrics that don't absorb sweat and remain warm even if wet. Avoid cotton as it absorbs sweat.

Middle layers need to be thick and duvet-like, but breathable and quick drying in case they get wet.

Outer layers should be windproof but breathable to allow sweat to escape. There should be openings to enable quick vapour release if you are exerting yourself. If sweat freezes, it will act like a fridge in your clothing.

Use drawstrings or string to block off the ends of your sleeves and trouser legs in order to trap warm air inside.

Wear layers of socks inside shoes or boots that fit you. If your socks and boots get wet, change the socks and keep changing them until the shoes or boots are dry.

them because the blood goes to the stomach after eating. You have to give it time to get back to the limbs.'

There are some other survival basics to remember, and Kamal Hyder has them all down to a T:

'One thing you should never take for granted is the weather. If you are going to the desert, it's going to be hot in the day, but freezing at night. Be ready for both extremes. Carry extra jackets if necessary. The weather is very unforgiving in Afghanistan and Pakistan. The one big thing is to have protection from rain, water or snow. If you are wet, you can't do very much.

'We were doing a trip up in the tribal territories as part of a peace caravan that was travelling from Pakistan into Afghanistan. It was so cold that I lost 7 kilos in 10 days. If it wasn't for my Gore-Tex jacket, I would have died on the trip.

'We took a four-wheel drive along with us, filled purely with wood, causing giggles amongst our fellow hardy trekkers. Whenever we had a chance, we would get together and have a big bonfire. The same people who had been laughing at us were all there enjoying its warmth. It is so important to bring basic things that keep you warm and dry.'

There are more hi-tech ways of keeping warm if you are staying for a long period. Shelley Thakral has some useful advice:

'We were revisiting the site of the 2005 Kashmir–Pakistan earthquake as the snows were coming in. People were still living in tents. We were there with the British Army, who had brought fantastic kit – tankers with ski-grips on them and things like that. But I'd never been so cold in my life. I was going to bed wearing every bit of clothing I possessed. But we had to go on. You have to use your frozen fingers and thumbs to work the computers.

'There are always going to be times when you are cold. Be prepared to be unprepared. There are tricks you can learn from the experts about kit – the right shoes, the best socks... Consider taking a small generator so you have heating and light at some point in the day. And most of all, if you can, always try to stay with the UN. Their camps are more long-term, and aimed at comfort-loving civilians.'

Finally, always assume that you might be forced to spend the night in the cold. Leith Mushtaq says: 'I was born in a furnace – I am Iraqi. In Afghanistan it was minus 20. I always travel with a sleeping bag.'

/HYPOTHERMIA

You are a small, warm thing competing with the huge, cold outdoors. You will be cooling by degrees all the time unless you take preventive measures.

Preventing hypothermia

- Keep clothing dry by wearing the appropriate protective layer – a wind-cheater, something waterproof but breathable.
- Wear a hat at all times.
- If you do have to go into water, take off as many clothes as possible and hold them above your head or wrap them in something waterproof while you make the crossing.
- If someone has an injury that means they cannot move, try to find a way of keeping them moving at least one limb or another with response games – like trying to slap a hand before it moves away.
- Watch for signs of hypothermia in yourself and your team (see below).

Signs of hypothermia

- Slowed responses and unnatural bursts and hollows of energy.
- Uncontrollable shivering and impaired eyesight.
- The sufferer will be making mistakes all the time.
- Dexterity will be low and the person will be stumbling while walking.

- Headaches and stomach-aches will develop before complete collapse and unconsciousness.
- The pulse will slow and eventually stop if not treated.

Treatment of hypothermia

- Protect the casualty from the elements, out of the wind and rain.
- Replace any wet clothes with dry ones.
- If the person is awake, feed them sugary foods and water. Hot tea, coffee or soup are ideal. Do not give alcohol – it will cool them down in the long run.
- Start to warm the person up. Separate them from the cold ground with clothing or a mat. Add your body warmth to theirs. Get inside a sleeping bag with them. Put heat sources, such as warm rocks or hot-water bottles, on any parts of the body where the blood is close to the skin – think pressure points (see page 116). If they are severely cold, their body might take hours to re-warm – it has lost the ability to do so itself. It must carry your warmth via their blood to their core.

Warning: Do not apply anything very hot to the body: it might cause burns that go unnoticed because the body is not able to react to protect itself as it normally would. Also, if you try to heat the body up too quickly, the cold blood will head into the core as a form of protection, making the problem worse.

/FROSTBITE

In extremely cold conditions a major concern is frostbite, which is when the skin actually freezes. The water in your cells expands, bursting the cell walls and ruining the affected area. The further a body part is away from the heart, the bigger the risk of it getting frostbitten. Nose, ears, feet and hands are all particularly vulnerable.

There is a hotel in Nepal called the Yak & Yeti. It's popular with climbers returning from ascents of Everest. One morning I went down to the hotel restaurant for breakfast after working through the night on a last-minute edit. I was starving. A group of Japanese climbers joined the queue behind me for a fry-up. I turned and looked at them, put down my still-empty plate and returned to my room. Their faces were black with frostbite. They reminded me of a Peruvian mummified woman I'd seen in the Andes. One of climbers had lost his nose, and two had bandages around the stump they had left for one arm; their other hand, bandaged too, was clearly missing fingers.

I am not going to provide gruesome drawings of frostbite. I hope you have all seen it before on television or in a textbook somewhere. Please read the description carefully to work out the level of seriousness.

Preventing frostbite

- Keep making regular checks of the vulnerable body parts. As the area numbs, it will be harder to feel what is happening.
- Keep the problematic areas moving. Wiggle your fingers, wiggle your toes, massage your face or pull faces.
- If someone is injured and can't move around much, massage their feet, hands and face. Keep all the mobile limbs moving.

Signs of frostbite

- Numbness or a prickly sensation in the skin.
- The affected part will go white, then harden.
- The part will swell with the frost, then break into blisters before turning black and dropping off.

Treatment for frostbite

The good news is that if you catch it early enough, frostbite is totally reversible.

The bad news is that the cure – thawing out – is very, very painful. Give the casualty painkillers to help take the edge off.

- If frostbite is at the first level (numbness or prickliness), you need to put the affected area somewhere warm to heat up slowly. Try your crotch or armpits. If you can't because your feet are affected, try someone else's crotch or armpits. Don't put the frostbitten part close to a fire – it will scream with pain.
- If the frostbite is deep and you cannot warm the area with body heat, warm up some water to just below body temperature, around 30°C – the temperature you bathe a baby in (test it with your elbow) – and put the affected area in it. If it is unbearable, let the water cool and try again, increasing the heat of the water gradually until the area is thawed.
- If the area has started to blister or turn grey or black, you need to protect it from further damage. Do not try to rub the area warm, or burst the blisters, or expose the area to extreme heat. Simply expose the area to body warmth, even if it takes hours. When it has no chance of getting better, blackened areas will just fall off.

Warning: If you are in an enclosed space and trying to warm up with a fire or any other uncovered flame, be aware of the threat of carbon monoxide poisoning. You must keep the area ventilated.

/TRENCH FOOT

When the feet have been exposed to damp and cold for too long, they develop a condition known as trench foot, which causes them to swell, blister and crack. This makes walking very painful, if not impossible.

One of the most important pieces of kit in a soldier's bag is a pair of clean socks. The priorities, after water, are feet, food, gun and feet – that's what you are taught in the British Army.

Preventing trench foot

- Change your socks every day, no matter how tired or wet and cold you are. This will give you a chance to inspect your feet.
- Socks need washing and drying as often as possible. Sleep with them on your hands inside a sleeping bag to help them dry. (It is amazing what you can dry inside a warm sleeping bag overnight.)
- Take plenty of socks if you want to avoid constant laundering.
- Take your shoes and socks off as often as possible and air your feet.

Signs of trench foot

- Feet start to feel numb.
- Pins and needles will develop.
- Sharp pain will rush through your feet.
- The feet will turn purple and blister and crack.

Treatment for trench foot

- Dry the feet and keep them dry.
- Protect the blisters with a dressing. Do not pop them.
- Do not rub or massage the affected area.
- Raise the feet and wrap them loosely in a dry rug or clothing.
- Rest. There is no quick cure for trench foot.

/COPING WITH HEAT

In a very hot environment, water is going to be your main concern. If you're in an arid desert and have none, the only places worth looking for some are dry streambeds and the lowest area you can find among the dunes. Dig at night, but be careful you are not losing more water (in the form of perspiration) than you are gaining in your efforts to find it. Wadis, oases and bore-holes will be dry and often covered up for most of the year, waiting for the rains to come, but it is worth digging in these places too if you come across them.

Any cuts or sores should be treated and bandaged immediately as they will quickly become infected.

Make a point of finding shelter because without it, your hard-won water will be in vain. Exposure to the heat of the day will soon cause health problems and see you dehydrated even more quickly. At night, when the temperature drops, use the shelter to keep warm.

/DEHYDRATION

You will not believe how much water you can get through under certain conditions. When I was in Basra in 2003 the temperature hit 63°C on a day of riots across the city. I was terrified and I was melting. That day I drank eight large bottles of water and I still felt dehydrated after all the kerfuffle was over. My clothes were soaked through, apart from the clear outline of my bra, which – as an extra layer – had absorbed some of the sweat and left a telltale dry patch on my top half. My friend Seb's trousers went from dark blue to white with salt over just a few days in Basra. My trousers eventually disintegrated from being constantly damp, ripping apart as I pulled myself out of a taxi for the tenth time that day. They are a very hardy lot, the Basrawi.

Caroline Hawley was the main BBC correspondent in Iraq while I was out there. I met her once and that was when I first learnt just how swan-like TV reporters really are – calm and authoritative on air, but paddling like crazy things underneath to make the broadcast on time and with the right information at their fingertips. The whole team is working at full speed. And when they're not working, they are travelling to the next story. As Caroline points out, it is easy to forget the simple parts of life in the rush:

'I got heatstroke in the summer of 2004. I think it was cumulative. After several days of going out in 45°C heat, I started to feel sick and dizzy. I became delirious and kept telling colleagues, "If my brain goes, put me down." I could see that what I was saying alarmed them, but I couldn't help myself repeating the same sentence again and again. I don't remember ever having felt so ill, and I wound up briefly in the American combat hospital in Iraq. After a break in the cool of the UK, we were out trying to film with an American medical air evacuation team and, unusually, a morning went by with no casualties. We twiddled our thumbs in a stifling pre-fab building with a broken air conditioner. Soon they were laughing at me as I became their first casualty of the day. Three bags of intra-venal fluid later, I was helicoptered back to central Baghdad. I definitely recommend the IV drip – it significantly shortened the recovery time.'

Back in Basra, Seb and I slept outside on the concrete floor, but it had been heated by the day's sun to around 40°C, so we continued to sweat and barely managed a doze. We experienced all possible heat disorders that week, from prickly heat, which makes you itch and can be relieved only by washing and putting on dry clothes – an impossible dream in Basra – to cramps from lack of salt, heat exhaustion and heatstroke.

Dehydration can happen in cold weather too. The dry air and the physical exertion of fighting the cold means you need to drink more than you otherwise would.

Remember too that diarrhoea, fever and vomiting (all symptoms of cholera, incidentally) can lead to dehydration, as can exercise.

Signs of dehydration

- Dizziness.
- Excessive sweating.
- Disorientation.
- Increasing lethargy.
- Weakened pulse.
- Nausea.
- Unconsciousness.

All these symptoms can be deadly if not treated immediately.

Treatment for dehydration

Almost all the symptoms can be cured by getting out of the sun and slowly drinking water with sugar and a pinch of salt dissolved in it.

Some people are like camels and seem to need very little water, while others need to drink every five minutes. If you are in charge of a team, you should monitor how much and how often people are drinking, and if it is not enough, ignore their protestations and force them to drink. As long as you are not water-boarding them, it is not the torture they claim it to be. In a dangerous situation you need to load up on your water reserves and drink as often as you can because you can never be certain when you might get another chance. Remember, if one colleague collapses from dehydration, it could put the whole team in danger.

Warning: I'm sure I do not need to tell you that alcohol will make all these conditions worse. If you are in a hot region and know you will be exposed to the sun over the next few days, avoid booze. You might want to enforce this rule within your team. Also note that drug-enhanced desert discos are not a good idea, though they always seem like one at the time. The drug Ecstasy can cause dehydration.

/HEATSTROKE

Although it often happens in conjunction with dehydration, heatstroke is different. It happens when the 'thermostat' in the brain that regulates body temperature breaks down.

Signs of heatstroke

- Headache.
- Dizziness.
- Sweating ceases.
- Hot red skin.
- Quickened and very strong pulse.
- Temperature rises above the normal 37°C.
- Unconsciousness can happen very quickly.

Treatment for heatstroke

- Move the person into the shade and remove their outer clothing.
- Prop up their head and shoulders.
- Wrap the casualty in a wet sheet or clothing and pour cool, but not cold, water on them until their temperature is back to normal.
- If the cooling process is not working, you might need to immerse the patient in cool water, slowly, massaging their limbs to move the cool blood back to the core of the body.
- Slowly feed the patient cool, but not cold, water when they are able to take it.

- Once the patient's temperature is normal, put dry clothes or a towel or sheet over them and keep them warm.

/SUNBURN

It is possible to avoid sunburn by staying out of the midday sun, in the shade, covering up with clothes and reapplying sunscreen as needed. You'll need up to factor 50 in the most extreme situations, such as deserts and snow. Minor sunburn is something most of us have dealt with before. But serious sunburn across more than 50 per cent of the body can be very dangerous, especially for children.

Treatment for sunburn

- Stay out of the sun and rest in a cool place.
- Drink plenty of cool water.
- Immerse the body in cool water whenever possible.
- Do not burst any blisters; protect them with a non-adhesive dressing, if necessary, and stop clothes rubbing where possible.

/SURVIVING IN MOUNTAINOUS TERRAIN

Most mountains provide little shelter, food or water. Unless you are with someone who knows how to live off the fat of that particular mountain, you need to get to a valley and water and safety as soon as possible.

When making a shelter, avoid steep areas or places directly under a large snowfall on a mountain, where there is a risk of an avalanche. The least steep slopes are the safest places. Also, trees provide a break in the event of an avalanche, so it is safe to shelter in front of them.

If you are walking along a ridge of snow and are worried about an avalanche threat ahead, test it by shouting and clapping your hands to see if it is set off. Ninety per cent of people killed in avalanches caused them in the first place by walking or skiing across them, or creating a noise to set them off.

If you're crossing a large area of snow with other people, tie yourselves together in case one of you falls into an unseen crevice.

If you are caught in an avalanche, use a swimming movement to stay on top of the snow – any stroke that works for you, except butterfly. And if you know which way is up, point your feet downhill.

/SURVIVING POTENTIAL FLOOD ZONES

If you are near the sea, never underestimate how far the water can move with the tide. You can never prepare for a tsunami, but you can look at where locals have their houses and place yourself there. When there is a full moon the tide can be dramatically larger.

Similarly, if you are near a river or lake after a big rainfall or snow melt, look to the locals for advice. Don't just plant yourself next to a river because it is pretty. Imagine what would happen if a dam was opened upstream. Pitch your camp away from the water, and walk to and fro to collect it for cooking and drinking rather than being right on top of it and in a likely flood zone.

And if, despite your best endeavours, you suddenly find yourself under water and disorientated? Blow a bubble to find the way up.

/SURVIVING IN JUNGLE TERRAIN

In tropical regions you are unlikely to starve or be thirsty once you have established what you can eat and drink. However, the risks are manifold – from the insects, leeches and other revolting things that want to feast on you, to the fact that it is easy to get lost and hard to find your bearings when surrounded by dense vegetation.

Making fire can be tough in the fertile and moist jungle. Find dead wood and strip off the damp outer layers. The inside should be good to fragment for tinder, to break up for kindling and to use as a whole for fuel.

Marc Laban is a founding partner of AsiaWorks, an independent production company, which is super-organized at taking teams into inhospitable terrain. I was playing a round of golf with Marc in the glorious warm rain outside Kathmandu when he had a call from base. There had been a typhoon, followed by flooding and mudslides, in the Philippines. Before we teed off at the next hole he had already deployed teams and chartered planes to the disaster. I was impressed. And he won the game too!

Large parts of Asia are dominated by jungle in all its various forms, and Marc has learnt the tricks of his trade marching through many of them:

'The jungle trips I've taken over the years have provided me with some of my best experiences and stories. But there was one story that beat them all. In 1997 I travelled with *Far Eastern Economic Review* journalist Nate Thayer and cameraman David McKaige to Anlong Veng, the final stronghold of the Khmer Rouge. Once there, we met the leadership of the Khmer Rouge, who had extended an invitation to interview Pol Pot. Nate and David had already filmed Pol Pot weeks before at a staged trial, but this would be his first "normal" interview in 18 years – and, as it turned out, his last.

'I spent a lot of time trudging through the jungle along the Thai–Burma and Cambodian borders in my early years in Asia. Normally, you're travelling with soldiers, and in the case of the Karen – an ethnic group that has been fighting the Burmese government for decades – hardened soldiers, who are not going to be spending any time worrying about how foreign journalists are holding up during a trek.'

One man's jungle can be another man's overgrown garden. Staying at a friend's house in the Seychelles one holiday, I found ants the size of small mice walking across plate-sized flower petals in his tumbling jungle garden. But he didn't think anything of it. There are many different types of terrain, and each one will have its own challenges. Equatorial rainforests, secondary jungle, subtropical rainforests, montane forests, saltwater swamps and freshwater swamps will all vary widely from kilometre to kilometre within their broad definitions. The best equipment for navigating a jungle is local knowledge and advice. But James Brabazon explains why you shouldn't take that for granted, and why you must stay in control of the situation:

'Jungle can be a misleading term. There is no one type of jungle. It can be primary, secondary or tertiary jungle, and each demands a different approach. Very few people indeed actually live in the jungle in West Africa – almost everyone lives in a village – so you won't find the same level of understanding about it locally that you would, say, in parts of the Amazon. In Liberia most villagers view the forest as malevolent, and stick to the forest paths. They sleep in huts and buildings.

'We were pursued by a ruthless government army for hundreds of miles through the jungle, and the best thing we could have done to shake them off would simply have been to step off the path – but the group of rebels we were with refused: they were more terrified of the jungle than the government army. In most other places, fighters use the jungle to their advantage, but in Liberia they don't. Local people there don't have any idea what lives in the forest either – they told us there were alligators and tigers, but those aren't even indigenous to Africa!

'You need to acquire your own set of survival skills and knowledge, and don't assume that just because someone lives in a place that they necessarily know what you need to know about it.'

Jungle clothing

In the jungle you have to stay covered up, and I mean *really* covered up. Ideally, you will be wearing a hat, a scarf up around your ears and tucked into your long-sleeved shirt, which should be taped tight around your wrists. Your shirt should be tucked into your tough trousers, which are, in turn, tucked into your socks.

Night and day you need to remain on constant vigil. Exercise strict mosquito-net discipline by making sure there are no gaps and none of the net is touching you. Close the net behind you every time you leave. You have to choose the right style, shape and size of net to fit your particular needs. In the jungle you will likely need a wedge net to fit over a hammock or a cot bed. The net should be strong enough to withstand weeks of use without ripping, and be able to keep out the larger creatures that might want to crawl into your warm bed. Bring a needle and thread to carry out repairs.

A bum exposed during a pee can be mottled with sandflies in a minute (I know – I have experienced it). A brush against the wrong plant or caterpillar could cause a violent allergic reaction. There is a risk every moment that some venomous insect will bite you with hideous consequences – malaria to name just one of them.

Fortunately, most snakes can't easily penetrate clothing. But you need to check for leeches on your legs and feet every hour – only for this are you allowed to be uncovered. If you find one, you need to remove it using salt, alcohol, or a lighter or a lit stick. Do not pull them off because there is a risk that the jaws or head could get stuck inside and cause an infection.

Travel together in a line in the jungle so that the person behind you can see if a spider drops from its web down the back of your shirt.

Avoiding creatures that bite

- Be careful about kicking rocks or picking up sticks and logs for a fire.
- Look where you are walking.
- Shake out your shoes and clothes before you put them on, even if you have taken them off for only a moment.
- Don't plunge your hand into your bag without taking a look to see what crawled inside first.

MARC LABAN'S TERRIFIC JUNGLE TIPS

/ Follow in your guide's footsteps and *never* wander off the jungle path. Landmines are strewn throughout conflict and post-conflict areas.

/ Make sure you know the route and how long it is going to take. Check on where you will be sleeping. It'll help you prepare.

/ Arrange to have a good translator. There's nothing worse than being caught in a changing situation and not understanding what is happening.

/ Take your own food. Soldiers generally carry what they eat and are not keen to share. I was on a trip where one of the soldiers was carrying a bag with a cat in it. The cat was dinner. So if you don't want to eat cat, bring your own grub. I keep it simple. Power bars, canned food and water.

/ Take a small medical kit with drugs. I always carry Imodium, medicinal charcoal, paracetamol and aspirin. Dry packages of electrolytes [rehydration salts] are helpful to stay hydrated.

/ Protect your feet and wear comfortable boots. If you wear new boots that haven't been broken in, they'll cause blisters and complicate your ability to walk.

/ Depending on the time of year, you will want to have leech socks that go all the way up to the knee. They're made out of quick-drying material that leeches can't stick to.

/ Take a flashlight and a head-torch (bring two in case one goes down). Also a knife, compass, GPS and wet-weather gear if it's the rainy season.

/ Cigarettes. Even if you don't smoke, take some and share them out. Cigarettes are a great ice-breaker, especially with soldiers and commanders.

/ Do not dress in camouflage. I am always puzzled by journos who insist on dressing in combat clothes. You are not a soldier and you certainly don't want to be mistaken for one in a conflict situation.

Treatment for bites

If bitten by a snake or scorpion, or any little vile beastie:

- Do not attempt to suck out the venom. Wash the wound and apply a compression bandage, but do not use a tourniquet.
- Immobilize the area bitten (see page 115) and keep the movement of your patient to a minimum.
- Do not try to kill the animal that bit your companion – just remember what it looked like in terms of markings and size.
- Don't give morphine or aspirin for pain – use paracetamol.
- Get to a hospital quick smart. A bite is a medical emergency.

/DEALING WITH NATURAL DISASTERS

There's danger, there's war and then there are the five-star disasters – hurricanes, earthquakes, wildfires, floods and tsunamis. There is nothing that can prepare you for these.

After one of these catastrophic events, the world as we know it stops. Man has lost to nature, and now he must return to nature to survive.

In a man-made disaster such as war there is usually still access to water and food, and international laws remain in place. And if the supplies run out, you should be able to find a way out. But these events remove your ability to choose. Your options are reduced, and your focus is narrowed to finding a way to respond to your most basic needs.

The fight for limited resources of water, food, shelter, heat and light will lead to riots. Fathers will trample over others' small children to get water for their own. A rumour can turn into a deadly stampede – either towards water or away from another feared disaster. If you have some water or food and it is only enough to keep you and the people around you going, do not tell anyone. Make yourself secure, safe and healthy; keep whatever you need to do your job. Then you can turn to helping others.

Your first thought after the immediate risk is gone should be communication with the people who know you are there – your colleagues, family and friends. Even if landlines and the Internet are down, the mobile networks will be working via the satellite link. Seek out an embassy or any connection to home. Establish a route for communication and use it.

When the norms of the world are turned on their head you can rely only on yourself. Be as self-sufficient as possible. Carry your tent, a sleeping bag, a medical kit, some cans of food, a torch, a means of communication, some chlorine or water purification tablets and some salt tablets (to be dissolved in water). This is especially true when there has been an earthquake – when all infrastructure is broken.

Sebastian Walker covered the Haiti earthquake in January 2010, and his principal piece of advice afterwards was not to sleep indoors...

'In many places in the world, a 7.0 magnitude earthquake lasting just 27 seconds wouldn't cause a huge amount of damage. In Haiti it levelled entire neighbourhoods, brought down the presidential palace and left more than 250,000 people dead. A major reason for this was cheap construction – building codes in developing countries are rarely stringent – but in Haiti, where the average wage is less than $2 a day, the average building is put together with the architectural equivalent of paper and glue, finished off with a ceiling of reinforced concrete.

'Driving through the blacked-out city the following evening was like witnessing the apocalypse. Pancaked three-storey buildings looming out of the darkness, cars crushed by masonry with limbs poking out, every Haitian in Port-au-Prince sleeping on the street just yards from body after body of relatives pulled from rubble and piled up on the pavement. I could understand how they were afraid to venture back inside any structure still left standing, but having never been in an earthquake zone myself, I put most of it down to shock.

'After an eerily quiet evening spent reporting on the dead, dying and dazed, our crew returned to base to file our story. We'd set up camp in the grounds of the Venezuelan embassy and it was starting to rain, so when all was done, I settled down for a nap underneath an arch.

'It was the sound of a Haitian subway train passing beneath my feet that woke me. It seemed to travel on and then return even closer to the surface. Finally, when the earth started juddering and the stone above my head made a cracking noise, I sprang awake and sprinted into the middle of the courtyard.

'The aftershock was 4.6 magnitude, but it didn't bring down the arch I had been lying under. Over the next few weeks, however, there were dozens more, some of which did collapse already weakened buildings. It was only after weeks of living in a tent that I felt confident enough to spend a night in a hotel – and I stared at the ceiling for a good few hours before falling asleep.'

/WATER

You can live for three weeks without food, but only three days without water. *In extremis*, you must make your own.

HOW TO PURIFY WATER

Basic filtration: This is the first step. Use a piece of tightly woven clothing – a cotton shirt will do – and filter out as much muck as possible. If you have a shop-bought filter, you should check how many times it can be used. Many are built for one use only.

Boiling: While this is the best method of sterilization, it requires heat and a metal container. If you have both, boil the water for five minutes, ideally with a lid on. Leave to cool, still with the lid on, then drink.

Chlorine bleach: Should be easily available and can be used if boiling is not possible. Try not to use a very old bottle or one that shows signs of having been moved around a lot. It depletes the force of the bleach. Use 2–4 drops of bleach per litre and leave to stand for 30 minutes. It should smell of chlorine when it is the right dosage. If not, add more. If the water is cold, you will need to add a couple more drops and leave to stand for three hours.

Iodine: *Do not use this if you are pregnant or have a thyroid problem.* You need to check the sell-by date on the iodine. Tablets last longer than liquid. Use two drops of 2% iodine for a litre of water – so that's three drops for your average 1.5-litre bottle. (If using 10% or 5% iodine, you actually need to add *more*, not less, to your bottle, but never more than 16 drops per litre. Shake and let it stand for 30 minutes before drinking. But if the water is cold or cloudy, you will need to let the water stand longer before drinking – nearer to an hour. If you are very suspicious of the water, add more iodine.

If you are still uncertain about the water after one treatment, try using two different treatments on it.

In extremes of hot and cold weather your body requires even more water than normal. Also, bleeding, injury or simple stress can all lead to dehydration. You need to find a drinkable water source as soon as possible.

> Watermelons are a fantastic source of safe water. And they have a few salts and sugars to help you rehydrate properly. **Peter Stevens**, freelance newsman

Water is also essential to maintain basic hygiene, as Nick Toksvig remembers: 'Moving into Kuwait after the coalition forces pushed the Iraqis out, we discovered there was no running water for the toilets. So we took it from the still full hotel swimming pool.'

You need to stay clean. You may be surrounded by death, broken water pipes or floodwater. Disasters are a festival for bacteria, so now would be a good time to become obsessive about being clean.

/PREPARE FOR THE WORST AND LIVE DEFENSIVELY

Aftershocks, newly broken riverbanks, a returning hurricane – all these things could happen. So stay away from potentially collapsible buildings if there has been an earthquake. Pitch your tent on high ground if there is the threat of a flood. And if there's a hurricane approaching, you need to seek shelter wherever local authorities are recommending. Basements are not always a good idea if there is a risk of flooding or your building collapsing.

> As a general rule, avoid getting into arguments with voodoo priests. **Mary O'Shea**

10/STAYING FIT AND BEATING STRESS

During a particularly exercise-happy phase, I took my dumb-bells on a trip to Eritrea. They pissed off my cameraman and hiked up my luggage overweight and didn't get used once. But at least the thought was there! **Jane Dutton**

'HAJIA, HAJIA!' This was my name for a month before I left Iraq. It means 'old woman', and was given to me because I developed a back problem that left me bent double like an ancient crone.

As I slid from my 50°C bed into a taxi every morning, longing for air conditioning or a shower that I'd gone without for up to six days, exercise was the last thing on my mind. I hadn't done anything to keep fit, and now my back, which I had broken four years earlier when I was 18, had broken itself again. With all my stomach muscles gone, there was nothing left to take the pressure off my spine. I regretted every step not walked over the last few months, and every muscle-using opportunity missed as I lay for 17 hours groaning in the back of a saloon car all the way from Basra to Amman to get myself home to a hospital.

Like most people, I'd used all the usual excuses for not exercising, but this time they included cultural sensitivity. As a woman in a Muslim country, it is difficult but not impossible to keep yourself fit. You can't just pop out for a run, even if you are covered from head to toe. You will be stared at or even followed in a car, as was my experience in relatively cosmopolitan Amman in Jordan. Gyms for women are rare and usually single-sex. It is just not expected that women will want to work out.

When I returned to Baghdad as a producer for Al Jazeera four years later I had learnt my lesson. I took one look at the stairs in my hotel and vowed to run up and down them every morning. Exercise helps with sleeping. It helps to burn off all those calories you eat and drink. It also helps to stop the body creaking, though it was tricky when you're not allowed to move more than a few metres from two charming bodyguards. (Bodyguards, by the way, can make excellent fitness instructors if you can keep up. I can't.)

For most people exercise is also invaluable as stress relief. It gives you a rush of that happy hormone endorphin. It burns up unused adrenalin that nutritionists say will end up giving you a fat tummy when it converts itself to sugar and sticks to your torso.

Ideally you should aim to be as fit as the people who are running the war zone – soldiers. You need to be able to move as fast as them. In an emergency evacuation you might find yourself carrying a lot of weight for miles on end, or flying in an army plane for 16 hours, or bumping over a long, long road. Damage will be done if your back isn't in top order. Also, what happens if you need to carry a friend to safety? It isn't your job to be that fit, but it will help you.

/SIMPLE WAYS TO STAY FIT

As your body prepares itself chemically for fight or flight, you should prepare it physically too. You can come up with all the excuses in the world – and I have used them all – but 15 minutes a day spent looking after your body will make a huge difference to how you are able to deal with your job.

Getting out of breath is the only way to keep your heart fit. Try to get your heart rate up and a sweat going three times a week for half an hour, or every day for 15 minutes. BBC correspondent Caroline Hawley has found her own way of achieving this: 'For entertainment and exercise when confined to a small area, I definitely rate ping pong. You can work up a surprising sweat if you move around the table enough!'

Stairs are your friend. Run up and walk down, unless you feel like running both ways. But be careful not to hurt your knees by overdoing it. Running uphill is great for your tummy muscles. We spend far too much time sitting down, so skip lifts whenever possible.

Fitness machines are great if you have them. Just make sure you use them, and don't let yourself get into a dull routine. Make it different each time. Your body will stop responding if it becomes predictable.

Skipping is easy. Do one minute skipping and one minute of another exercise 10 times and you will be done for the day.

Leg lunges strengthen your legs. They'll be most effective when you have run out of breath already. Make sure your knee doesn't go forward of your foot and your tummy is pulled in. Add weights (see box overleaf) in your hands if it is getting too easy.

Step exercise can be done with a bench, chair or stairs. Start with both feet on the floor and step up to your chosen height, being careful to keep your back straight and your knees no further than 90 degrees from your torso. Bring the other foot up and stand straight on your bench or whatever, then step down again. Go as fast as you can without losing control, and switch legs every 10 repetitions.

Shadow boxing is also pretty easy. Keep your legs still, one foot forward of the other. Look straight ahead at a point on the wall and start punching, keeping your

EXERCISE EQUIPMENT ON THE CHEAP

There's no need to spend a lot of money on equipment. With a little imagination, you can create everything you need.

/ For weights, use tins of beans or full water bottles (1 litre of water weighs 1 kilogram).

/ If working out in a swimming pool where there are no floats, use empty plastic bottles with the caps on. Pushing them under the water is a great resistance exercise.

/ For a makeshift medicine ball, put some books in a small backpack and stuff it tight with newspaper.

/ If you have no stairs, try running on the spot on a mattress.

arms at that height. Now try moving your legs back and forth too.

Samantha Bolton recommends Kegel exercises: 'These strengthen the pelvic floor and can be done sitting down – just pull in as if holding in a wee, tighten the butt muscles, then release. Do it 20 times. Good for both men and women are yoga sun salutations and sit-ups; also tricep dips for the backs of the arms, which you can do while sitting on the toilet, bath or bidet [see page 213]. Dancing is also good exercise, as is having a good laugh!'

/STEPPING UP THE PACE

In this section are basic Pilates exercises, which are easy to follow without expert help being at hand. Once you've mastered them, a quick search on the Internet will throw up plenty more complicated ones to keep you interested.

Go through the exercises as slowly as possible. It is not the number or size or speed of repetitions that will help. It is keeping your tummy 'zipped up' (held still with your core muscles) that will maximize the effect.

The key is to keep your core still and tight throughout. Feel those muscles you hardly ever use at the bottom of your stomach. Pull them in and imagine they are trying to touch your spine. You should be able to feel they are tense to your hand, but don't suck in your stomach. You need to be able to breathe and have your muscles engaged throughout. When lying down, your spine should be as flat to the floor as you can make it without it being uncomfortable – anchored not pressed. Don't let that feeling go while you work your core muscles in these exercises.

All of the following exercises can be done in the privacy of a small room – on the space of a towel in fact – preferably on a carpeted floor so that you don't get a bruised bottom.

Unless stated otherwise, you should aim for about 10 repetitions of each exercise. Just be careful – if it hurts, stop.

Don't forget to breathe!

Keep breathing slowly and evenly during each exercise, and try to exhale whenever you lift a leg or move your body away from the floor in any way. However, with lunges and press-ups you should exhale as you move towards the floor.

Stomach and back exercises

I cannot emphasize enough the importance of keeping your back healthy when you spend days or weeks on end hunched over a computer or stuck in a tiny hotel room watching TV. However, being confined is no excuse for not exercising, as Monique Nagelkerke reminded me: 'Watch the movie *In the Name of the Father* and pay close attention to what Daniel Day-Lewis does when locked up in a cell for years. He got a great six-pack. You can do that, but you will need to rearrange the furniture, though!'

Leg circles

Lie on the ground and raise one leg at right angles to the body. The aim is to keep your body still as you make circles with one leg, then the other. The size of the circle is determined by what you can do while keeping the rest of your body anchored to the ground. I can do only grapefruit-sized circles, but you can go as large as you like provided you aren't rocking one way and another. Reverse the circles after 10 reps.

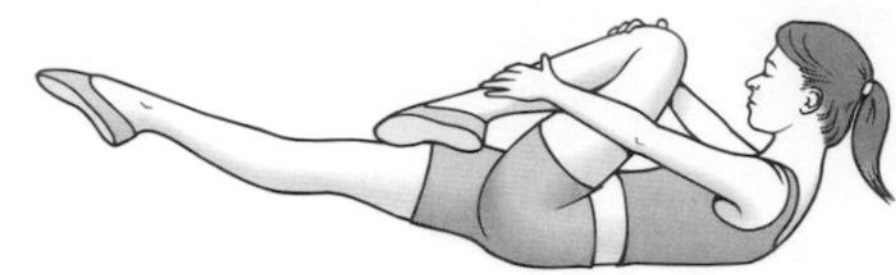

Single leg stretch

This is a great one to do in the morning while you are still warm from bed – a good soft stretch for your lower back. Lie on your back and keep your neck lifted, then bend one knee and pull it towards you, hugging it to your body. Leave the other leg suspended a few inches off the ground. Then switch sides. The body should be still, anchored and even as you move through the exercise. Start slowly holding the leg for a couple of seconds, but then fall to whatever your natural rhythm might be as long as your core is still held tight. It is a slow exercise, though – you are not aiming to build up a sweat.

Straight leg stretch

A good stretch for highly strung hamstrings, this is the same as the single leg stretch but with two straight legs. Hold your leg just below the knee on your thigh as you look at your leg. Keep it straight and pull it close until it's at a right angle to your body. Don't hold on too tight. It is an exercise for your core, not your arms. Move in a natural rhythm, changing legs after 10 reps. But again, don't aim to go fast. Your body should not wobble. This is the most effective way of doing the exercise.

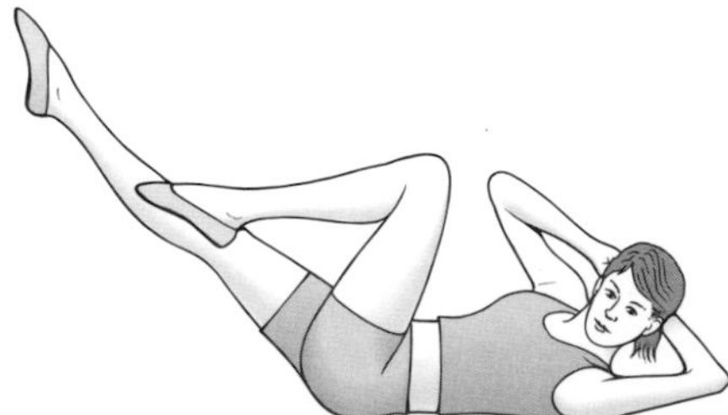

Elbow to knee twist

Proceed even more slowly with this one. Support your head with the tips of your fingers. Slowly, slowly, keeping your lower torso anchored to the ground, raise your upper back and touch your right elbow to your left knee. The movement is a lifted twist, not a lift. Do the same with the left elbow and right knee. Follow the twisting movement with your eyes, first to the left, then to the right. The straight leg should be active – the muscles kept tight to keep you from rocking from one hip to another.

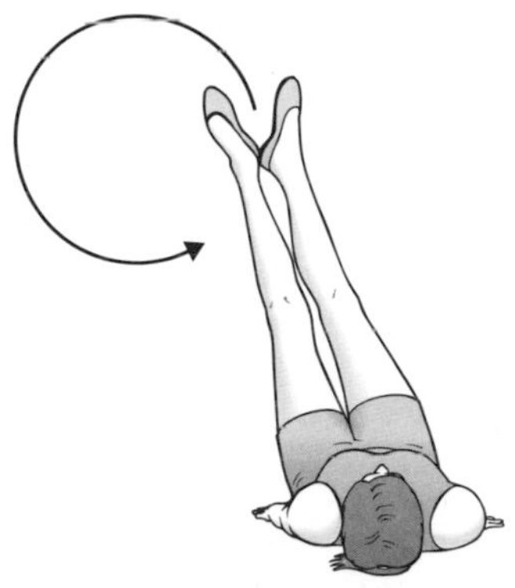

Cocktail stick

With legs tight together and as straight up in the air as possible, make slow, even circles, as though stirring a cocktail glass. Keep the torso still, circling only as far as you can without moving it. Aim to do beach ball-sized circles.

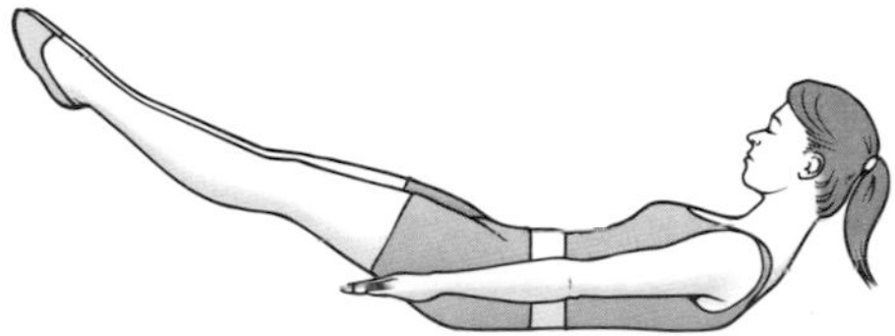

The hundred

Lie on the floor with your stomach zipped up and your arms by your sides. With your head and shoulders raised slightly, raise your legs at right angles to your body, then lower them as far as you can without losing control of the core. Mine stay straight up in the air even though I have been doing this exercise for years. If it hurts like this, bend your legs.

Hold this position, breathing slowly, and start pumping your arms like a seal out of water. They should be moving about 20 cm up and down. Count to 50 while doing this, and if you are still feeling that your stomach muscles are properly engaged, go all the way to 100...hence the name of the exercise.

Gradually lowering your legs will make this exercise harder, but in the end it will make your muscles stronger. When lowering your legs, make sure your back doesn't come away from the ground.

Rag doll

Sit with your legs apart, heels pushed out: they are your new anchor. With arms straight out to your sides, twist your body around to touch the right hand as near to your left toe as possible. Don't bounce or push too far – go just as far as is comfortable. Now do the other side. Keep those stomach muscles strong and engaged.

Twist

This is the same as the rag doll, but without leaning down. You can actually feel air being forced out of your lungs as you twist around with a strong lower back and no movement in your anchored hips and legs.

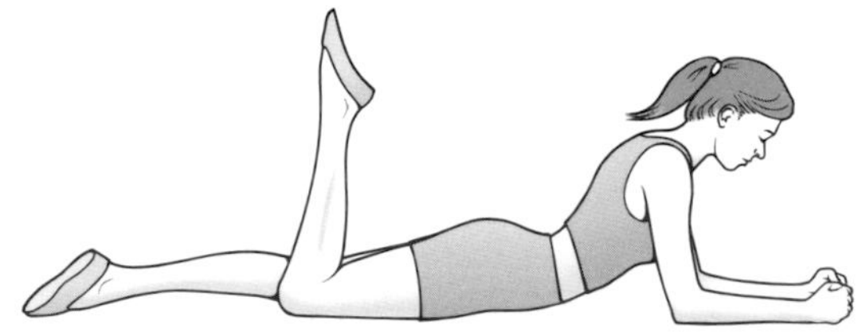

Buns of steel

This is as simple as it looks. The only important thing to remember is that your stomach needs to be lifted off the floor, supporting your lower back. If you let it drop, you will hurt your back. Stick to 10 reps for one leg, then move to the other. Relax your shoulders away from your ears.

Bridge

Avoid this one if you have a bad back, wrists or knees. Otherwise, lie on your back with your knees up, hip-width apart. Lift your bum off the mat and support your hips with your arms, straight up and directly under each side. If this feels like you are pushing yourself up, stop immediately. If it feels comfortable, imagine you are being held up by a swing under your bum. That swing should be still as you lift first one leg, then the other. Again, go only as far as you can without moving that swing. Keep those stomach muscles strong.

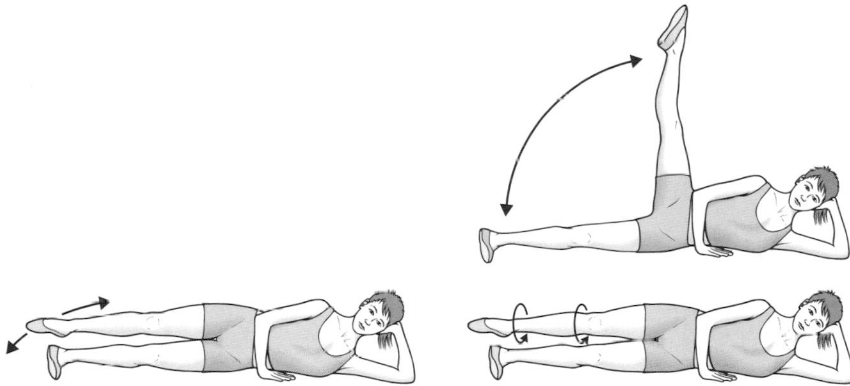

Side kicks

Imagine you are a model lying on a car bonnet, casually leaning on your elbow: if you move your torso, you will fall off. Your top arm positioned out in front of you acts as a balance rather than a support. The torso remains still as you perform a series of kicks. Start small with your movements until you can go big without collapsing the top half of your body. Once you have the body sorted, try the following:

- Move your straight top leg forward and then behind your bottom leg – as far as you can go without losing control of your top half. It's like walking with one straight leg, except you are on your side and going nowhere.
- With the toe pointed, move the leg up and down.

- Make apple-sized circles a few inches above your bottom leg.
- Make slow bicycling movements – 10 reps each side, then switch.

Arm exercises

The plank

This is your starting position for all the following exercises. Look back at your feet: is your bum in the air or your stomach on the ground? They shouldn't be. Your body should be straight, in the basic press-up position. Now move your neck to a neutral position, looking straight down. If your wrists hurt, move onto your elbows, fists straight out in front of you.

Leg lift

Start in a strong plank position and, without wiggling from side to side, lift each leg a little off the floor – never above bum height. Hold for about two seconds and then switch.

The crab

This is the same as the leg lift, but in reverse. This time there should be a straight line down from your chest to your toes. It is a backwards press-up position.

After you have finished this exercise, try bending your knees and your elbows a little and walking around like an awkward crab. A few steps forward, back and side to side. It's great for your triceps.

> Exercise your chest – stress tends to build up there. Push-ups, racket sports...just moving your arms around a lot will help. **Marc DuBois**

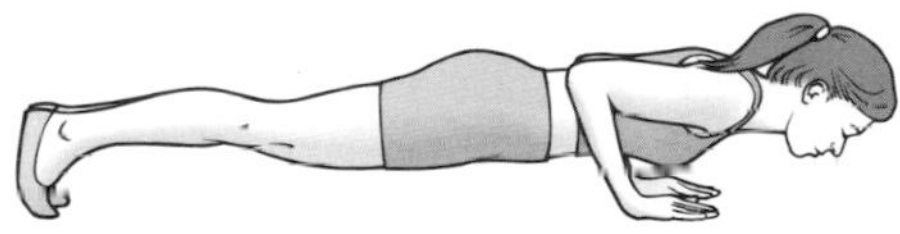

Press-ups

There should be a straight line from your head down to your ankles – no bottom sticking up or tummy scraping the ground. If you struggle in a straight press-up position, as many people do, bend your knees and put them on the ground, or stay on your toes and move your top half up so it is at an angle by leaning on a window ledge or the wall. Use this trick only until you build your strength up. Vary the distance your arms are apart to work different muscles.

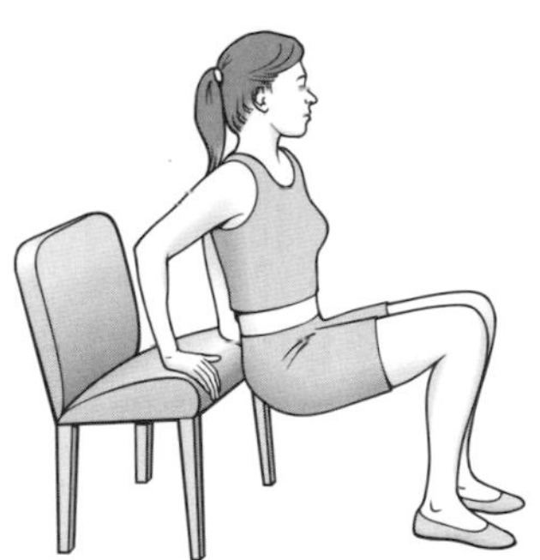

Tricep dips

Sit on a seat, bed or ledge with your hands holding onto the sides. Move your feet forward and drop your bum over the edge. Now your tricep muscles on the back of your arms are supporting you. Dip down and up again, keeping an even weight on both your arms. Keep going until failure.

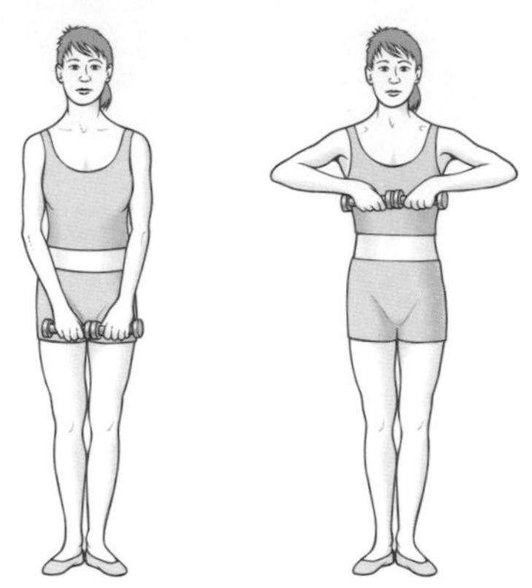

Front weight lifts

Take your weights (see page 206) and lift them up to chest height while keeping your shoulders down. Lower them and repeat.

Skiing nowhere

Keeping your stomach muscles strong, move your arms from bent to straight in line with your body in deliberate movements, not a swing.

Shoulders together

With your arms falling towards the floor, move your shoulder blades together. This is a great reliever of repetitive strain injury (RSI) if you have been sitting hunched up at a computer all day.

> Exercise is very important. It's stress relieving. Even in the middle of Darfur, you find logisticians who built their own homemade gym. It helped them and it will help you.
> **Dr Carl Hallam**

/SLEEPING IN TIMES OF STRESS

For many people under pressure, the first things they turn to when they want to relax, sleep or forget the horrors of war are alcohol or drugs. While these might work to get you off to sleep, the body is just sleeping off the effects of them rather than getting the rest it actually needs. The same goes for your mind too. Scientists all agree that the brain processes the events and thoughts of a day during the deepest part of a night's sleep. That means you can file away all the awful things you have seen, delete unnecessary worries and find calm space...but you need to hit that deep level of sleep first.

My friend Hoda Abdel-Hamid knows all about this: 'You always sleep badly in a war zone. I cannot sleep without my lavender oil, which I sprinkle on my pillow at night. And I take my own pillow too if I can. It feels so luxurious.'

Lack of sleep plus a hangover will:

- Worsen depression.
- Lead to accidents.
- Make you more vulnerable to illness.
- Make you less productive.
- Make you irrational and grumpy.
- Kill your appetite for sex.
- Make you fat as you overeat to compensate.
- Make you thin because of all the extra hours spent awake.

All these things make you less able to cope in an emergency.

Remember too that lack of sleep can be as dangerous as being drunk or drugged on the job. Make it a priority to get some proper shut-eye.

> The most important things in my bag relate to sleep – which I do very badly. I absolutely insist on earplugs, and I always carry multiple eye masks. The most important piece of embed kit is a very thin inflatable mattress. An American soldier gave me an excellent one, which I still use. **Tom Coghlan**

Everyone has their own tricks for helping themselves to nod off. As a lifelong insomniac, these are the ones I have picked up over time, though I often find a glass of red wine helps too.

- Routine – stick to a pattern before you go to bed. Always read, or always have a bath, or always listen to a certain song, or always delete unwanted e-mails in your inbox. Whatever it is, find one that works for you and stick to it. Monique Nagelkerke told her winning formula: 'Have one stiff drink, and watch re-runs of *Grey's Anatomy* every night. Guaranteed to make you fall asleep.'
- Don't smoke or eat right before you go to bed. You might find it relaxing, but it will actually be waking up your body.
- Avoid caffeine or chocolate late at night. Resist, resist.
- Eat bran or wholewheat-based cereal with milk about an hour before you go to bed. There are elements of the sleep-inducing hormone melatonin in both the grains and the milk, which will help shut your eyes.
- Try to get some sunshine during the day; then, when it is dark, your body will know it is time to sleep.
- Have a very dull but worthy book to read in bed, and force yourself to read that rather than a page-turner.
- Avoid using your computer or watching television while in bed.
- If you wake up, don't move or turn on the light – just lie and wait until you can get back to sleep.
- Control your breathing and slow it down to sleeping pace.
- Let your mind move out of the present to a safe place.
- Concentrate on relaxing your muscles, moving from the toes all the way up to your jaw (see page 218).
- Don't count the hours until you have to get up. Try not to look at your clock or watch.
- Don't worry about not sleeping. Even lying still and quiet with your eyes closed is restful if not healing.

Samantha Bolton tells me: 'Sex and a spliff works for many. But deep, calm breathing and making sure you are not sleeping in the same tent as a smelly, snoring logistician or cameraman really helps. Lock doors and push furniture around as need be to feel extra safe. Try to think of somewhere peaceful on a beach. If mentally exhausted, make sure you are also physically dead and then the body takes over.'

SIGNS OF STRESS

/ Putting on weight or losing it suddenly.

/ Abnormal insomnia.

/ Low or high blood sugar.

/ Fleeting sharp pains in the chest.

/ Pain in the lower back, shoulder or neck unrelated to exercise or injury.

/ Sudden hair loss or menstrual problems.

/ Withdrawal from social life.

/ Stomach-aches and acid taste in the throat after eating.

/ Abnormal nail-biting or teeth-grinding.

/ Abnormal skin irritations.

/ Repeated minor illnesses and headaches.

/STRESS RELIEF

Your natural fight or flight response fills your body with chemicals that will tire you out if left unattended. Exercise and sex help, as do reading and other relaxing hobbies, but if they are not possible, it is worth looking at a few other types of relaxation. Samantha Bolton recommends sharing jokes, war stories and funny childhood experiences. She also says: 'If being bombed and under severe stress with nowhere to move, talk about the perfect meal you will have when you get out. Imagine what family or others are doing at that particular moment. Pray to God and promise never to get yourself in that situation again: promise to go to church and be good, just as long as He gives you just one more break until the next time...'

Breathing exercises

Find a calm, quiet place. If this isn't possible, turn on some calming music to block out the distracting noise.

- Sit or lie comfortably. Put one hand on your stomach and the other on your chest.

- Inhaling through your nose, take a long, deep breath that feels as if it is coming from your stomach, counting slowly to six as you do so. You should feel the hand on your stomach moving the most.
- Breathe out through your mouth, again counting slowly to six.
- Continue breathing in this way and you will find that the oxygen relieves stress and helps settle your mind. Simply concentrating on your breathing will rest your brain for a minute. It is a type of meditation.

Once you have learnt this basic technique, you can play around. For example, lie down with a book on your stomach and watch it rise up and down; breathe through one nostril, then the other; hold your breath, keeping the nostrils shut with your fingers, and count to six before breathing out again. Use your imagination to think of other ways to keep the exercise interesting. Mary O'Shea tells me that her stress antidote is to recite *The Wasteland*.

Muscle exercises

Lie down in a comfortable position and think your way through your body from toes to head or vice versa, systematically tensing and then relaxing your muscles. Hold each muscle tense for around eight seconds before letting go.

This exercise will also help you to learn what your muscles feel like when they are tense. This means that when you feel the signs you can take a moment to relax.

Meditation

I am useless at meditation, but many close friends and colleagues swear by it. Some of them have two kids and two jobs, yet they still manage to find half an hour a day for themselves. It's just a question of making it a priority, they tell me. They say they have their best ideas after their mind has been cleared by meditation.

Meditation is not about staring into the middle distance: it is an intense form of concentration on something that would normally pass you by. You are aiming for a mind-full-ness rather than an empty mind. It's all about finding something peaceful and positive to concentrate on. You don't even have to be still.

- Go for a walk and concentrate on your breathing, the wind and smells and sights. Be aware of each step.
- When you eat turn off the television and put down the book; try to focus your attention on the meal and how each bite feels inside your mouth.
- Try thinking your way up or down your body, considering each individual part and how it feels.

- For more intense meditation, turn off all distractions, put a 'Do not disturb' sign on your door and find a comfortable position.
- Pick something to concentrate on, whether it is your breath, a scene in your mind or a word or phrase. Close your eyes and keep your mind on your chosen thing for as long as you can.
- If your mind drifts off, don't worry – just bring it back to your focus and carry on.

Never try to use a dangerous trip as a chance to diet. Eat. You will lose weight anyway, believe me.
Dr Carl Hallam

11/SURVIVING WITH AND WITHOUT WEAPONS

I don't have a weapon. I just carry a camera. **Leith Mushtaq**

IN MANY PARTS OF THE WORLD you can buy small arms along with your bread at the market. I remember taking one BBC reporter to the Basra black market, where, for $100, he 'bought' a tank that had surrendered during the invasion. 'It's in full working order,' he told me proudly. I didn't tell him that every reporter who came through went down to the market and posed for the same snapshot – 'Me and My Tank'. The tale was worth the $100 alone. The old man to whom the tank 'belonged' had a toothless grin as big as his wallet as he waved off his buyers and waxed the barrel of his gun for another day.

There is little doubt that carrying a weapon can give you more confidence in a dangerous world – especially if you know how to use it.

Patrick Hennessey, a former British army officer, says: 'Survival in a war zone is obviously a little different for a soldier than it is for a civilian. I got a taste of that difference when I returned to Helmand a few months after finishing my five years' service with the British Army as an infantry officer and found myself ambushed on patrol, only this time as a freelance journalist embedded with my former comrades. The adrenalin rush was the same, as was the heightened sense of awareness, the noise and noticing the absurd details (this time a bright pink rose that minutes earlier I had been given by a local farmer and which had fallen into the muddy water at the bottom of the ditch into which we'd jumped for cover). One thing, however, was worryingly different, and that was having a camera in my hands instead of a rifle. It was the most naked and useless I've felt in a long time.'

Some people don't have a choice in whether or not they should carry a weapon 'just in case'. Most NGOs, medical personnel and others working or visiting a highly armed society won't be allowed one, and won't want to touch one.

Dr Carl Hallam, who works for MSF, told me: 'Having been on both sides of a gun, I advise never to underestimate the confidence and swagger it gives if you are the one with the weapon. If you don't have a gun, you are a very small guy compared to the one who does. As aid workers, we are always unarmed. Therefore it's difficult for most to imagine the difference between being unarmed and armed.'

Producer Shelley Thakral says: 'At the BBC we don't have weapons, and of course it's better that way. As a journalist working in a dangerous place, you change the job dynamic the moment you start arming yourself.'

As well as the risks to your independence, just having a gun on your person can be a dangerous thing. In a draw, the one with most experience is going to win.

My colleague Jane Dutton, who lives in South Africa, told me: 'My dad lent me a small handgun after a family friend was shot and another friend of ours was broken into, but I gave it back after a week. I knew it would get used if I found someone breaking into my house. I was angry and scared enough. But nine times out of 10 the criminal will end up using your handgun against you. I didn't want that risk.'

Warning: If you use a weapon in a war zone, it can change your legal status to 'mercenary' under the Geneva Convention (see page 40]) – not a particularly good idea if you are captured.

Chris Cobb-Smith, who has contributed to earlier parts of this book, generously offers his security expertise here too. I asked him for advice about guns, and for a few basic instructions on how to work a weapon if you really need to use one.

/IS THE SAFETY ON?

Few subjects cause as much controversy as that of firearms. However, it is unavoidable, an ever-present fact of life, and encountered continually in the high-risk regions so much in the news today.

For some, carrying a firearm is as natural as carrying a mobile phone, almost a natural extension of the arm – a comforting and continually present friend. For others they are objects of bewilderment and revulsion: 'Why on earth would I want a gun?' Whatever stand you take, some rudimentary knowledge is necessary, and here is some advice:

Never touch a firearm unless you are totally confident in its operation. But if you have to, avoid any contact with the trigger as some are extremely sensitive.

Always keep the barrel pointing away from people. Direct it up in the air or, if the ground is soft, downwards.

Remember, firearms can be 'attractive' items and in some scenarios could be booby-trapped, so again, do not touch them unless it's imperative to do so.

/IF YOU MUST USE A GUN...

Should you ultimately be driven to use a gun in a life or death situation, try to remain calm and take the following steps:

Look for the safety catch – internationally, 'S' stands for 'Safe'.

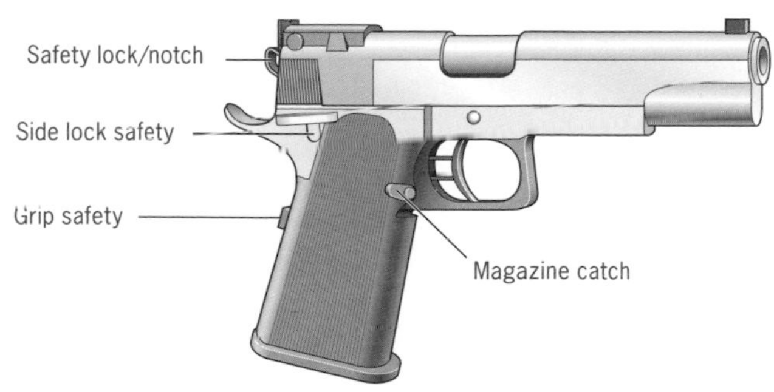

Choose a setting – 'R' for 'Repeat' and 'A' for 'Automatic'. For accuracy and control, select 'R', allow the weapon to point naturally, aim at the centre of mass of your target and squeeze (don't pull) the trigger.

/SECURITY

My advice is that if you feel the need to be armed, you should leave the weapons in the hands of experts like Chris. But the process of finding the right kind of security is a delicate one. Do you go local or do you outsource? It depends on the task at hand.

Let's start with a few observations about Western 'security contractors'. I don't mean to generalize – I have worked with some incredibly professional (and handsome) bodyguards – but all too often 'security' means a bunch of pasty, tattooed, slightly overweight men who have arrived in a country for the first time with few or no local contacts. They tend to charge a fortune to tell you that you can't do what you need to do in order to keep your job. However highly trained and excellent they are, they stick out like a sore thumb, and so will you.

Shadi Alkasim advises: 'Avoid hiring a muscly bodyguard: it could draw attention to you and might lead to you getting kidnapped or killed. People might attack you, believing that you are working as a spy with the forces of the armies stationed there. Or they could hijack you for a ransom demand in the belief that you are someone important and rich, and you could end up dead.'

But if you are heading into an unknown area or disaster zone, the bodyguard's knowledge, experience and ability to adapt to any situation is invaluable. What they don't know when they turn up they make it their job to learn. There is a network that spans the world, and they will tap into it for the best local knowledge.

Film-maker James Brabazon told me: 'In Liberia I employed a South African ex-mercenary as a bodyguard – the only time I have used an expat as an armed guard. He was dressed in a military uniform and carried a gun, which is an entirely different thing from a journalist carrying a gun. If he had been arrested, he would have been tried as a mercenary and probably shot. They wouldn't have done that to me. He understood that.'

James has made it his business to mix in worlds where most people wouldn't dare to go. Even the ballsiest people I know look at work by James and wonder why he decided to put himself at such risk. The first film I saw of his was a documentary made in Liberia during the war there in 2003. While filming with the rebels, a notoriously nasty bunch, James got to know them and understand their impulses. After that he was chosen as the official documenter of the failed coup in Equatorial Guinea. His book and film about the man behind that coup, Simon Mann, is called *My Friend the Mercenary*. James says good security is not just about finding the right man for the job – it's about learning to listen to him too:

'In Liberia in 2002 I was filming rebel soldiers fighting against government troops at close range. I wanted to stay in the position where I was filming from, but a rebel commander wanted me to move back. It had taken me about two hours to get there crawling on my hands and knees under fire. I was very reluctant to move back. The South African mercenary I had hired to protect me, Nick du Toit, insisted I move back. I still said no, but he grabbed me and dragged me to one side. An RPG [rocket-propelled grenade] hit the spot where I had been standing. The group of people I had been standing with were all killed or injured. Deafened by the blast, we were shouting at each other, trying to work out what to do next. Our noses were two or three inches apart and a bullet passed between us. He grabbed me again and we ran back into cover. My advice is this: if you have employed someone because of their expertise and value them for it, listen to them – even if it is inconvenient.'

On the other hand – and here I risk a sweeping generalization – foreign security guards tend to err on the side of caution. You have to learn when to listen to them and when to follow your own instincts. Nick Toksvig agrees:

'There had been a terrible bombing at Qurna, in Lebanon. It was the second by the Israelis in a number of years. It was highly contentious and the Israelis were on high alert. Rumour said that they were targeting cars going along the road from Beirut to the south. Our security guy told us not to go. I listened to him, but I also knew we were in the country to cover stories exactly like this. I decided we should risk it. We got there and they were still pulling children's bodies out of the rubble. It was awful.'

If you can find good local security guards, you are onto a winner. Look for discipline and, if they are in a team, a clear hierarchy. You need to be able to communicate clearly with them. They need to be clear on your objectives, what you need to do each day, but you also have to trust that they will know when to say no. At other times you might need to push them for a little more caution because the land and people are so familiar to them. Take time to get to know them and even their families if you can. They could be risking their life for you. Their partnership with you will be noted by the local community. They will be judged one way or another long after you have moved onto the next job.

According to Nick Toksvig, local hire can be a hit and miss affair: 'We drove from Peshawar through the Khyber Pass into Jallalabad in November 2001. The hunt for Bin Laden was under way and we were making our way to Tora Bora. We travelled by convoy and hired local armed guards throughout the time we were there. They were OK, but it's always a risk hiring someone carrying a gun. Their loyalty is to the money rather than you. If someone pays them more, they can stab you in the back.'

For some, such as Zeina Khodr, the idea of hired security is never a good one. She advises: 'Keep a low profile. I never travel with bodyguards because armed escorts set you apart. My life is not more important than the life of anyone else here. In the end you won't get the support of the people.'

/SELF-DEFENCE WITHOUT WEAPONS

The idea of self-defence is to avoid getting hurt, not to hurt your attacker. It is great to learn a few techniques, but in reality they are not going to save you if you are taken by surprise, or overwhelmed by someone who is hugely stronger than you.

But if you have time, take some self-defence or martial arts classes. At the very least, get fit and strong. Knowing what it feels like to punch and kick might give you the confidence you need for that extra edge in a fight.

Remember, though, your aim is to avoid engaging altogether – run!

Warning: When faced with someone who is armed, comply and do nothing to aggravate them if you think they might use their weapon.

/AVOIDING ATTACK

Many fights can be won before they start. If you can convince your attacker that you are not worth the effort before they begin their assault, that is the better option.

If someone is stalking you or you think you are about to be attacked, pretend to be on the phone to the police.

Confront your stalker loudly. Ask what they are doing. Make sure they know you have seen them and will be able to identify them at a later date.

Monique Nagelkerke advises: 'In countries where men feel they can just grab, pinch and say anything they want to a lone woman, be prepared to hit before you get hit, grabbed or pinched. Hold a soft drinks bottle in your hand at hip level when walking the street so that men cannot bump into your hip "by accident". The bottle can also serve as a weapon. Hit them hard on the hand and shout: "How dare you!" It nearly always works.

'When being hit on or grabbed, look the man sternly in the eye and – if you speak the same language – put on your schoolteacher voice and say: "Would you like your wife/sister/mother to be treated like this?" This has worked well for me in the past.'

/IF YOU ARE ATTACKED

Surprise is your first weapon. Your attacker might not expect you to fight, so use every last ounce of your energy and strength, and direct it at his weakest parts – the eyes and genitals.

Distract him. Throw coins in his face. Spray perfume in his eyes.

If you are grabbed or assaulted, scream and kick and shout as much as you can in the early stages.

Use your strongest parts to hit him – your feet, your knees, your elbows, your fists. A palm strike (see below) in the face or nose will hurt like hell.

Find a weapon in your surroundings. Use anything you can to keep the attacker away – an umbrella, a handbag, a windscreen wiper, a mop, bricks, park benches, walls and railings...anything. Your mobile phone held in your fist and aimed at his temple would hurt him, as would 'stabbing' him with pens or bottles. The end of a rolled-up newspaper hurts if it hits an eye. Hold it close to the end and use the last 5 cm or so as an extension of your fist. Use your clothes or a bag cord to strangle, whip or tie him down.

If you are in your car, use the car as a weapon.

/SELF-DEFENCE MOVES

The palm is stronger than the fist.

Palm strike

Use the flat palm of your hand rather than your fist or fingers to strike directly.

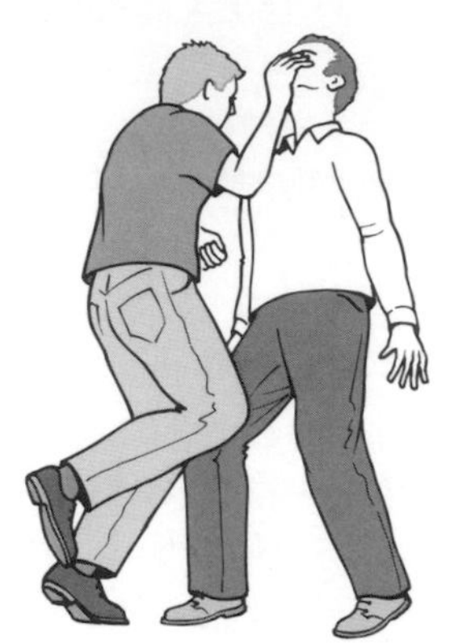

Aim for the most vulnerable points – the eyes and genitals.

Knee strike

Hold onto your attacker and aim for his testicles any which way you can. Take him by surprise.

Punch

Keep your thumb protected when you punch. Don't have it inside the fingers or sitting like a lid on top of your fist.

Elbow strike

Use your elbow to hit directly. It is less easy to grab and has more force.

Follow up these moves with hit after hit, cut, crush, break, rip or (if you have no other choice) bite…whatever it takes. Once you have the advantage, use it and don't give up till you can make your escape.

/RAPE

There is no knowing what position your attacker will get you in, but these four pieces of advice can be used in most situations.

Stab his hands with any weapon you can find. Bite them if necessary.

Put him off balance in any way you can and follow this up with violent strikes directed at his weakest parts.

Try to bend your knees and place them or your feet between you and your attacker to keep a distance. If you can do this, use the chance to kick him away.

If you are physically overcome, use your last weapon – appeal to his emotions.

Samantha Bolton told me some encouraging stories about the effectiveness of this last technique:

'I know two women who have talked their way out of a rape. One Canadian aid worker was attacked by some young Croat soldiers. She stayed calm and appealed to them: "Look at me. I am blonde, like your sister." So they backed down.

'Another woman, much older than her attacker, started slowly to stroke his head when he was on top of her, telling him it would be all right, that she knew how hard the war was. It reminded him of his mother, he started crying and stopped the attack.

'And if they are going to rape you anyway, follow the example of a nurse who was attacked in the DRC. She told her attackers that she had Aids and gave them condoms to wear. It probably saved her life, though not from the attack.'

In the British Royal Marines they force you to run 10 kilometres before you learn self-defence. The message being that it is always best to run before getting into a fight. You are relying on the fact you are stronger than the other person. Avoid fighting somebody at all costs.
Dr Carl Hallam

12/SURVIVING LANDMINES, IEDS AND CHEMICAL PERILS

Sometimes I can't control myself when I work in a war zone.
I feel ready to die for the job. It's not work – it's making history.
Leith Mushtaq

RALPH HASSALL is a friend and former employer of mine at the *Baghdad Bulletin* newspaper in Iraq. He has since become a specialist in disaster management, but his main area of expertise is landmines, and he has worked in a number of mine action programmes around the world. He's a truly independent spirit with a hidden love of sensible jumpers. And that's what shines through in his advice below.

He explains that mines planted during wartime are not the only problem. Areas where unexploded weapons have fallen may be unmarked.

/EXPLOSIVE REMNANTS OF WAR

Conflict areas will invariably be littered with explosive remnants of war (ERW), which includes landmines and unexploded ordnance (UXO). The latter refers to weapons systems that have been deployed on the battlefield but did not activate as intended. It includes ammunition for light weapons, artillery shells, mortars, grenades, fuses and rockets. UXO can detonate if disturbed, unleashing the full lethal force that it was intended to deliver.

Cluster munitions are also a prevalent menace. These are air-dropped or artillery-fired weapons that disburse hundreds of smaller submunitions over an area. They are usually designed to detonate on impact with the ground. Each cluster weapon can carry up to 2000 small bomblets, but they have a failure rate of up to 10 per cent, so can leave a sizeable and explosive contamination problem for years to come.

Even just a short time after a conflict, cluster munitions that scattered but did not detonate can become buried under sand or vegetation. No longer visible, they can have a similar impact to landmines that have been deliberately planted. Countries such as Laos have an enormous number of unexploded bomblets littering the countryside. More recent conflicts in Lebanon, Gaza, Iraq and Afghanistan are all characterized by cluster-bomb contamination.

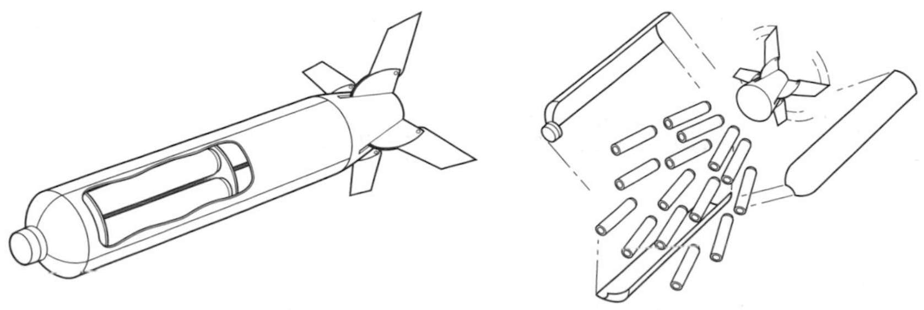

Cluster bombs come in all shapes, sizes and colours – all highly attractive to children.

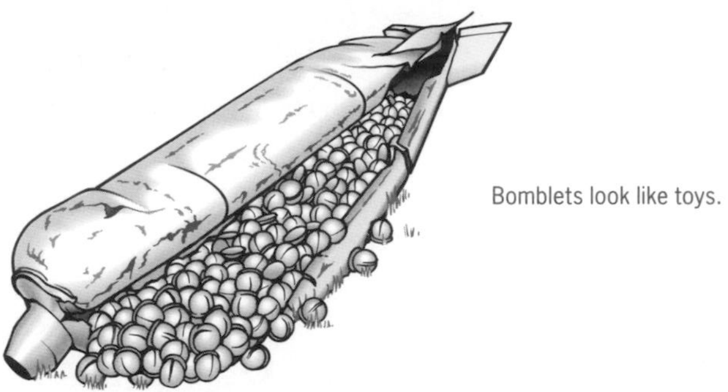

Bomblets look like toys.

/DON'T TOUCH

Never be tempted to touch anything or pick up 'souvenirs' from a battle area. In the summer of 2003 Hiroki Gomi, a Japanese reporter working in Iraq, picked up an unexpended cluster munition without realizing what it was. He packed it in his bag to take home as a souvenir from the war. While it was going through the X-ray scanner at Amman airport in Jordan, the cluster munition exploded, killing the security guard making the inspection.

If you find yourself close on the heels of conflict or in the conflict itself, there may be a temptation to take souvenirs, or to poke around in abandoned buildings and military emplacements. Do not do this. You could well activate unstable UXO, or trigger a booby trap (see page 237) designed specifically to attract your attention.

Taking souvenir photographs of people sitting on tanks or other destroyed military equipment may also expose you to depleted uranium (DU). Shells made from the extremely dense material DU, which is used to destroy armour, might vaporize on impact, contaminating the surrounding area with radioactive dust particles that could be absorbed into the body through inhalation, for example. Unnecessary exposure to toxic DU can lead to long-term health effects.

/THE LANDMINE THREAT

Landmines have been a favourite tool of warring parties precisely because they are easy to deploy while being difficult to detect and remove. Most countries that experience conflict will have a legacy, great or small, of mine warfare. Landmines can stay active almost indefinitely, just as potent and deadly as the day they were laid, or perhaps even more so as triggering mechanisms might have frayed or decomposed.

Anti-personnel (AP) mines are designed to kill or maim individuals. Warring parties prefer the latter as the care and treatment of victims will absorb manpower that would otherwise have been used for operations.

Anti-tank mines are specifically designed to destroy or disable vehicles or armour, *not* individual personnel. The most common form of activation for mines is by pressure (from a foot or car tyre). However, tripwires and other forms of activation – proximity sensors, tilt-switches, magnetic attraction, and specifically designed anti-handling systems – can be used too.

There is a common myth that there is a delay between activating a landmine and it exploding: the reality is that the explosion is instantaneous.

Landmines and booby traps can be found anywhere that conflict has occurred. They can, for example, be laid as a 'nuisance' for advancing forces in houses, gun placements, trenches, rest-stops by the side of the road or at water sources. They can also be laid in patterned arrangements in clearly identified locations.

Nick Toksvig recalls a frightening experience during the Kosovo War: 'We were in a village and found the mayor's house, which had been abandoned. There was a path leading to the front door, but I chose to make my way across the lawn. I knew it was an official's house and had probably been booby-trapped as the Serbs retreated, but I didn't really pay enough attention to that. At one point a colleague told me to stand very still. A couple of centimetres from my heel was a small landmine that, had I stepped on it, would have taken off at least my leg. We had no security with us, and I had certainly advanced without the necessary caution.'

Understanding the mine threat in a particular area or location requires an understanding of the conflict that has taken place there, preferably learnt from witnesses (civilian or military). It's also important to have some knowledge of mine-related incidents or accidents that have occurred. It is standard practice for UN agencies, host governments, specialist NGOs and commercial companies to collect this data in a systematic way.

If you are embedded with military forces, they will provide you with their own guidelines for safe conduct. However, the level of acceptable risk for military personnel is higher than that usually tolerated by civilians during either conflict or peacetime. If you are not working with the military but will be operating in an area that has or might have experienced conflict, you should contact the local UN or governmental Mine Action Centre (MAC), or an agency that you know is concerned with demining or mine action. Mine action is the provision of an integrated set of

BEFORE HEADING INTO A MINED AREA...

/ Locate the nearest hospitals.

/ Understand access routes and discuss them with local specialists.

/ Know the history of conflict in the area: ask the specialists.

/ Seek training in what to do if you get stuck in a minefield.

/ Sort out your medical kit with trained personnel.

/ Check your radios and communications equipment. Establish a communication protocol.

services designed to reduce the impact of landmines and UXO working to a commonly accepted set of international standards.

Remember that understanding of the mine threat can change as better information becomes available. Make sure always to check the latest information when planning field missions. If there is an area that you know or suspect to be mined, avoid it – do not even go near it.

/HOW TO SPOT A MINEFIELD

A minefield will often look indistinguishable from any other piece of land. However, there may be telltale signs.

- Locals might be avoiding the area, despite its obvious use for agriculture or for transport access.
- Dead animals might be seen in the area.
- Waxed packaging used to store the mines may be littering the ground.
- The area may be overgrown.
- Locals or organizations might have tried to mark out the area of the minefield using sticks, stones or more formal markings (see opposite). Always be conscious of your surroundings.

Signs of mines

There are dozens of different signs used to mark mined areas. They go far beyond the more traditional skull and crossbones. Mary O'Shea reports that: 'In Sudan the minefields are apparently marked by red Coca-Cola cans. I am unsure if Pepsi and Diet Coke have any significance.'

Some of the more formal signs are illustrated below.

/IF YOU FIND YOURSELF IN A MINEFIELD...

Remember the following mnemonic – MINED – from *The UN Landmine and UXO Safety Handbook*.

Movement stops immediately. Remain still and do not move your feet. If you are in a vehicle, do not try to reverse through your tracks. Do not move the steering wheel. Stay inside the vehicle. Keep calm.
Inform others immediately. Warn those around you. Call for help, but keep others away. If you are in a car, use the horn to summon help.
Note the area. What else can you see: mines, tripwires, mine signs? Visually locate the nearest safe area – the last place you knew you were on a safe surface, such as a paved road, well-used path, or concrete or steel structure.
Evaluate your course of action. Be prepared to take control.
Do not move if there is no indication of a safe area, or you can't reach it without stepping on unknown ground. Wait for help to arrive.

/WHEN NO HELP IS AVAILABLE...

According to the *National Technical Standards and Guidelines* for mine action in Sudan, 'It is better to spend two days in a minefield than a lifetime as an amputee.'

However, if there is genuinely no possibility of getting outside help, you might be forced to take action. There could also be exceptional circumstances when faster action is forced upon an individual or group of people, such as when someone is injured and the others must clear a path to reach the victim.

If your footsteps show clearly in snow, sand or wet mud, you can follow them back. However, they must be clear enough for you to know with certainty where you are treading. If you are in a car, climb onto the roof and walk back along the car tracks if they are entirely clear.

Prodding the ground and retracing your steps is an extremely risky business if not taught properly by certified professionals, so you are strongly advised against attempting it. If you know in advance that you're heading into regions or countries where mines are considered a threat, it could be worth getting professional instruction and practical exercises in the technique of prodding before you go. At the very least, read the following information first.

Prodding is the traditional technique used by military and civilian landmine clearance agencies alike, and ordinarily used in conjunction with other tools, such as metal detectors. The technique involves using a sharp, pointed, long-bladed instrument, such as a knife, to prod the ground at a shallow angle (no more than 30 degrees) and at short intervals (no more than 20–25 mm) to detect the presence of objects hidden under the surface and clear a safer passage through a dangerous area. The depth to which it will be possible to prod will depend on the ground conditions. Some mines may be located fairly deep beneath the surface and beyond the range of the prodder.

/IF SOMEONE IS INJURED BY A LANDMINE

The time period during which the casualty should be delivered to hospital is sometimes called the 'golden hour' because for about 60 minutes the blood vessels and capillaries around the wound site constrict in response to the trauma, restrict the bleeding and naturally compress the damaged tissue. This gives paramedics and any others assisting critical minutes to get the casualty to where transfusions and proper surgical help are available.

While you are waiting for help to arrive, take the following steps:

- Ensure that you are not in danger yourself.
- Apply first aid and stem the bleeding.
- Stabilize the casualty and prepare for transportation.
- Select a safe route to the closest hospital with transfusion and surgery facilities.
- Call or radio ahead to prepare the hospital for the arrival of the casualty.

/IMPROVISED EXPLOSIVE DEVICES

The aftermath of improvised explosive devices (IEDs) – namely, people with devastating injuries and graves at every turn – can be seen in numerous places around the world. They have been around for more than a century and used in all the wars within living memory. Perhaps because of media coverage, or maybe because at one point there were dozens a day, the improvised explosive device seems to be the weapon that defines the war in Iraq. The whole convoy of US vehicles in Iraq has been adapted and re-adapted to make them IED-proof, and still the bomb-makers are inventing new devices. The struggle to beat them has even been immortalized in the multi award-winning film *The Hurt Locker*.

The picture that won me a job at Reuters was taken three days after I arrived in Baghdad, when a roadside bomb hit a convoy of armed Humvees 50 metres in front of me. Iraqis jumped into action, pulling wounded, burnt and broken soldiers from the flaming vehicle. On a busy day in relatively quiet Basra I once visited three roadside bombs that went off during one hour, all within half a kilometre of each other.

The journalist Imad Shihab says: 'I think there is no way IEDS can be avoided by ordinary people, without sophisticated devices like the ones the US Army has. They can be anywhere and any shape. They could be under the pavement, even in the corpses of men and animals. Like what happened to my friend and her mother when kidnappers planted IEDs inside their bodies after they killed them. When people tried to move the dead bodies the triggers went off, killing many more people.'

IEDs are not just roadside bombs, and not just in Iraq. They are found in every war zone – attached to cars, hidden inside pianos and even, as Imad said, inside dead bodies. They can be targeted or random. Sometimes you get a warning and sometimes you don't. If the locals are not actually the target of the devices, they usually know where they are, but sometimes they won't be told. IEDs are intended to cause chaos and fear for everyone.

My advice is to avoid being blown up as best you can, and to heed the following tips from Imad:

- Stay away from possible targets – army vehicles and obviously armoured or brand new-looking cars.
- Take routes that possible targets don't usually use.
- Sometimes locals get news about an IED being planted somewhere for a particular target. They pass the news around the community and people avoid the area. You need to tap into this sort of information whenever possible.
- If an IED goes off, you should hit the ground, facing away from the blast; cross your legs and cover your head with your hands.

/ADVICE FROM AN EXPERT

I also offer the following advice from an explosives expert in the British Army. He works for a regiment that specializes in disarming IEDs. Due to his position within the forces, he has provided his advice anonymously.

'IEDs differ from conventional bombs and mines in that they will always be placed by a perpetrator in an area of their choosing as opposed to being in a minefield or former bombing range. This means that it is potentially more difficult to determine where you might stumble upon them. The question you need to ask yourself is, "Who is likely to have placed an IED and why?"

'An IED can take many forms and will always be designed to blend in with its background so that it is difficult to identify what is or isn't an IED. For example, is that shopping bag in a crowded supermarket out of place or just someone's shopping that has inadvertently been forgotten? That is what the perpetrator is hoping you will think, but before paranoia sets in that every bag is an IED, you have to ask the question you asked before: "Who is likely to have placed an IED and why?"

'Before carrying out an IED attack the perpetrator will study their target and look for a weakness they can exploit, or something they can do that will go unnoticed in normal life. Now look at where you are and what the conflict you are following is trying to achieve: that will give you the best indication if you are in an area where someone might wish to use an IED.

'If you have been in an area for some time, you will know what normal life is like, so look out for what is not normal. Are children who normally play in the streets missing from view? Is a usually bustling hive of activity oddly quiet? These can be indications that something might be about to happen.

'So what should you do if you happen to stumble across what you believe to be an IED? First, stay calm. If it hasn't actually exploded, don't do anything to it. Simply retire to a safe distance and take others with you, making sure there isn't another IED where you move to. Report your findings and stay back.

'Remember, IEDs are indiscriminate and your best chance of identifying a threat is by knowing who the perpetrator is trying to target and then making sure you don't present yourself as that target.'

/CHEMICALS AND RADIATION

The threat from chemicals, radiation spillage and depleted uranium can also be high in war zones long after the battles are over.

BBC correspondent Caroline Hawley advises: 'Be aware that hazards can lurk where you're not expecting them. I still regret not being better prepared for a visit to Iraq's nuclear site at Tuwaitha, which was extensively looted just after the war that toppled Saddam Hussein. People living in the area had taken away barrels used for storing uranium, tipping the 'yellow cake' out first so that they could use them to store rice and water. They were becoming ill and wanted international help. As we filmed on the site with an Iraqi armed with a Geiger counter, the needle of the machine suddenly pinged past its highest reading and the man shouted, "Off scale!" As a dusty wind blew, laden with I hate to think what, we jumped back into the car and covered our faces with scarves. Call me a hypochondriac, but I have always worried that future health problems might be traced back to that former nuclear site.'

Avoiding contamination

Ask around locally to find out which are the danger areas. Avoid poking around blown-up vehicles, as they could be covered in depleted uranium. Don't be afraid to use protective clothing and masks yourself, even if the locals don't use them.

Treating contamination

If you think you have been contaminated, avoid touching your eyes and face with hands. You need to take off your clothes and shoes before you enter your house or hotel and rinse yourself thoroughly under cold running water. Don't use soap unless the contamination is of an oily consistency. You will need to call for new clothes. Put the ones you were wearing in a plastic bag and throw them away as they might contaminate other items, or even the water supply if you wash them. If you were wearing protective clothing, throw it away in a plastic bag, writing some kind of warning on the bag in the local language.

/EXPERT ADVICE AND FURTHER READING

For further advice on chemical contamination you can call the following companies:

Avon Technical Products: +44 1225 896 375
Remploy: +44 151 631 5017
Sema: +33 147 819 521

Before going out in the field, it is strongly recommended that you read the *UN Landmine and UXO Safety Handbook*, available as a download from ngosecurity.googlepages.com/UN_Landmine_UXO_Safety_Handbook.pdf. It will provide you with accepted good practice for safer operations in landmine-affected states.

> You can be the most experienced journalist in the world, but the minute you stop caring about what you are doing, you have to stop. **Shelley Thakral**

13/SURVIVING A KIDNAPPING

Be prepared to smile into the faces of your kidnappers and agree enthusiastically with their ideas. But you must also be prepared to kill them if necessary. You owe them nothing.
James Brandon

I HAVE NEVER BEEN kidnapped, but I have been an outside force working to get someone released.

I'll never forget waking up one Friday morning to a message from a friend: 'James has been kidnapped in Basra.' It was the height of the hostage-killing season in Iraq, late 2004, and I'd just learnt that a few days after I'd left my former house, also in Basra, a group had come and kidnapped the housekeeper. He was a university student I had lived every moment with for five months. His father, an unemployed fisherman, cleared out his life savings and more to get his son back. The kidnappers had been looking for me. I was full of guilt.

James Brandon hadn't been taken by the ad hoc groups we saw on telly every day. Instead, it was the increasingly dangerous and well-organized Shia militia who had stormed his hotel in the city of Basra, beaten him up on camera and then dragged him off without a word about their demands. The pictures of his violent seizure were made public, but the British Foreign Office wanted to keep his kidnapping quiet.

Choices, choices, urgent choices to be made. Do we – his friends with contacts across Iraq – stay quiet as recommended by the Foreign Office, or go large, make him front-page news? Against the advice of the experts, we decided to go public. Our aim was to get a renegade 'enemy of America' Shia cleric – the infamous Moqtada al Sadr – to stand up at Friday prayers and ask the kidnapping group, who claimed allegiance to his Mehdi army, for James's release.

I ran to the BBC newsroom – not such an effort since I was working at BBC Current Affairs at the time – tapped on a reporter's shoulder and told her the story. The BBC crew then jumped into action. Three hours later James's bruised and battered face was plastered all over the afternoon edition of London's *Evening Standard* newspaper.

The story was out. James's value as a hostage was up, but so was the danger to the kidnappers. All the stakes were higher. It was a risky gamble, but it worked. Moqtada al Sadr called for the group to release James, and some days later he was freed. We were lucky and so was he.

/TIPS FROM TERRY WAITE

Terry Waite became famous for his work in helping to negotiate the release of hostages in the early 1980s, then he became one himself. Held for five years in Lebanon, most of it in isolation, he explains that advance preparation isn't really possible, but you must do everything in your power to remain strong.

'Having worked for several years as a hostage negotiator, I was always aware that one day things might go wrong and I would either be captured or, worse still, killed. The first thing to say is that if one is captured, nothing can really prepare one for the experience. I had secured the release of many hostages and listened to their stories, but when eventually I was captured I had to learn, and learn pretty quickly, how to manage.

'Each situation is different, but probably a good rule of thumb is to remember that when one is captured it is likely that the captors will be excited and nervous, so one must be aware of making sudden movements that might cause one of the group to pull a trigger. You want to preserve your life, so it is wise to be compliant.

'Once under their control, keep your wits about you. Listen carefully to what is said and remember it if you can. If you are blindfolded, listen for sounds around you so that at a later date it might be possible to locate where you were kept. Remember smells too.

'Treat your captors with respect. Being aggressive will not help you. There is no need to be unduly submissive, but remember that at this stage they have most of the cards, and until you have a better idea of who they are and what they want, you had better go along with what they request.

'If they require you to write a message, introduce into that message a deliberate mistake that only your immediate family might know. This will convey to those outside that you are speaking under duress.

'It is essential at all times that you maintain your self-respect. This is where those who have had military training ought to have a slight advantage as they will have been taught to keep themselves smart. I was in captivity for five years, four of which were in strict solitary confinement, and for the first week, when I had my own clothes, I put my trousers under my mattress on the floor to keep them pressed! My captors thought I was mad, especially when I requested shoe polish. After a week my clothes were taken from me.

'I had no books or papers for many years, so had to keep myself alive mentally. Do not allow yourself to be over-depressed by the situation. Use it as an opportunity to explore your inner self and to use your imagination in a creative manner by writing in your head or composing music if you have that ability.

'I was chained by the hands and feet, but managed to do regular exercise, like what you can do when confined to an airline seat for many hours. It is important to keep your health as best you can.

'Don't demean yourself by pleading with your captors, and don't say any more than you have to. There is no need to be aggressive, and it's pointless, as it will get you nowhere.

'Keep hope alive. Remember that most hostages are released eventually. There is much, much more that I could say, but that is enough for the moment. Let's hope you never need the tips that I have given.

'Happy travelling!'

/ADVICE FROM OTHER KIDNAP EXPERTS

Sue Williams works at the very top of the mysterious business of hostage negotiation. She has been involved in hundreds of kidnap incidents, and not all of them have ended happily. She says there are two things to remember if you are ever taken hostage:

1. Do everything within your power to maximize your chances of survival.

2. Don't underestimate the outside influences working tirelessly on your behalf.

/HOW TO MAXIMIZE YOUR CHANCES OF SURVIVAL

The information here is all about staying strong and able despite the strains that kidnapping will be having on you mentally and physically.

Sue Williams advises: 'During the extended periods of boredom and increasing feelings of hopelessness, it is crucial to remain focused. A daily routine can provide structure to an otherwise vacuous day. If exercise forms part of this programme, improvement may occur physically and that achievement can also improve your state of mind.'

Chapter 10 is devoted to exercises that you can do in the confined space of a hotel room in a war zone, but they can also be done in the average prison cell. The importance of physical fitness, and its effect on your mental stability and levels of stress, cannot be overstated. It will also help you to sleep away the long hours.

Your captors might use food as a bargaining chip for good behaviour or information. On the other hand, starving you could be their chosen means of torture. But remember, a dead hostage is worth little to your kidnappers. You too can use food to your advantage, but use it to build ties rather than break them. According to Sue Williams, the trade-off for refusing food is not worth it. 'All offers of food should be accepted, not only due to its scarcity, but also to avoid offence, increase bonding and encourage rapport during mealtimes.'

But James Brandon, the hostage and friend I introduced you to at the beginning of this chapter, offers a word of caution: 'If your kidnappers give you food or water, it can seem like generosity. It isn't. Your kidnappers are feeding you because you are more valuable to them alive than dead, not because they like you.'

Another way to maximize your chances of surviving is to make your incarceration about more than just survival. Sue Williams advises trying to build as much of your normal life into your caged world as you can: 'Do not be afraid of asking for things, particularly medicines, reading material and items that will assist in maintaining personal hygiene. Remember, it is in the kidnappers' interest for you to remain alive and in good health.'

Note that the more human you are, the easier it will be to build those key bonds with your kidnappers. James Brandon told me: 'If you get kidnapped, you must get your kidnappers to empathize with you. My kidnappers accused me of being a soldier and a member of the CIA. In an effort to make me "confess", they alternated mock executions with punching me in the head. After hours of this they stopped and one of them offered me a cigarette. I don't smoke, but I took one anyway, hoping it would in some way break the ice. As I smoked it down to the butt, still blindfolded, a kidnapper reached down and gently took the smoking cigarette from my fingers before I burnt myself. In a small way it seemed like progress. A man who had been willing to kill me was now stopping me from giving myself a cigarette burn. He was being forced to recognize my humanity.'

Jacky Rowland, a reporter based in Jerusalem, has a simple tip: 'Always carry a photograph of you with your children. Or with someone else's children. When push comes to shove, if you can connect with your captors or kidnappers on a human level (everyone loves their kids), it might just save your life.'

Finally, no matter how isolated you feel, never forget that people in the outside world are working on your behalf. Sue Williams advises: 'Hostages should never underestimate the wealth of activity being undertaken by those on the outside who are trying to ensure a speedy and safe release. It is easy for hostages to believe they have been forgotten and that nobody cares about their plight, but that couldn't be further from the truth.'

/WHAT HOSTAGES SHOULDN'T DO

Everyone I have consulted agrees that there are no absolutes when it comes to kidnapping situations, but many concur with the following:

Don't be a hero. Accept your position as a prisoner and behave like one. Any attempt to show authority or rebel will result in the kidnappers picking you out from the group. If you are alone, 'stroppiness' might distinguish you as annoying, possibly easier to kill than the last person they held captive.

Do not make any threats or promises based on your position in the outside world. You are no longer that person. You are now a hostage with a certain value. You have no authority any more. Claiming that you do will alter the kidnappers' perception of you and might have bad consequences.

Don't escape unless you are certain that you can. Getting caught will simply put you or others in danger. Work out what you are gambling.

Not everyone agrees with that advice. James Brandon told me: 'I decided early on I would rather escape than wait for my kidnappers to decide what they wanted to do with me. I would rather die in an escape attempt than be slaughtered like a sheep with my final moments immortalized forever on YouTube.'

Do not let on that you know your kidnappers. If they are trying to hide their identity but you recognize them anyway, play along with their disguise.

Do not sustain eye contact with your kidnappers. Many people find this threatening.

Don't get too frustrated with deliberate attempts to confuse you. Keep to a routine to orientate yourself in place and time.

Do not behave aggressively. It will make it harder for the kidnappers to empathize with you.

Do not try to form genuine friendships with your captors. It might result in them exploiting you. It is also the road to Stockholm syndrome, where a hostage falls in love with and eventually aids their kidnapper.

/GOVERNMENTS DO NEGOTIATE

The resolution of almost all kidnappings involves an exchange of money. If kidnap negotiation were a science rather than a delicate art, your price or political value would be determined as shown on the following graph:

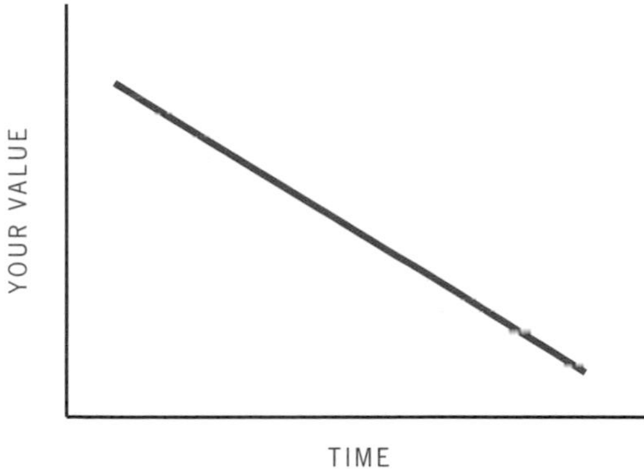

The initial price demanded by a group of kidnappers is likely to be unacceptable to the government, company or family negotiating for the hostage. The negotiators therefore have to weigh the risk of your being killed against the figure they think the kidnappers will accept for a ransom. It is a delicate balance because the price must also be high enough for the kidnappers to take the risk of returning you.

As the period of incarceration increases, so does the danger that the kidnappers will get caught. Likewise, as their fear increases, the price on your head will fall. The same is broadly true if your value is political rather than monetary. Media glare eventually falls away, making it less likely that the kidnappers will get the attention they seek.

But negotiation is rarely as simple as an equation involving value versus time. There are many more factors that come into play.

Imad Shihab advises: 'Be grateful for a negotiation in today's world. So often in Iraq in the past it has been impossible to negotiate. They were simply not interested in money or in the welfare of their victim. If they are willing to negotiate, you need to come to them open-handed.'

After the Iraq war in 2003 kidnapping became the favourite weapon of many small groups of fighters. Money was earned passing a hostage up the chain from criminal gangs to those with a political agenda. It became common to watch the pixillated videos of hostages in distress in the moments leading up to their horrible murders. The media coverage had become an incentive for kidnappers. Since around 2005 there has been an unwritten agreement within the media not to broadcast the manipulation and revolting treatment of hostages. The media decided that broadcasting kidnap videos was increasing the value of the hostages – and audiences were telling them that they did not like seeing the videos.

Since then the kidnapping has not stopped, and the pictures keep coming into newsrooms, but the agreement not to broadcast has removed the glamour. The publicity has gone away and so have the excesses of 2004–5.

/WHAT OTHERS CAN DO

There are very few organizations that offer help for hostages and their families, but www.HostageUK.com can give you support and point you in the right direction. The government or company your relative or friend is working for should also be making efforts to get them out. But at the end of the day it's the families and friends who will be the real drivers of the negotiation. Sue Williams says you should never underestimate the power of their work:

'The families, ordinary people, will become extraordinary, finding an inner strength to keep fighting for freedom. They will be supported by and seek comfort within their social network and local community. Everyone will be watching the media. Friends who have not spoken for years will be in touch. Prayers, vigils, concerts, petitions and many similar activities will be taking place.

'Board members will be chairing crisis meetings and making difficult decisions against the backdrop of "getting it wrong". Co-workers will be circulating updates.

'Governments will be applying diplomatic pressure directly or indirectly and searching for the individual or group that wields influence and will be key to a hostage release.

'Many people who have never met the hostage will be making his or her release a priority and letting the safety of a stranger take over their own lives.'

/WHAT ARE THE KIDNAPPERS THINKING?

If you know how to approach your captors, you can do as much work on getting released from the inside as people can do on your behalf on the outside. Imad Shihab recommends: 'Know who your kidnappers are. The fine details of their politics and their history are vital to any negotiation. Know why they targeted you. Is your value political or financial?'

Qais Azimy is one of the best journalists I have ever met. He works in Kabul for Al Jazeera English, but could put his skills to use anywhere in the world. His ability to negotiate himself into and out of anything has saved his life several times. He recalls: 'I was kidnapped by the Taliban in 2007 and what I learnt is not to give up. At that time, when we were kidnapped for 38 hours, they said every hour that they would kill us in the next hour. But we didn't give up; we tried and tried to win them over. They were open to understanding. We opened their brains to the idea that every foreigner was not a George Bush.

'I was with a British journalist at the time and he put my life at threat because of his race, his non-Muslim status. I was praying all the time. My belief at that time grew. Whatever religion you are, you become more religious because you see all other roads blocked. You are waiting for magic to happen. Then it did – the kidnappers changed their opinion. They released us. When we left we wanted to send off the story, but there was another truck waiting to kidnap us again. I learnt to expect the unexpected, not to let my guard down.'

Sue Williams stresses the need to find common ground with your kidnappers: 'You need to get them to see things from your point of view. They are scared too. They have families too. This can be used to your advantage.

'Attempting to change your status from hostage or commodity to human being is essential. This is achieved by personalization. Talk about your family and home; use your first name and theirs. It is less likely for them to hurt someone who has become a personality.'

Part of that is standing your ground, as Qais Azimy illustrates: 'In 2009 I was arrested by the Afghan Army. It felt like I was kidnapped. I had no contact with the outside world. I was blindfolded and they took me to a ditch, and I could hear gun noises, like they were going to kill me. They were pretending, but I didn't give up. If you give up they will think you are guilty and that they are doing the right thing. Fight for your life.'

In most cases kidnappers will be balancing your value against the danger that they will be caught. When this calculation tips far enough in either direction you are likely to be released. It is worth the wait. You need to sit tight. The advice from everyone I have spoken to in the writing of this chapter is that rushed rescues often lead to disaster.

This softly, softly approach is supported by Qais Azimy, who told me a sad story: 'Sultan Munadi was a close friend of mine. He was kidnapped with *New York Times* reporter Stephen Farrell in 2009. He had such experience in the field and had never been kidnapped, but he died in the rescue by special forces. They killed him even though he shouted "Journalist! Journalist!" They should have fought for his release before the operation was carried out. In my opinion, they wanted to downplay the importance of the hostages to the Taliban.'

Mohammed Hersi has played both sides of the kidnap game – as a pirate, and now as part of the fledgling Somalian anti-piracy force. He advises hostages to stand their ground: 'My advice to anyone passing through the Gulf of Aden is to carry a weapon and defend yourself. Do not make it easy for the pirates. Resist handing over a ransom. It is keeping the pirate business alive.

/HOW TO AVOID BEING KIDNAPPED

There is actually little you can do to prepare, but keeping your wits about you never goes amiss.

Enlist someone local to help you negotiate a safe route to wherever you are going. Someone who can tell you how to dress, how to act and what car to drive. In Iraq at one point there was a single 'ruler' of each area, or each street in some cases. If he wasn't happy for you to pass through, you were in danger of being kidnapped or killed. Sometimes safe passage will take a cup of tea and a handshake; at other times it could involve hundreds of dollars. You might think it unreasonable, but far worse would be for them to think *you* unreasonable.

Avoid making yourself a target. If you are exceptionally rich or working for a rich company, or if you are carrying a lot of cash, never let it be known unless necessary. If you have kidnap and ransom (K & R) insurance, or you have been told that your company has, do not let anyone around you know.

Be aware of new people around you, new cogs in the wheels that keep you safe as you move from A to B. Make sure you have someone you trust in charge of vetting the people close to you.

Try to look and act as if you are not worth much. This is most important when meeting new people so that they do not know you have any kidnap value.

Always let trusted people know your movements: where you are going, when you will be back, or when you are likely to call in to let them know you are safe.
Give your call list (see page 23) to someone you can trust.

If you are lucky and your organization has taken out K & R insurance, a whole team of trained negotiators will kick into action. You might even have Sue Williams looking after you. However, you are unlikely to know if this insurance is in place, and it's better that you don't. If you are kidnapped, you might reveal it to your kidnappers, and suddenly you are more valuable. For the same reason, nobody else should know if you have K & R insurance; they will understand the value it carries in potential ransom payout.

If the insurance is in place, it is the insurance company's job to get you out alive, and that often means throwing money at the problem – money that a family or company might not otherwise have been able to afford.

It is worth pointing out the possibility of K & R insurance to your boss if you think you might be in real danger. It is also possible to take out such insurance yourself.

If you find yourself in the horrible position of being a hostage, James Brandon offers the following advice about how to conduct yourself: 'During my interrogation, every minute or so a man cocked a gun, put it against my head and pulled the trigger. I never knew if there would be a bullet in the next chamber. When my feet started shaking I pushed down hard to hide it from the kidnappers. I knew that if they knew I was afraid it would give them more power – and make them contemptuous of me.'

Sadly, the stress of being kidnapped can have long-lasting traumatic effects even when it's all over. And this can affect not only the hostage, but family and friends too. Everyone will have been through hell. Chapter 15 offers advice on how to handle and treat trauma.

> Be aware of propaganda. Be aware how you might be used to manipulate a story. As an aid worker, I was always aware that I might be killed and used by the other side as propaganda. **Dr Carl Hallam**

14/SURVIVING IN POTENTIAL TROUBLE SPOTS

Approach people with innocence and a confident manner. Never assume a group you are approaching will be against you. If you go in with fear or expecting trouble, you will get into trouble. **Wadah Khanfar**, director-general of Al Jazeera

SO FAR THIS BOOK has focused on places where war is actively being waged. Now it's time to look at some other potential trouble spots.

Among my colleagues it's become a cliché to talk about holidaying in George W. Bush's 'axis of evil'. After all, it's where many of them spend most of their working lives. However, countries such as Iran, Myanmar, North Korea and Yemen are places of mystery and rumour to many people, and what they see of them in the news can make them seem a little scary.

Whenever I'm going somewhere new I always find a little advice from people in the know helps me to dismiss preconceptions and begin to root my understanding in the culture of a place rather than its politics. So let's take a look at some of the less well-known trouble spots and get some insight from people who know them.

/IRAN

Nazanin Sadri was working as a journalist in Tehran during the 2009 post-election riots. They were violent, and dozens of journalists were targeted by the government and thrown into prison during and even after the demonstrations. It took brave protesters and bold journalism to bring the story to the world via the Internet and other means. For Naz it involved an even more careful balancing act. Her family is Iranian and she did not want to put any of them at risk. As a woman too it was far harder for her to go unnoticed.

For men, Iran is a relatively simple place – difficult from a surveillance and legal point of view, but basically a safe place if you stick to the rules, which are mostly to do with paperwork and deference to the right people. One of the rules is to avoid body contact with women. Be aware of this if you have women around you. You will not be allowed to enter some places because there are women present. Make sure you ask before walking around someone's house or office. And be patient: the bureaucracy will lead you somewhere...eventually. Don't expect things to move at a normal pace, or for anything to be open when you expect it to be.

This is Naz's advice for other women planning on travelling to the Islamic Republic of Iran:

'Of course, the most important thing for a woman is to remember her headscarf. This does not have to be anything heavy duty. Nowadays it's easy, given the popularity of pashminas and other scarves. People spend a lot of time worrying that they are showing too much hair, but that's not normally a big problem, unless you are in one of the more religious towns or government buildings. Scarves can be any colour or style, but it's a good idea always to have a conservative black one on hand. And make sure it's cotton, not silk or any other material. You will be running round, stuck in traffic, eating and working in it the whole time, so it's best that it doesn't bother you too much. You just want it to stick on your head and cover your neck. If you want, you could get a bib-type of thing, like nuns wear. Have a look in the local market when you get there.

'As for the rest of the body – cover the arms and bum, and the legs at least down to your knees. In winter, you can wear a normal winter coat (I once saw a woman stitch two airline blankets together to make a poncho for herself before she landed as she had forgotten to bring a coat). In summer pick something loose, cotton and easy to walk around in. For obvious reasons it should not be too tight or skimpy. Some people get away with a long shirt over some baggy trousers, like a *shawa khameez*.

'For attending government events, mosques and funerals and visiting the holy city of Qom you will need a *chador* – a massive piece of black cloth. You can buy or borrow this once you're in the country. They give them out at mosques before you enter. Just drape it over you and keep your normal scarf and coat on underneath. It's uncomfortable and a pain, but you'll get used to it.

'Generally speaking, try not to show your legs or ankles. Even in the summer when it is hot, if I'm wearing flat shoes, I always carry a pair of black socks in case I'm going somewhere that's a bit more conservative. Avoid bare feet.

'Don't shake hands with official figures and government types unless they put their hand out. Don't initiate a handshake yourself. In public don't hold hands, hug or kiss members of the opposite sex on the cheek. You will see Iranian people do this, but if you're just working there, I think it's best to keep safe and generally give an air of modesty.

'In working situations you will be surrounded by men and spending a lot of time drinking small cups of tea as you gather information, permissions and so forth. Stay patient – it's quite bureaucratic. Take tea if it's offered – it breaks the ice.

'Being a woman can actually be an advantage. For example, if I find myself surrounded by a lot of men, as in government departments, I tend to flatter them, ask them about their wives and children. There are few places where you can't go – but make sure you ask before going anywhere, just in case. You don't want to wander into a politically or religiously sensitive place.

'Iranians like foreigners a lot and are very hospitable towards them. Don't take it as a threat if someone chats to you in the street or opens up the subject of politics. They are just interested in what you're doing there.'

/MYANMAR

The country formerly known as Burma is a difficult place to work in or visit. The government is especially hostile towards their old colonizers, the British, but they are equally harsh on their own people if they consider them to have been disloyal to the country. It takes very little for them to leap to judgement. So whether you are travelling as a tourist or otherwise, you need to be extra cautious in your behaviour. If you get caught doing something the authorities don't like, the chances are that you will have tainted everyone you came into contact with along the way.

A former colleague of mine is now an NGO worker in Myanmar. He has been there for years – through the government suppression of the monk-led riots of 2007, and cyclone Nargis a year later, which killed an estimated 134,000 people and devastated the most fertile parts of the country. He has chosen to remain anonymous because he wants to be as honest as possible in explaining why, despite the repressive government, everyone should visit the beautiful country that has become his home and, to him at least, is 'the safest country on Earth'.

'According to George W. Bush's administration, Myanmar is an "outpost of tyranny", not quite an "axis of evil", but a badass place nonetheless. It is indeed true that the country has a less than charming military dictatorship that is hopelessly inadequate at governing, and is sometimes described by expats as a "kleptocracy" or "ineptocracy" whose sole aim is to strip the country of its abundant natural resources, pocketing what they can and putting nothing back into the "Union". These sad old men in green, paranoid to a fault, bicker and quibble amongst themselves in their malarial jungle lair while stuffing their Singapore bank accounts with ill-gotten gains and waxing lyrical about democracy and a "discipline flourishing nation".

'Here are a few pointers to keep you out of the local prisons and on the straight and narrow. First and foremost you have to know who to trust. When you step off the banana boat, all fresh faced and doughy eyed, you cannot help but be charmed and seduced by the long-suffering and repressed locals. Their hospitality is second to none, their charm is engaging, their smiles are enough to melt the polar ice-caps, their devotion to Buddhism undeniable. But be warned, for beneath a veneer of all these qualities lurk some of the most conniving, double-crossing, two-faced backstabbers ever encountered. They would sell their soul and that of their mother for a few thousand kyat. Fortunately, most of the people aren't like that – they are the loveliest you are likely to meet. But when they are bad, they are really bad.

'Corruption is rife. It is impossible to do anything in Myanmar without having to pay "outside money" or "tea money". Accept this and you will not be driven mad at having to pay a bribe so that your telephone line is not routinely cut by the very people who are meant to be maintaining it. Fight against it and you will age at an alarmingly fast rate. In this respect the country is rotten to the core, which to my mind is the single largest obstacle holding the country back, preventing it from joining the rest of Asia in "developing".

'Do not talk politics. Most importantly, do not discuss politics with a local unless they bring it up with you. This is potentially a fast-track way for the local to head straight to jail. It is also the best way for you to get thrown out of the country and never be allowed back.

'Expect numerous power cuts, the local telephones not to work, the Internet connection to be woefully inadequate, and the general infrastructure to be nothing short of hopeless. There was a joke when the capital moved from Yangon to Nay Pyi Taw a few years back that there had been a "shift in power" quite literally, as all the electricity was moved to the new jungle lair of the junta. Take a torch.

'The city abounds with rumours. Did you hear this, did you hear that? When you first arrive you'll be seduced by these rumours. They flesh out the life of a country that few people know little about. However, it will not take long for you to gather that roughly 90 per cent of them are simply hot air.

'I have lived through a civil protest where hundreds of thousands of people took to the streets in a peaceful demonstration and were cruelly beaten down. I endured a cyclone that claimed the lives of many thousands of people and left swathes of the country utterly devastated. Yet for me, Myanmar is still the safest country on Earth. Arriving here feels like stepping back in time. This is obviously a nuisance for the locals, who would like their country to develop a little more to ensure a better life for them and their children, but from a visitor's point of view, it does not get any better than Myanmar.'

/NORTH KOREA

Donald Kirk first visited Seoul, the capital of South Korea, in 1972 for the *Chicago Tribune*, and has been reporting on the region for international media outlets ever since. He has a unique ability to cut through the dense rhetoric and misunderstanding surrounding news from North Korea. At the moment he is the Korea correspondent for the *Christian Science Monitor*. He offers the following insights.

'North Korea is undoubtedly one of the most dangerous countries on Earth, but that's only if you're a citizen of it and living in constant fear of the dictatorship of "Dear Leader" Kim Jong-il. About 200,000 people live in a vast gulag for political prisoners, and thousands more are imprisoned for lesser crimes. Public executions and torture are common, and millions are suffering from hunger and disease. As a visitor, however, you will see none of this while spending a few nights in a luxury hotel and dining out in fine restaurants in the capital city of Pyongyang.

'The real difficulty in writing about North Korea is posed by tour guides, who monitor your every move and will not let you out of their sight. I had my most trying encounter in September 2008, when I taped a brief conversation with a guide in which he insisted that Kim Jong-il was not sick, had not suffered a stroke and that all the reports about his illness were "lies" spread by CNN and the BBC. He knew that I was taping the conversation, but a few hours later asked me to delete the recording or give him the tape as he was not "authorized" to speak for the regime. I refused. That evening, at a meeting of the members of my group, he and his superior again asked for the tape, and again I refused. They reminded me of the severity of the "security agency" and said agents might stop me from leaving when I got to the airport the next morning at the end of my standard four-day visit. I decided to take my chances. When I got to the airport the next morning, no one said anything, and I was able to leave without a problem.

'The threat, however, was a reminder of the difficulties of covering North Korea even when all you have done is to record a conversation with a tour guide who merely repeated the propaganda of the regime. Tour guides also warned us of expulsion from the country if members of the group went on their own in search of interviews.

'On one of my four visits to Pyongyang they had us list our occupations and the names of the companies for which we worked. Since American journalists were banned, I had told the tour organizer in Australia to list me as a teacher, even though he knew I was a correspondent. I said I worked for "The School of Hard Knocks". Nobody questioned that affiliation.

'On my longest trip to Pyongyang, in 1995, I accompanied a group of Korean–Canadians, who were there ostensibly to attend a sports festival. They actually hoped to see long-lost relatives whom they had last seen in 1950, before fleeing from invading North Korean forces with their parents.

'In North Korea all foreign visitors, however they list their professions, are targets for propaganda. Visits get to be repetitious since you're escorted to many of the same sights every time. Day one, your group will have to pay respects before the great bronze statue of Kim Il-sung, Kim Jong-il's father, who died in 1994. You're expected to bow respectfully while a member of your group tosses a bouquet at the base of the statue looming atop Mansudae, the hill that rises in the centre of Pyongyang. You'll then visit the home where the late Great Leader grew up, and probably go to Panmunjom, the "truce village" that straddles the line with South

Korea. From the North Korean side you'll see tour groups on the South Korean side, while a North Korean officer tells you how the South Koreans and the Americans started the Korean War. And you'll learn that North Korea inflicted terrible defeat on the "enemy" before they had to "surrender" in the armistice signed at Panmunjom in July 1953. You'll also hear more about the "crimes" committed by the vanquished Americans during a visit to the war museum in Pyongyang, another standard stop.

'The highway to Panmunjom is an eye-opener. It's four lanes wide, but you'll see hardly any traffic on the four-hour journey – just the occasional oxen pulling ploughs in distant fields. You're likely to notice only one or two tractors, most likely manned by soldiers, as you pass by whitewashed buildings with few visible signs of life and no evidence of manufacturing or commerce. You won't be able to get close to any of these, and you're constantly warned not to take photographs anywhere that might seem to present a negative view of life in the country. Again, that's the type of offence that could bring about expulsion along with confiscation of your film or videotape and possibly your equipment.

'You get your first taste of the hazards of visiting Pyongyang when you're told on arrival to hand over your cell phone. You're sure to get it back before your departure, but until then you can forget about phone calls unless you want to spend inflated fees on a hotel landline, which you can be sure is tapped. After your tour guide meets your group and you're seated in the van at the airport, you're told to be sure not to throw away any newspapers and magazines. That's because they all feature photographs of Kim Jong-il and Kim Il-sung, and it would be an act of extreme disrespect to sully either of their images by crumpling them up and tossing them into a waste-paper basket. Tourists get expelled for just this offence, and ordinary citizens have gone to jail for years for such a heinous crime.

'Before you ever are exposed to these difficulties, however, you will have had to go through the hassle of getting a visa. You must apply through a travel agency in Beijing or possibly Australia, and there's no certainty you will be able to take the trip at a time that's convenient. All four of my visits were for special occasions. In 1992 I accompanied a large group on a tour by train to the special economic zone at Rajin and Songbon in the northeast. The zone has been a failure, but at the time North Korean authorities wanted to publicize the zone's potential. On my three subsequent visits, I attended lavish festivals. The most spectacular is the Arirang festival, a display of 100,000 performers, half of them in the stands forming images with flash cards, the other half on the field going through an amazing series of routines. They perform night and day for weeks.

'At one time tourists were able to go to Kumkang Mountain on regular visits arranged by travel agencies, crossing the border from South Korea by bus and van, after an elaborate customs procedure. However, the tours ended tragically in July 2008 when North Korean guards shot and killed a middle-aged South Korean woman who had wandered outside the tourist area to look at the sunrise. There could have been no better evidence of the horrors of life in North Korea – and the hazards of visiting the country even on a tightly constricted, organized tour.'

/YEMEN

When one of my colleagues at the *Baghdad Bulletin* went to Yemen to brush up her Arabic, I decided to pay her a visit and had my preconceptions about Yemen blown out of the water. Little is widely known or written about this magical country, an ancient world struggling to adapt to modern times. Recently, it has achieved notoriety because most of the Guantanamo detainees were Yemeni, many picked up in Iraq and Afghanistan. Also, the 2009 'Christmas bomber' was trained in Yemen. But the extreme views of those men, born out of uneducated, crippling poverty that is the wider fight in Yemen, hold sway with only a minority of the population.

Mystery and fear mean that the country has few foreign visitors, but my friend was accepted and embraced by the local population, her boyfriend too. I had just a peek, but they really lived in a medieval world. Due to the sensitivity of her current role in the region, she has decided to give her advice anonymously.

'The first thing most visitors to Yemen have to survive is the landing at Sana'a international airport. At an altitude of around 2400 metres and ringed by jagged peaks, it's rumoured to be one of the trickiest landings in the world. For the eager first-timer craning to get a glimpse of Yemen, the rusting Tupolev carcasses beached casually by the side of the runway provide scant reassurance.

'A pin-cushion of minarets, the tiny walled city of Old Sana'a is straight out of *A Thousand and One Nights*: wedding-cake houses, turbaned men dancing with daggers, camels grinding corn, and the deafening call to prayer as each muezzin tries to drown out his neighbour with throat-searing flourishes. And many of the dangers are equally archaic. Acid has been thrown at women wearing the trendy, black, Saudi *burka* because the silhouette of their chest is more visible than under the traditional multi-coloured *chador*. A boy who lived near me was horrifically scarred after his father set fire to him for talking to a girl who wasn't a relative. There are also the never-ending tribal skirmishes, which are often lethal in a country where almost every man and boy has a gun. But these are dangers faced mainly by Yemenis.

'The increasing terrorist threat aside, most visitors encounter few problems. You should take advice from a local tour agent and your embassy before arriving, but generally the north is off limits to foreigners. The situation in the rest of the country is very variable. Yemen still abides by the old codes of honour and hospitality, and discourtesy to a visitor is a shame on the community. Standards of conduct are rigorously imposed on the young, as I learnt from one twinkling old woman on a bus. "Young men are wild beasts these days," she said, lifting her voluminous *chador* to show me a stash of rocks that she would hurl from the mini-bus window at any young man she saw behaving inappropriately. Even modern problems have old-fashioned solutions in Sana'a. With the same logic, while many female visitors don't wear a headscarf, if you do, you'll gain respect and be given greater protection.

'No introduction to Yemen would be complete without a mention of *qat*, the mild amphetamine that many Yemeni men spend their days ruminating. Your cheeks may never be quite the same after a good *qat* hamstering, nor will you probably sleep for a day afterwards, but most casual users experience very little. With *qat* you have to cultivate addiction. And for most, one evening with a mouth rammed full of leafy cud while suffering insatiable thirst is enough.'

Do not ride roller-coasters in Sudan. **Mary O'Shea**

15/ARMING YOURSELF AGAINST TRAUMA

For people who've worked in war zones there will always be a sense that peacetime is life with the volume turned down. More than anything, I miss the sense of camaraderie, of shared purpose, of optimism. I also miss the excitement that comes from living for the moment. Slowly, however, I have realized that it's not the war that I pine for, but rather that youthful sense of being able to go anywhere and do anything.
James Brandon

LEAVING A WAR ZONE ALIVE is one thing. Leaving behind the worst of your experiences is quite another. This chapter offers you ways to prepare and work that will help you to avoid experiencing trauma – basic know-how that I was missing on my first entry into Iraq.

Fresh from my finals at university, I arrived in Jordan on the promise of a job if I could make it to Baghdad. The man who was going to get me there met me at the airport. He was a fellow recent graduate from Oxford, where he had survived three years of alcohol, kebabs, dancing, no sleep, last-minute, bullshit-crammed essays and still walked out with a First. I thought that was more than enough of a qualification to start up a newspaper in post-war Iraq. My new job.

I was taken to meet Mr Feras. He was the owner of the Soraya Hotel – a favourite hang-out at that time for NGO workers, human shields, Peace Corps people and freelance journalists. He poured tea and showed me photos of people, dead and alive, whom he had helped to find a reliable driver for the trip to Baghdad.

He told me that the suitcase at my feet was full of a dead man's clothes. More tea. They belonged to a young photographer who had been shot dead at a protest in Iraq the week before. The suitcase was following his body home to his parents. He had been sitting in my seat looking for a ride into Baghdad only weeks earlier. I was told he had a shaved head and had been wearing combat kit. He had been mistaken for an off-duty soldier. 'That wouldn't happen to me,' I told my mum. Overnight, Western visitors to Baghdad threw away their combat trousers and boots and started to grow their hair because of the tragic murder of Richard Wild.

A car would be available at four in the morning. And would I like another tea? He just needed another $500 and then we would go. I was told to expect a five-hour drive to the border, then another six hours, non-stop, all the way to Baghdad. Four o'clock came and went without a wake-up call. A convoy of Japanese missionaries had been car-jacked along the road. 'It isn't safe for the driver,' I was told. And me, I thought.

Days passed. More tea. More convoys were attacked. Kidnappings and robberies took place in crowded petrol stations. The drivers refused to go without more money and more tea. And all the time Mr Feras was spooning sugar into my cup and telling me stories of the people he had helped in and out of Baghdad.

Every night I would pack my bag and head to his office at midnight. 'Are you prepared?' he would ask.

'As much as I can be.'

Mr Feras would shake his head. 'If you were my daughter...' Then more tea. More advice.

One night I knocked on his door to find him sitting with a grin on his face. Mr Feras was not a smiley man.

'I can help you prepare,' he said. 'Stand up.' He clicked his fingers and a worker came in with a measuring tape.

A bulletproof vest, I thought. Excellent.

'For your coffin,' he said, licking his finger to turn a page and note down my measurements. I was in a car heading to Baghdad four hours later.

At the time my lack of preparation seemed romantic. Exciting. I had done as much as any wannabe war junkie could do to warm up for the journey, I thought. Having survived a major car crash and all the pain that entailed, I was hardened to the possibility of death or injury; afraid of almost nothing. I was dangerous.

I didn't know the risks and neither did my family. Within a month I, like many others around me, began to think my job was worth more than my life. I also thought that fear-clouded, snap decision-making based on instinct alone was the best way to operate.

I was not prepared for entering a war zone. But there are ways to get ready. Tricks to help you keep sane. And if you are sane, you will be able to do your job more effectively. If you understand that your job is just that, a job, it will help you in the early days of your new life. And eventually it will help you return to the life you had before you went to war, without experiencing trauma.

/WHAT IS TRAUMA?

The medical name for the long-term after-effects of trauma is post-traumatic stress disorder (PTSD), but there is nothing 'post' about trauma. It can happen at any time. The dictionary calls it 'emotional shock'. Don't underestimate shock. The physical kind can kill you. The emotional kind can manifest in a thousand different ways.

It didn't hit Samantha Bolton until years after the event that caused it – the Rwandan genocide in 1994, when 800,000 Tutsis and moderate Hutus were slaughtered by extremist Hutu forces. Two million refugees fled over the border into Zaire, now called the Democratic Republic of Congo, and Sam was there to meet them.

'Two years after the Rwandan genocide, and after a trip to Russia for a campaign on Chechnya, I had a severe PTSD attack that lasted a year. I was supposed to have gone into Grozny on a convoy, but a colleague went instead and was kidnapped and gang-raped. I felt guilty and afraid for her, and this triggered the attack. I was living in a fancy apartment in New York. Every time I went home I would get the shakes, convinced a Hutu axe-murderer was behind the door. I would search the whole flat for people – check the windows, check under the bed. It was a paranoid routine.

Sometimes it comes back for a few days when I go back to insecure situations in the field. I can become paranoid about intruders and unable to relax. I just want to lock the door and curl up in as small a space as possible. A safe place.

'You need to recognize the signs and work through it in your own way. I worked through it myself as I was too scared I would go completely insane if I spoke to someone. To each their own.'

James Brandon agrees with Samantha's philosophy of self-help: 'I think the golden rule when recovering from PTSD is to do what feels right and not to let people push you into doing things, such as therapy or counselling, that do not feel right to you. PTSD is your body's defence mechanism: it is warning you against putting yourself in future danger – and telling you to give yourself time and space to recover.'

There is nothing cut and dried about avoiding trauma. But the experts I have spoken to tell me that it's all about retaining normality and routine from your pre-conflict days in your war-zone life. And also, despite what James and Samantha say, being prepared to get proper help if you're not coping on your own. Obviously, everything changes in a war zone, but if, for instance, you like getting a bagel from the corner shop in the morning to have with your coffee, try to find an equivalent to your corner shop in your war zone. If you normally like a bath before bedtime but that's out of the question in your war zone, boil a pan of water and have a thorough head-to-toe wash before carrying on with your evening. Whatever your normal habit at home – reading for a while before going to sleep, listening to the radio while getting dressed – try to replicate it wherever you are. It is all about remembering the life you had outside of the war zone.

For Hoda Abdel-Hamid, who's been in and out of Iraq for around 10 years, normality means indulging in small pleasures, such as smuggled Parma ham and

SYMPTOMS OF TRAUMA

/ Recurrent and intrusive memories, such as flashbacks or nightmares.

/ Emotional numbing and avoidance of people and places that are reminders of the event. And/or sometimes avoidance of anyone who *isn't* a reminder of an event.

/ Persistent physiological arousal, which may include irritability, poor concentration, sleep disturbances, stomach cramps or sweating.

/ An exaggerated startled response to anything unexpected.

Parmesan cheese, and having a pampering session when the gunfire is over: 'I take face-masks, and even boys enjoy having them. We had parties in the war zone where I was doing facial scrubs and facials for big burly cameramen.'

The American Psychiatric Association defines trauma as the impact of 'direct personal experience or the witnessing of an event involving actual or threatened death or serious injury, or other threat to a person's physical integrity; or learning about unexpected or violent death, serious harm, or threat of death or injury experienced by a family member or close associate'.

I arrived back in the UK on Bonfire Night and found the fireworks overwhelming. I sat under my table, telling myself how stupid I was being, but I had to stay there until the bangs stopped.

For years I couldn't smell pork without thinking of the burnt bodies I had been sent to check every day in the morgue.

The week after I left Iraq my housekeeper was kidnapped by armed men who raided the house. It was my fault. I had known it was coming. A week before I left I had hailed a taxi as usual to get home, but before I could begin to pidgin my way through the directions, he said he already knew where I lived. He then told me how much he hated the British and that he supported the attack made on the army earlier that day. He had friends who didn't like me either. Despite this hostility – and despite having a loving family and boyfriend back in England – all I wanted to do was go back to Iraq. I resented people at home for making me feel so guilty. I felt trapped in London.

Mine were pretty everyday experiences. But it took me years to admit them.

Others never really leave the war zone or disaster – it follows them for years, or becomes the only place they feel comfortable.

/COPING STARTS BEFORE YOU GO

Think about what you are about to do and calculate all the risks. Involve your family and friends in those thought processes and decisions. Know why you are going. As Dr Carl Hallam says: 'War zones are terrifying. Bullets flying everywhere. Try to think about that – what it might be like – before you go. It will help you prepare your emotions.'

For those you leave at home it's difficult too. Their imagination is going wild. They aren't sleeping. They need your support as much as you need theirs.

- Make sure your friends and family know what you are doing and what you will be experiencing.
- Make sure you know how to contact them and they know how to contact you.
- Make sure the person who will be looking out for you in the war zone has their details and vice versa.
- Try to give them an end date – something to look forward to. But make sure it is realistic and doesn't keep shifting.

Mothers, fathers, lovers and friends will be torn between wanting to be supportive, understanding why you want to go and feeling hurt and left out.

During my short stint in Iraq my mother, Vicki, was in touch with another Vicki, the mother of one of my friends out there, Sebastian Walker. They struck up a Dear Vicki, Love Vicki e-mail relationship that helped fill in the blanks when Seb and I weren't able or willing to talk about things. I know it helped my family to hear about others in the same confusing place. My mother didn't sleep more than a few hours at a time for all six months that I was away. But she didn't tell me that until about four years later. Talking to friends and family back home, I know that they are often in the more difficult position. It is hard to know how to get it right, how to 'be the mother of a war correspondent'. Seb's mother, Vicki Woods, explains her own struggle:

'My son had been at the *Evening Standard* for a year or so when he rang me from their offices on a May afternoon in 2003. "Turn on BBC2 now. *Now!*" We both watched George W. Bush give his swaggering speech – "Mission accomplished" – on our separate tellies, and when he'd finished I said this thing was not accomplished at all. My son said, "No. It's still the biggest story of my generation and I've got to get out there." I did not demur. Nor did his father. This is a journalists' household; it's how we make our living. If I'd been 25 in May 2003, I'd have wanted to write the biggest story of my generation too. Neither of us ever said, "Don't go, don't go, we love you so."

'When he made contact with a couple of "young British entrepreneurs" who were setting up an English-language newspaper in Baghdad [the *Baghdad Bulletin*], we were very admiring that he quit his job immediately. Girls were going out there to join it, for heaven's sake. The author of this book was one of them, and much younger than Sebastian. When people said, "Iraq? Are you nuts?" we said bracing things like, "Well, at least the shooting war is over," or "Well, that new guy Bremer is making the right noises about the reconstruction." How insane that sounds now. Not only did I not demur, I cheered him on, almost to the extent where his father could have legitimately blamed me for the rest of our lives if he'd been killed. I just didn't think he could be killed. I didn't think he'd be in danger. I just thought he'd be hot, hungry, dusty, uncomfortable, driven mad by electricity shortages, erratic transport and iffy communications, and asking himself whether he should have stayed in the high cappuccino country of Kensington High Street.

'We bought things that would be useful: Tubigrip, rehydration salts, water purification tablets. I kept issuing reminders: "Don't forget paracetamol, toothpaste, batteries." I wondered fleetingly if he should take a couple of pints of his own blood. My daughter grew very sardonic as I rolled socks and packed sunscreen. "Hmm, I wonder if John Simpson's mummy does his packing for him?"

'He flew to Amman, Jordan, in late June 2003 and sent a long, chatty e-mail headed "To Baghdad…!" I looked at a map for the first time and thought, bloody hell! That's a long drive over the desert. I knew there wouldn't be another e-mail for about 36 hours. When it came, it said: "Am in Baghdad. Am fine. Will e-mail later cos this place is v expensive."

'Iraq was the first Internet war. In the Gulf War of 1991 (only 12 years earlier) wives and mothers waited for airmail, not e-mail. Whether that made things harder for them is arguable, I think. The shrunken time-gap between seeing something hideous on the telly news and reading words from one's loved one in real time is disconcerting. My son's e-mails were sent from Baghdad's Internet cafés, which I airily imagined would look a bit like the Greek Internet cafés I'd used on holiday, but fronded by date palms instead of olives. They read exactly like the ones he'd sent from his office: laconic, factual, properly spelt and punctuated, jokey, sometimes sarcastic. "Oops, getting close to curfew, better run," he'd write. I would think, "Oh bugger, I wanted to tell you what your sister's doing in Spain." I didn't think, "Oh Lord, keep him safe as he slips through nervy streets packed with a) gun-toting teenage American troops, b) Ba'athist bitter-enders and c) Shia militiamen."

'Looking back, I don't understand my blithe Pollyanna-ism. I was skimming enough websites, watching enough news, reading enough online reports to understand what a war zone was, surely? Sometimes his e-mails actually beat the news. In late August of 2003 I didn't get to my computer until after lunch, having spent the morning at the dentist. His first e-mail (received at 8 a.m., which was midday in Baghdad) was a brief moan about his broken laptop. The second (received at 2.30 p.m., i.e. 6.30 in Baghdad) said, "Don't worry, I wasn't at the press conference that was taking place just as the car bomb exploded at the UN building this afternoon..." I pinged back, "Bloody hell, was anybody else, d'you know?" – a response so unspeakably mindless that it makes my armpits prickle. Then I saw the horror on the evening news. Even so, I didn't know until a year later that his colleagues had thought he *was* at that press conference. He'd set off in the office car, but was held up. They'd thought he was blown to pieces. That was his point; I might have too. That's why he e-mailed.

'When the *Baghdad Bulletin* folded, he stayed on in Iraq and became a stringer for Reuters, who sent him to Mosul in the hope that he might find Saddam Hussein. Agence France-Presse and AP both had stringers there, but they were both native Arabic speakers from the Middle East. He was the only Western journalist for miles, living in a rented room on his own. He e-mailed that Mosul was "very quiet" and he wouldn't have much to report, but Black Hawks started falling out of the sky almost immediately, and it became more and more dangerous. A man I knew who worked for a security company started sending me alerts about the "Ramadan offensive", which I passed on. Ansar al Islam began targeting Westerners (oilmen, contractors, Red Cross workers, as well as the military), and also the Iraqis who worked with them – drivers, translators. I began to be really, really scared when I didn't get e-mails every day.

'I would send jokey e-mails, links to stuff I'd seen on the Net, political news. I didn't send anything that I thought would make him miserable. In January I got a terse message saying, "Am on a fleeting visit to Internet café" and a link to a really chilling piece he'd done about targeted assassinations all over Mosul, of academics, newspaper editors, broadcasters, prominent businessmen. Then nothing for 48 hours, after which he was back in Baghdad.

'He came home in February 2004 for a couple of weeks. We hadn't seen him for months and months. He woke up all through the night every time the beams creaked. I was quite surprised he didn't pile furniture against the door.

'Few people in the UK have ever seen a dead body, even the tidily dressed body of a family member, let alone witnessed violent, multiple deaths. I was in Auberon Waugh's Soho club once, when he was talking to a 20-something war correspondent just back from his first war zone. Waugh (who'd covered the 1960s' Biafran war) said: "It is extraordinary, the smell of death. Rank, sweetish. You'll never forget it." What's extraordinary to me is that my son, half my age, knows the smell of death – lived with it daily, like the hundreds and thousands of Iraqis living under the occupation. He told me, "The threat in Iraq is not being ignorant of what to do if a firefight kicks off around you. That threat exists, but it's dwarfed by the threat of being targeted, for which neither experience nor training is a great deal of help. Hardened war hacks who have survived the Balkans, Chechnya, Afghanistan, etc. have been killed here." Yes – I know.

'A hardened war hack greeted me with, "How's it going? He still over there?" When I said yes, he laughed. "My mother has only just told me that she didn't sleep for 20 years."'

/HOW TO REMAIN SANE

Jonny Harris, a captain in the Light Dragoon regiment of the British Army, works closely alongside the Afghan Army. In fact, he wrote his advice for this book from an Afghan Army compound somewhere near Lashkar Gah. After some sad and bad times, he has found various ways to put his mind at peace in the midst of chaos.

'On my first tour in Afghanistan I witnessed at first hand the effect of the stress of combat on people: one of my soldiers suffered a breakdown, was returned home from theatre, and was eventually, sadly, invalided out of the army. While I wouldn't claim that my advice could, or would, have prevented such a mental collapse, I have developed some personal tactics that have kept me going through some fairly dark times.

'**Escapism.** Each day, take some time that is exclusively yours, be it five minutes or 30. Do something that takes your mind completely away from what you are doing. Small luxuries from home can provide great comfort – fresh coffee, a cup of decent tea, a cigar, a dram of whisky, olives, favourite sweets – and the associations of taste and smell can offer a mental sanctuary in the most inhospitable places.

'**Understanding**. Make an effort to understand the context of the situation you are in – historical, social, cultural – and interact with the local population wherever possible. It can be easy to lose perspective when there are elements of that population trying to kill you, but it is important to realize that there are a great number of people in the local area who are just trying to get on with life.

'**Discussion.** The sensations experienced in dangerous situations, especially in combat, combine to create a heady cocktail of emotions that, if left unexamined, can cause great confusion. You can be certain, however, that someone else has experienced thoughts and emotions not dissimilar to your own. Talk.

'**Exertion.** Exercise is a great reliever of tension. Even in a confined space and with minimal equipment, you're limited only by your own imagination. The simplest exercises are those that use your own body weight, such as press-ups, sit-ups and chin-ups.

'**Anticipation.** If you find yourself in a war zone, you will almost certainly find yourself in some rather unpleasant situations. It is important to remember that the unpleasantness will cease eventually, and that the state of affairs will most likely improve. You must maintain the ability to look beyond the immediate circumstances to a more pleasant time.'

/HEALTHY BODY, HEALTHY MIND

This is the advice your mother would give you. But that doesn't mean it should be ignored. If you eat well and sleep well, you are more likely to be able to deal with your extraordinary everyday experiences in an ordinary way. So I'll say it again – eat well, sleep well. And in order to do that, it's a good idea to stay as active as you can, especially if you are stuck indoors all day (see page 205).

Stick to a routine

The routine you follow in a war zone might not be the same as the one you follow at home, but it is yours and you have chosen it. The important thing is to find one and stick to it. Ring a friend at the same time every day. Take a break – chocolate or cigarette or water – after every dangerous drive across town. Have a sleep after eating. Watch the terrible local music channel while you drink your coffee in the morning. Pray, smoke, walk, arrange flowers, do your neighbour's laundry, build paper planes – everything and anything in moderation.

Regular visitors to war zones each seem to find their own poison. The key is to choose a healthy one.

Leith Mushtaq told me: 'I was born in a war in Iraq. This is my natural background. I saw people killed when I was a schoolboy, and only 12 of us out of 2400 people who went to fight the resistance returned. I write about my experience. That helps me a lot. My writing is my doctor. Damage happens inside. It is difficult for me to be happy now. I have travelled the world for work and holidays. Seen everything...but nothing compares to that experience.'

Know when you need to say no

How much sleep do you need to function on a regular basis? How long can you go without food and still be able to do your job? What situations can you cope with and which ones are a step too far? Which rules don't you want to break? Where do you draw the line when it comes to people? What lies won't you tell? Which people don't you trust? How much alcohol is too much?

These are decisions we make every day in the normal world, but when it's falling apart we sometimes forget our limits – push ourselves beyond what we are prepared for.

Talk

According to Dr Carl Hallam, talking is vital: 'Conversation, conversation, conversation…even if you all end up speaking at once. It is when people stop talking about what awful things happened to them that day that you have to worry.'

Develop friendships within work and outside. Find people you can talk to. Before an event talk about what you are expecting to see and feel. You can learn from others' experience or teach people who don't have any. After an event tell people if there were any surprises. How did everyone cope? If something went wrong, why did it go wrong? There is a reason the military put such an emphasis on preparation and debriefing. Dealing with events in the present is a lot more effective than when clarity has faded a little. Learning how to talk and make decisions under stress is vital to being able to do your job in a disaster area or war zone.

Hoda Abdel-Hamid says: 'When I know it's going to be a bad day in the news I call my family early and tell them I am fine. Then I call immediately after the bad news and I tell my mum and husband I am OK. It's very difficult talking to your loved ones because you are in such different realities. You have to play the game, put on an act.'

There is one exception to this, pointed out by Laura Tyson, who has spent most of the last 10 years working with children recovering from one disaster or another: 'Children who have been through extreme situations just want to get back to being children again. Take some pencils and small notebooks, yoyos or bouncy balls to give out. If you're a journalist, don't push them to describe their experiences, even through play. You could have a negative impact on their recovery.'

Know when you are stressed and find a way to deal with it

This is about awareness. How do you respond to stress? Do you go quiet or become manic? Look at your sleep pattern – it's usually a good indicator. Getting less sleep than you need means you are less able to cope with stress. It's a vicious cycle.

Learn what triggers your stress and what you need to change in your life to cope with it. Maybe it means giving up that quick glass of wine before bedtime rather than taking it up with you. Maybe it means putting on the radio so you can hear a calm voice above the rest of the noise outside. Maybe it means keeping some music with you that you know will calm you down if you have a long time to wait.

Listen to your body when it says slow down

Journalist Giles Trendle says it took him a long time to recognize when he was under stress and to admit what was behind it. Now, more than 20 years after he first went to a war zone, his advice is to pick your battles, really understand that you are not invincible and know what that means.

'After two years on the front line as a journalist in the Lebanon war, I went home to London, going via Cyprus to visit a friend. There I sat on my first safe beach in two years and realized that the whole left side of my body was paralysed. It felt tight, like it might be a heart attack, but I sort of knew it was driven by my recent experience.

'I stayed in bed for a week in Cyprus and went straight to a doctor when I got to the UK. All my physical tests were clear. The doctor said it was post-traumatic stress disorder. It took me another three years and another huge emotional breakdown to really understand what that meant and how to deal with it.

'The reverse culture shock of moving back home to London was what did it. I spent the first eight months huddled in a corner of my room. Sometimes crying and sometimes in a foetal position, I felt like a waste of space. I felt that no one else understood what was really happening in the world. And if they did understand, they didn't care. People around me were angry about the new government budget adding another penny on the price of a pint. Where I had just come from people were worried about bombs and dying.

'Then, on a weekend away in Dublin, it all stopped. I realized that everything was going to be OK. I accepted my mortality. I understood that the risks I had been taking were putting me in unnecessary danger for no reward. When shells started dropping on Beirut most people would seek shelter, but I would go out looking for a story – or something. I would come back with nothing but adrenalin. Somehow fate kept me alive when I should have been dead. But to anyone thinking of doing something similar, as some test of their manhood, I would say don't – it's not worth it. Whatever you are chasing is not worth it.'

Breathe

Breathing properly is good for your heart and good for your head. By 'properly' I mean taking long, deep breaths from your belly, not your chest. This technique is described more fully in Chapter 10, but you can also read about yoga and Pilates breathing online. Pick the one that works for you.

Imagination

There's no doubt that imagination can play tricks on you when you're under pressure, especially at night when fear has no distraction. But imagination can also be a powerful tool in helping to relieve stress. Imagine a 'safe place' – a room filled with your closest family, a bed somewhere else, a favourite garden or beach, a boat, a cloud – and go there in your mind when you are stressed or unable to sleep.

Your mind computes its experiences via dreams when you are in your deepest slumber. So nightmares can be expected and are a healthy way of filing away experiences. But entering sleep through the window of your safe place could help to ward off those bad dreams *and* help you get to sleep.

Hoda Abdel-Hamid makes a good point that the less you see, the less nastiness your mind has to deal with:

'In Sarajevo in 1993 I had been seeing constant misery. I had to travel down the famous "sniper avenue" to work. It was well named – a road where you took your chances against gunmen who did not hesitate to target the press or civilians. It created a feeling of excitement. Then, when the excitement was over, I was immediately bored. I didn't feel very good. I found everyone around me boring and trivial. I looked around for a solution that didn't involve talking to anyone. I stayed in bed for a month, staring at the ceiling. I cut off all contact. In those days there were no mobiles, so it was easy.

'Over time I have learnt to protect myself. There is no need for you to see everything first hand. There is only so much your head can take.'

Your imagination can work against you as well as for you when under stress. I know mine can. I am the queen of sleep-talking and sleep-walking when the pressure is on.

One cold November in southern England I was the officer in command during an exercise at Sandhurst army training college. We were all prepared for an attack by the Gurkhas, who were pretending to be the enemy. The troop had been on the go for three days in the field, so I made sure that 'stag' (the watch) was strictly assigned so that everyone could get a few hours' sleep. But at four in the morning there was panic. I shouted for everyone to 'Wake up' and 'Stand by for enemy fire'. Everyone rushed out of their sleeping bags, tied their boots and prepared for a blank-fire battle. Then a friend tapped me on the shoulder – I was in my sleeping bag, eyes firmly closed, crawling around in the mud like a soggy slug, holding my rifle and barking instructions into the dark. My team was not happy the next morning.

I have never understood why the army teaches you to sleep with your rifle in your sleeping bag. Surely there are better bedfellows.

Alcohol and drugs

How much is too much for you normally? Have you upped your intake? It is very easy to turn to alcohol, nicotine or drugs as an apparent solution to stress or to help you 'wind down' before you go to sleep. But be aware what you are doing to your body. You are actually making it more difficult for your mind and your system to deal with stress. Feeling numb is not good when you need your wits about you. The hallucinogenic properties of marijuana and other drugs mean that your brain is not able to deal with its experiences. It needs rest – clear-minded rest – to file those experiences away. So know your limits.

Documentary-maker Leigh Page says: 'There is great value in knowing how many bloody Marys it takes to appease a stonking hangover. The Afrikaans have a saying, *N klam lap word gou nat*, which means, "A damp cloth gets wet quickly".'

There is a vast difference between an alcohol abuser and an alcoholic. Alcoholism is an illness, while abuse can be controlled with help.

Alcoholism is a physical dependence with real physical withdrawal symptoms. Abuse is when you roll your Saturday night into a four- or five-day stretch, but then it comes to an end.

Alcohol abusers drink for all sorts of reasons: they like the taste, they see it as a way to release stress, they want to sign off from life. Alcoholics drink because they have to.

SIGNS OF ALCOHOLISM

/ Alcoholics will be able to drink you and all your friends under the table and still seem sober, or at least functioning.

/ That high tolerance of alcohol will increase with time as they need more and more to feel the effect of the booze.

/ One drink will always lead to another until oblivion. There is no such thing as 'a quick one'.

/ Alcoholics *need* a drink first thing in the morning 'to wake up'.

/ Alcoholics drink in secret and go to great lengths to hide it.

Look out for warning signs of trauma

Delayed reactions, unexpected feelings, small events that overwhelm all of a sudden – don't dismiss those fears or feelings just because they are the product of relatively minor events compared to other things you have seen or coped with. Passing a traffic accident back home when you have been dealing for months with untangling people from molten tank shells; a conker falling onto your head after living through repeated earthquake aftershocks in Pakistan; the smell of a butcher's shop after experiencing the aftermath of a tsunami...all these incidents have been enough to tip my colleagues and friends into reliving a trauma.

SIGNS OF TRAUMA-RELATED DISTRESS

According to the British Royal Marine stress test, the following signs are those to look out for:

/ You experience upsetting thoughts or memories about a traumatic event, which come into your mind against your will.

/ You are having upsetting dreams about what happened.

/ You sometimes act or feel as if bad things are happening again.

/ You feel upset by reminders of past events.

/ You are having physical reactions, e.g. rapid heartbeat, nausea, upset stomach, sweatiness, dizziness, when you are reminded about an event.

/ You are finding it difficult to fall asleep or stay asleep.

/ You are uncharacteristically irritable or angry.

/ You find it difficult to concentrate.

/ You are overly aware of potential dangers to yourself and others.

/ You are jumpy or easily startled by something unexpected.

If you are still experiencing any or many of these symptoms months after an event, you need to seek professional help. And don't be frightened of the therapist. Chances are, they've been around the block themselves, maybe even in war zones. However, if you just don't click, find someone else. It's your money, and your time, so you have every right to be choosy.

Remember why you're in a war zone in the first place

BBC correspondent John Simpson is clear-eyed in his sense of purpose: 'I don't feel you can stand by when people are being killed and say, "I'm just an observer, I can't get involved." So there have been a couple of times, once at Tiananmen Square and once in the Romanian revolution, when I waded in.'

Why are *you* in a war zone? This is, arguably, the most important thing you must know and remember. It is easy to get attached to people and places and unfamiliar but now urgent driving feelings in times of stress. It would be unnatural if you didn't feel a particular bond with others who are going through the same experience as you. But never forget the reason you came in the first place. Write it at the front of your notebook, on your rear-view mirror, on your medical kit, your toothbrush – wherever you might look during the day. It's your *raison d'être*. It might develop over time, but be aware if it slips far away from your original intentions. Assess if that is what you want, or if you are being propelled in that direction by other forces. If so, bring it back under control.

Caroline Hawley observes: 'Foreigners who have gone to a war zone have usually chosen to be there and can get out. We're lucky. We have another home to go to. But working under pressure in dangerous circumstances can take a toll that you're not aware of until it's too late. After nearly three years living in post-war Baghdad, I was physically and mentally exhausted. Bombs, kidnap threats and the daily adrenalin rushes caused by tight deadlines and reporting live on television had left me feeling what I can only describe as complete adrenal fatigue.

'It was when I moved to Jerusalem in the spring of 2006 that the emotional fall-out caught up with me. I realized I had put up mental defences in response to what we were witnessing – the lives lost and torn apart day after day after day. When I left Iraq and brought those barriers down, feelings of sadness flooded in, coupled with an anxiety I had never felt in Jerusalem before, even back in 2001 and 2002 when the city was the target of regular suicide bombings. It wasn't long before a diagnosis and treatment for post-traumatic stress followed. Sadly, there's no magic bullet to sort you out, but I found EMDR [eye movement desensitization and reprocessing therapy] helpful, as well as the opinion that I – and several others I knew in Baghdad – didn't have a disorder, but a "very normal reaction to very abnormal circumstances".

'Don't underestimate the silent toll that living in a war zone is putting on you.'

Know how and when to leave

Making sure you know how you are going to get out before you go in should be a condition of your making the journey.

Similarly, making sure your family and friends have all the information they will need in the event that you are injured, kidnapped or killed will also give you peace of mind. (For more detail about this see page 21.)

As part of your exit plan, it's a good idea to have something to look forward to. It might help push you to leave at the right time. Monique Nagelkerke has some interesting ideas about this: 'Take long breaks in between contracts. I honestly believe that back-to-back missions are killing. I have taken regular breaks of six months and more. Try to work somewhere completely different – with orang-utans

IF YOU DIE ABROAD...

/ The company you were working for is under a legal, if not moral, obligation to sort things out on your behalf. They should kick into action. Check your contract for details on this before you go anywhere.

/ Your tour company (if you were using one) will also be responsible for looking after the arrangements. They should work with your employers if you have one.

/ If you travelled independently or as a freelancer, your next of kin or whoever has taken charge of the process locally (e.g. the owner of the place where you died, or just a friend who met you the day before) needs to take the following steps:

- Get in touch with your embassy in said country to help register the death locally. They will need your date of birth, passport number, where it was registered and your full name. Some nationalities will be able to register directly with the embassy for the death certificate.
- The body will need to be embalmed and placed in a zinc-lined coffin before it can go anywhere.
- To bring the body back home you will need the locally issued death certificate (officially translated into the language of the country where your body is going), a certificate of embalming and authorization to remove the body from the country where you died.

in Borneo, as a Jilla-roo [cowgirl] on a farm in Australia. There are plenty of options. Just get away from the war zones, and avoid turning into a war-zone junkie.'

/COMING BACK HOME

You've been living a high-octane life in a dangerous environment, so peace can be difficult to handle.

You'll be yearning for that buzz, that sense of the unexpected that your war-zone life used to offer.

Conversations will seem trivial. You will smile when you want to shout, 'I'm bored! Who cares which dress you wear tonight; whether we eat steak or fish for dinner; which flowers should go where in the garden…'

You are likely to question why you ever fitted in back home. Or what you have in common with your friends and family.

You are likely to find it harder and harder to come home each time you go away. You might want to return to the field immediately.

Your new job and surroundings are likely to disappoint. The lights will seem too bright. The food too rich. The smiles too broad. The parties, bland. The shops too trivial. The world, apathetic. But it is the same place you left – no different.

It's tough, but there are things you can do to get over these difficulties. Just don't expect instant results.

- Talk, even though it is often the last thing you feel like doing.
- Connect with colleagues or friends who have had similar experiences. Try to involve your family in those conversations where possible.
- Ask your family and friends how they feel. What their worst moments were when you were away.
- Take on a new project, something challenging but different and involving, not isolating. Build a tree-house. Take up a language. Plan a holiday. Redecorate a room.

Note: If your feelings of alienation don't go away over a period of 6–8 weeks, you need to seek professional help.

Marc DuBois, executive director of MSF, recommends: 'If you are travelling as an employee of a company, you should insist they put a support network in place. At MSF we have in-house counsellors and it's obligatory to see them when you get back. Then, once you are settled, there's a team of people dedicated to calling you up and checking you're OK. It's vital to have people you can talk to back home who have gone through the same things. It is important that organizations don't make you believe that's what sissies do. My induction to MSF was carried out by a really tough guy who admitted up front that he'd been reduced to tears by the work and that he sought counselling to help him out. Once you know that, it creates a culture where seeking help is normal.

'It's important to understand that trauma is normal and positive behaviour. In Angola in 2002 I was going into these areas where the level of starvation, malnutrition and death was horrid. I went through a few nights of being unable to sleep, having bad dreams, intrusive images, panic attacks. What the counsellor said afterwards was, "Thank God you went through that. You are a human being. It is a positive reaction to a situation – a human reaction based on human compassion. It's natural to be affected by these people. It's like experiencing a fever: it doesn't feel good at the time, but in reality it's burning up bad germs inside your body. It is a positive thing. Imagine seeing that sort of suffering and degradation and not having it affect you deeply. That's the thing to worry about."

'It's also not unusual to have an overwhelming feeling of pointlessness. Looking at the big picture can be depressing. Humanitarian aid doesn't fix a political crisis. But it can fix lives. So remember the individual instances where you helped people or affected their lives for the better. Forget the overall picture if it isn't a positive one. Try to remember what would happen if you weren't there.'

/ANETA'S CHOICE

Alina Gracheva is a stellar human being and camerawoman. She has many impressive achievements to her name, but it is her report 'Aneta's Choice', about a Beslan mother, that stands out. It is a story that has affected her deeply ever since:

'By September 2004 I thought I'd seen it all and could give advice to a rookie like Rosie any day.

'But then came the Beslan school siege.

'It was getting dark outside when Aneta Godjieva made tea for us and finally agreed to record an interview. It was hard to believe that this prematurely aged woman was in her thirties – about my age.

'The day before she had been a hostage stuck inside School Number 1 with her daughters – two-year-old Milena and nine-year-old Alana. And now we wanted her to tell us what had happened. She spoke enough English to tell it in her own words:

"Chechen gunmen had seized the school on the first day of classes. Hundreds of children and parents had been trapped inside for days in stifling heat with no food, water or clothes. Russian forces outside had the building under siege. The children were terrified and exhausted."

'Aneta continued in a simple, dispassionate tone that betrayed no emotion. "The terrorists said all the women with all the infants can go. I asked if my older daughter could take my younger daughter out, and I would stay behind instead. They said no. Either I had to stay and risk all of our lives, or leave Alana behind and save two lives. The terrorists were yelling and rushing us."

'Aneta had a few minutes to make her choice. Save herself and one child, leaving the other alone and scared, or stay behind and risk the lives of all three of them. She left the school carrying the infant Milena, and told her older daughter Alana to keep close to her friends.

"What would you do in my situation?" Aneta asked me, breaking the unwritten rule that the person with the camera is not supposed to be a person at all.

'Alana was killed by a bullet in her neck, one of 186 schoolchildren who died during an armed battle that ended the siege.

"Every day I go to my dead daughter's grave to ask her for forgiveness," Aneta said.

'Tears were welling up in my own eyes, but I had to keep the camera focused on Aneta. It was good material.

'We drove back through the hot, empty streets of Beslan. They were full of the sound of human wailing; it came from behind every fence in town. What would I do if I had to make this choice? I have only one son.

'In situations like this my brain and body go onto autopilot. I still have to finish the job – get back to the hotel, tape-edit the report and send it via satellite to CNN studios in the States in time for a prime-time show.

'The report played out that night, and we moved on to our next story – about survivors from the siege being sent by train to a sea resort far away from the grief-stricken town to recover. But somehow the further I was getting away from Beslan, the more I felt Aneta's pain. By the time I got to London I was a wreck. Aneta's words kept sounding in my head. London didn't feel like the fun party town I left just a few weeks ago.

'It was not for the first time I'd reacted like this. I was familiar with stress and had had similar reactions to events I'd covered in the past. Most vividly I remember a scene we had filmed in the middle of the jungle near Kisangani in Congo, then still called Zaire, during the uprising that led to the fall of the dictator Mobutu Sese Seko. Rebels had blocked the approach to a refugee camp. There were reports of killings. Two weeks later the journalists and UN were allowed to drive on the narrow jungle road into the camps. The site looked like a horror movie: there were wounded and dead bodies on both sides of the road. A woman lying on a rug was trying to tell us something. It was not clear what she was saying, but she was pointing at the top of her head. When the camera zoomed in, instead of hair there was a round gash. It was crawling with maggots. In my mind, and in my banter with colleagues, she became 'Mrs Maggots'. For months afterwards her image would come to me at night and keep me awake.

'Another ghost who had haunted me was a Chechen mother, begging to borrow my driver to take her son to a hospital. A cluster bomb had blown up next to her house in a rebel-held town called Shali that was coming under regular attack from advancing Russian troops. On this sunny winter afternoon a spray of shrapnel had pierced a thousand holes in her fence, hitting her 15-year-old son. His body, still warm but clearly dead, was lying in the middle of the yard and there was no point in taking him anywhere.

"Please take him to the hospital, he is wounded," she was insisting. Her husband shook his head and told us to leave.

"Stop it, Fatima. We don't need a car. He is dead."

'Back in the 1990s I lived in or near the war zones I would cover. My husband and virtually all my friends were war reporters. It seemed the most normal sort of life. We would respond to the traumatic things we saw by drinking harder, popping Valium, making wild jokes and driving too fast. Mostly, we would respond to the pressure of work with more work – the relentless logistical task of creating television in the most remote and dangerous parts of the world. We became hyper-competitive, almost manic. And if we couldn't stop the war or protect its vulnerable victims, we could still achieve victories by getting video images to air faster than the competition, track down a guerrilla commander for an exclusive interview, take an extra risk, go someplace the other guys wouldn't go. Some of my friends got killed doing the job, some of them cracked up and quit. Some of them are still out there, living life in just the same way.

'By the time I met Aneta, I was older and perhaps wiser, now living in London with a child of my own. I'd still go out into the field on assignment, but I'd struggle to summon the same mad passion to get the story at all costs. In between missions I'd be back at home with a mortgage to pay, schoolteachers to meet, rose bushes to prune and a leaking roof to fix. There isn't much point in talking about Aneta's choice at parties I go to. It would ruin the atmosphere. But Aneta's story is still present in my life of buying groceries and walking the dog.

'I kept recalling many other terrible events as a tool to get Aneta's words and pain out of my head. It was not working. I must have gone soft with age. Or possibly since I had become a mother I appreciated more the value of human life: now I knew what it takes to make and raise a person. I also projected what would it be like to lose my own child. How helpless, stupid and humiliating it would feel not being able to protect your kid from the dangers of the world. The unforgettable look of a parent who lost their kids and basically their future would stay with me forever.

'I analysed my reaction over and over again. The fact was, I had trouble handling Aneta's pain. It had now become mine. So I contacted CNN's psychiatrist on call, who told me that it was a normal reaction to a traumatic event. And if the symptoms continued after three weeks, I should call him back.

'Aneta's story was nominated for prizes, including an Emmy. It felt nothing like the victories we achieved in the old days in the field, standing out in the cold rejoicing after transmitting exclusive pictures of a gun battle that our competitors couldn't match. The Emmy awards ceremony, attended by rich executives and TV personalities in Manhattan, left me dazed and feeling guilty. Aneta had been forced to abandon her child to die, and here I was being fêted at one of the TV world's most prestigious parties. Producers from New York studios were credited in our nomination, as if it was some kind of outstanding accomplishment to include in their nightly news broadcast the report we sent them about Aneta's grief.

'In New York I recounted Aneta's story to an old friend. Her six-year-old son overheard us and asked his mother whether she would save him or his sister if it happened to them. The question, asked in a quiet Brooklyn townhouse, seemed meaningless and bizarre.

'Some months after the siege, I went back to Beslan to do a follow-up report. Watching the town come to grips with its enormous grief helped me to heal my own wound. But it took a few more years for me to stop crying every time I told the story. I still have Aneta Godjieva's mobile number in my phone and we talk occasionally, about once a year.

'Although her hair is now completely grey, she looks good. And little Milena, the infant she saved that day she made her choice, has grown a lot.'

> When the trauma experienced after leaving a war zone or disaster doesn't resolve, it can become what doctors like to call a mental disorder. But thinking in advance about what might happen can make it worse. It's a bit like taking magic mushrooms: if you worry about having a bad trip, this will increase the odds of that bad trip becoming a reality. **James Brandon**

/POSTSCRIPT BY JON SWAIN

IT WAS JON SWAIN'S stark account of his time covering the wars in Vietnam and Cambodia from 1970 to 1975 that sent me catapulting into journalism. I wanted to see the world through his eyes, as depicted in his book *River of Time*. Within a month of my moving to Basra, he turned up and I was assigned by the *Sunday Times* to be his local fixer. I would have fixed anything for this man, but he knew when a story was a story, and he knew when to say no. He told me to trust my instincts and if I was going to be brave, to write brave journalism – don't be stupid. His early support and advice have stayed with me ever since. He offers the following insights:

'It was my godfather, who had won a Military Cross with the Eighth Army in North Africa, who warned me that the most dangerous time in war was nearly always the first few weeks. The newcomer was prone to inordinate risk-taking, convinced he was invincible and that the bullets splitting the air were always intended for someone else.

'I have never forgotten his advice and even now, decades and many wars later, I try to apply it every time I go into a new combat zone. Each conflict is different and has its own lethal idiosyncrasies. Because you have become a veteran of one battle zone does not equip you to be competent in handling the risks of another.

'The best example of this was the war in Cambodia between 1970 and 1975, when the press corps, of which I was a part, lost a higher percentage of its own than in any other conflict, and that includes Iraq and Afghanistan. In 1970, 26 foreign reporters and photographers were killed out of a tiny press corps of about 60. Between 1971 and the war's end (with the Khmer Rouge capture of Phnom Penh) a further 12 foreign and local Cambodian journalists were killed, and a further 32 were killed or disappeared under the Khmer Rouge.

'Quite a number of the 26 foreign reporters and photographers who were killed in the first months of 1970 were seasoned in conflict, having come from covering the war in Vietnam. But although Cambodia was just next door, the war was very different. In Vietnam we usually attached ourselves to an American or South Vietnamese military unit and travelled to military operations by helicopter. The helicopter was the taxi to the war, and the conflict was less fluid than in Cambodia, where there were no front lines.

'In Cambodia the usual way to see the war was to go by car down roads that could change almost at any time from government to Khmer Rouge control. So timing and being aware of danger signs were critical to survival.

'Of course, one was careful not to drive through pot-holes, which might conceal landmines. But sometimes that was unavoidable. It was important not to be the first vehicle down the road in the morning, when you were more likely to hit a mine or be ambushed. It was important to talk to local people and get a feel for what lay ahead.

'And the golden rule was not to push it too hard, particularly if the peasants working in the fields on either side of the road were no longer there. This was a sure sign of a danger.

'In addition, one learnt never to be on the road too late in the day. As the afternoons wore on, government troops would melt away, back to their outposts, and the insurgent Khmer Rouge and Vietnamese communists would move in.

'In 1970, fresh from the big war in Vietnam, some reporters and photographers were perhaps ill equipped to judge these risks and were killed. On one black day – 31 May 1970 – television crews for CBS and NBC, with eight foreigners and one Cambodian, were killed on Route Three, 34 miles from Phnom Penh. The first CBS vehicle was hit by a rocket-propelled grenade, and one of the journalists was shot trying to get out of the burning car. The occupants in the second CBS car and the entire NBC crew were taken prisoner and later beaten and shot to death

'And so it went on.

'For me, one of the lessons of these tragedies was that none of us is safe. In recent wars, like those in Iraq and Afghanistan, Western journalists have decided that they are being targeted in a way that never happened before, and that somehow the notion that their job as non-combatant observers should protect them has been violated. My experience in Cambodia meant I have never held to this view. I have always assumed that we could be targets for a whole variety of reasons, and have been prepared to act accordingly. You have to be prepared to accept that there is someone out there who wants to kill you.

'I don't think that having a white skin or being a journalist accords one any special protection or privileges in a war zone. But I have found that being a white man has on occasions saved my skin. In East Timor, renegade militia hesitated to shoot me and a colleague because they realized it was a big thing to kill a white man rather than one of their own. It gave us enough time to make a bolt for it and survive. Obviously, in Cambodia that did not apply. Indeed, on the day that Phnom Penh fell I and two other Western journalists were on the point of being executed by the Khmer Rouge, who had captured us for the very reason that we were Westerners. Our lives were saved by a Cambodian interpreter, Dith Pran – the story told in the movie *The Killing Fields*.

In Ethiopia, where I was kidnapped for three months, it also helped that I was a Westerner, I think. And there was a horrible occasion once in the Congo, when an angry Angolan major pushed an AK-47 rifle hard into my neck but hesitated to squeeze the trigger long enough for others to calm him down and allow me to get away.

'So you have to follow your instincts. Be prepared for each situation to be different.

'If you are in a soft-skin car that is under sustained fire, like in an ambush, get out of it quickly, as I did in East Timor. It is difficult, but staying inside will certainly get you killed.

'Listen to those more experienced than you. I was fortunate in Cambodia and Vietnam to have around me very experienced journalists, some of whom had fought as soldiers in World War II, and they were generous with their advice of what to look out for in the field, where to go, where to hide in a firefight, all these things.

'I tended to drive myself to war because I did not want to put my life in the hands of another colleague. Also, travelling in a car with other journalists can sometimes be more dangerous, as being together can turn them into courage snobs and they lose perspective. I know of incidents of this, some fatal. No one wants to be the first to buckle and say we have gone too far, this is too dangerous, admit he or she is afraid and say to the others, "Let's get out of here".

'Much better to know your own capabilities. The drawback is that if something happens to you, there may be nobody to help or tell the tale.

'Never lose your temper with locals who are threatening you, but at the same time do not be so craven that it is easy for them to shoot you before any others. And don't argue if you are held up over trivial things. I remember a German who was shot dead by rebels in the Congo because he refused to hand over the keys to his Mercedes, which he had saved up for and just bought. It was brand new, but he was silly. He would be alive now to buy another if he had given up the keys. He had lost his perspective and it proved fatal.

'There is no special talisman I take into the field. But I do generally have some personal photographs with me. These pictures are anchoring. They attach you to your real life, and they can also help to break the ice with potential enemies. They show that you too are a human being, not just a cipher to get rid of with a bullet or a bash on the head. When I was kidnapped in Ethiopia the first thing I did was to step out and very deliberately shake the hand of my kidnapper, who was training his AK-47 on me. It made him deflect his weapon and helped break the ice. Later I showed my kidnappers a picture of my girlfriend. It all helped.

'There is no point in being a journalist if it destroys your humanity so that you put the story above everything, even a person's life. You cannot help everyone, of course, in a war situation or a natural disaster. But you should always be ready to help with a little money or food.

'I constantly marvel at how the poorest and most desperate people, say the victims of an earthquake who have lost absolutely everything, including their family and homes, talk to you, a complete stranger, and ask for nothing in return. It is very humbling and good to help them.

'On occasion, I have made some mistakes, pushed the envelope too far, especially when I was in Cambodia and Vietnam, but fortunately not to the point of being wounded or getting a colleague wounded or killed. Such situations remind me of my mortality. I vow never to put myself in such a situation again, but inevitably it can happen, and I must always steel myself for it and be prepared.

'Coming back from a combat zone is tricky. Usually, I have to write a story, so am under a lot of pressure. That is a good thing. I isolate myself so that I can retain the authenticity of the experience, even to the point when I was in Vietnam or Cambodia of not washing the muck off myself or changing my clothes until I had written the piece. It's no good making oneself too comfortable.

'You feel exhilarated to be alive after going through so much fear. Perhaps broken too because of what you have seen and experienced. It's important to realize that these things are natural reactions to the exceptional situations you have gone through. Living on the edge of death can also make love and sex more real and intense. It isn't necessarily true, but making love certainly helps.

'I think that no one who sees a lot of combat and misery comes back from it in one piece. Trauma is cumulative. See the signs before it really damages you and, if necessary, get help.'

/INDEX

Page numbers in **bold** refer to illustrations.

D

G

H

I

J

K

L

M

N

O

P

Z

A NOTE ON THE AUTHOR

Rosie Garthwaite is an Al Jazeera journalist with six years' experience working in the Middle East. She began her career as a reporter for *The Baghdad Bulletin*, the first English-language newspaper in post-invasion Iraq, before becoming a freelance reporter for Reuters, *The Times* and the BBC. She lives in Doha, Qatar. This is her first book.